Dostoyevsky
Reads Hegel
in Siberia and
Bursts into Tears

Dostoyevsky Reads Hegel in Siberia and Bursts into Tears

LÁSZLÓ F. FÖLDÉNYI

TRANSLATED FROM THE HUNGARIAN

BY OTTILIE MULZET

YALE UNIVERSITY PRESS ■ NEW HAVEN & LONDON

A MARGELLOS
WORLD REPUBLIC OF LETTERS BOOK

English translation copyright © 2020 by Ottilie Mulzet.
© Földényi F. László.
English-language edition published by arrangement with Eulama International Literary Agency.
Earlier versions of these essays were originally published in Hungarian.
For details, see the credits page.
The credits page constitutes a continuation of the copyright page.

Yale University Press books may be purchased in quantity for educational, business, or promotional use. For information, please e-mail sales.press@yale.edu (U.S. office) or sales@yaleup.co.uk (U.K. office).

Set in Electra and Nobel types by Tseng Information Systems, Inc.
Printed in the United States of America.

Library of Congress Control Number: 2019947285
ISBN 978-0-300-16749-8 (hardcover : alk. paper)

A catalogue record for this book is available from the British Library.

This paper meets the requirements of ANSI/NISO Z39.48-1992 (Permanence of Paper).

CONTENTS

"There are more mysteries contained in the shadow of a person who walks in the sunlight than in all the religions of mankind, past, present, and future," wrote Giorgio de Chirico, sometime shortly after 1910. In his works of that period, which he termed "metaphysical paintings," he grants a prominent role to the shadows cast by the monuments and the campanili on the piazzas, by the people and the columns of the arcades. And yet everything in these pictures swims in blinding sunlight; the light illuminating the spaces of these piazzas is as sharp and penetrating as the light in an operating room, where it is a question of life and death. But it is the shadows that are the main actors in de Chirico's paintings. And no matter how paradoxical it may seem, these shadows also cast their darkness on the light above. Because it is in vain that light creates the impression that it will last forever, that nothing can ever extinguish it—in these images, obscurity, darkness, the shadows have succeeded in rebelling against it. Even so, they have not succeeded in eliminating light; they could not liquidate it—instead, the shadows have become its equal, emancipated.

The belief in the omnipotence of reason that illuminates all phenomena—similar to the sun—is the great inheritance of the Enlightenment. Thinking, of course, ever since humans have existed, has always tried to disperse the darkness. Earlier individuals did not cherish the illusion that here on earth they would be able to liquidate every shadow and every darkness. During the Enlightenment, however, the conviction that only time and intellectual preparation were required in order to eventually cast light upon all things—with no dark corners remaining anywhere unilluminated by the light of reason—became ever more resolute. Nothing less was at stake than capturing the positions previously occupied by God. In the history of human cultures until that point, only God (or the gods) had the right to absolute autonomy. Humans could only compete for this right when they themselves had begun to consider themselves gods—or, at the very least, had begun to entertain the thought that their own power was divine (that is to say, unbounded). As a result of the process of secularization of the modern age, nondivine beings (humans) began to act as gods, believing themselves, in their restricted existence, omnipotent, believing that they would never have to confront the fragile condition of their seemingly absolute power.

As with all great thoughts and aspirations, this too had its own shadow. William Blake had already written in 1791: "God, so long worshipp'd, departs as a lamp / Without oil." Ever since the Romantic period, because of God's absence an ever strengthening disquietude has predominated, not only in individuals but in the entirety of Western civilization. Those who sense this disquietude justifiably pose the question: What is the point of oil if there is no longer a lamp into which it can be poured? What remains to fill the place of God when God has been exiled, and history and progress have also proved undeserving of trust? How shall we practice freedom if there is no longer a transcendental shelter in the heavens above us? And if we no longer trust in a being whose blinding light can illuminate even the darkest corners, then how shall we deal with the darkness and its many shadows which have loomed continuously, ever since the Enlightenment, over our civilization? From the age of Romanticism on, if someone were to observe the vulnerability of obstinate trust in reason and historical progress, an observation exposing history as a mere construction, a mechanism of self-defensive blinding (and the protagonists of the following essays, including Dostoyevsky, Kleist, Caspar David Friedrich, Antonin Artaud, Nietzsche, and Canetti, among others, did make this observation), then at the same time the increase of that shadow could be observed; the same shadow in which de Chirico glimpsed that mystery which is a priori connected to existence itself.

When God, at the beginning of creation, created light, after the heaven and the earth, the darkness was born alongside it. It is true that Moses claims a previous existence for this when he says, "Darkness was upon the face of the deep." But this was not what we call the darkness of humans. Darkness, to exist, requires light. And vice versa. Neither can be imagined without the other. Illumination existing without darkness is not a part of the human world, just as darkness without illumination is not. Moreover, the two cannot truly be differentiated from each other. "If there were only darkness, all would be clear." This statement was made not by Moses but by Samuel Beckett, according to whom, because of the existence of this duality of darkness and light, nothing in human existence is clear, but all remains obscure, "inexplicable."

The following essays circle around this duality. More precisely they examine the experience of *inscrutability* to be found in the depths of all cultural phenomena. They deal with aspects of our culture which have been pushed into the background, or have remained unobserved by us, suppressed and concealed, or exiled to the very depths of consciousness. Often they have been considered dark, although certain German Romantics designated them *Nachtseite*, "the side of night, of darkness." And yet this discussion is not really about darkness and the night, but rather about that mysteriousness of which de Chirico and Beckett both spoke. This mystery is not far away from us, residing at some unknown distance. On the contrary, it is here, in our immediate proximity. It makes itself felt in the most ordinary daily phenomena, as there is no situation in our lives which does not contain this latency, this possibility of genuine mystery. We do not necessarily have to think of the great enigmas of birth or death; from day to day, we live among mysteries. And they occur precisely when we are most likely barely to notice them. If you love someone, the world becomes a great enigma to you. If your love is consummated, everything becomes even more enigmatic. And if you suffer disappointment in your love, then a true mystery commences, as when, in the ancient mythologies, the death of the god is repeated in a contemporary setting. What happens when I concentrate on the work of art or listen to music during a recital, or if I observe another human being, trying to grasp the essence of that person's face, or if I begin to wonder at something, if I am sunk in contemplation of the veins on a leaf, or if I simply forget myself? Or, for that matter, if I become immeasurably bored? At such times I am overpowered by the feeling that there is something incomparably greater than my own self. And without realizing it, I step out of my own self. I cross my own boundaries, and at the same time something begins to become clear. And yet this is not the light of reason, strictly segregated from darkness, but the light of a much deeper clarity. Carson McCullers called it illumination, a moment of epiphany that comes to us "in a flash, as a religious phenomenon."

Indeed, these religious phenomena are experienced in countless situations in their lives by those who are otherwise not religious and not believers. There are mysteries which even those who are religious are not able to reach, wrote de Chirico in relation to shadows. The essays contained in this volume explore phenomena which perhaps could best be termed atheistic religiosities. What does this mean? It means that even if someone is not a believer in God, every human being undergoes certain recurrent experiences during which human life is revealed as deeply embedded in a series of profound coherencies pointing well beyond the manufactured structures (social, political and economic); these states, therefore, can reliably be designated metaphysical.

Historically, the disposition of God from his throne began during the Enlightenment. Humans tried to base their foundation upon their own self, seeking no further external reference points. But the Enlightenment—while bidding farewell to traditional metaphysics—nonetheless preserved its own belief in a final Rationality, to be achieved in an unknown future, in which everyone would take part. This belief, as demonstrated by the *Culte de la Raison* introduced in Paris in the last decade of the eighteenth century, was the equivalent of a new faith. When André Breton and Marcel Duchamp organized the large exhibit they called *Le Surréalisme en 1947*, Georges Bataille wrote the text for the catalogue, "The Absence of Myth." In this piece he writes, "The decisive absence of faith is resolute faith." This thought practically rhymed with the idea, expressed in Theodor Adorno and Max Horkheimer's *Dialectic of Enlightenment* (published a couple of years earlier), that the Enlightenment, while claiming to expose everything as a myth, itself towered over everything as a colossal unavoidable myth.

Enlightenment, while depriving the world of its so-called metaphysical dimensions, applied newer metaphysical categories to it—and this was due to the simple reason that we cannot exist without metaphysics. Even in a secularized age, a sense for metaphysics can be maintained and nurtured: this is the sense for the uniqueness of our life, for the exceptionality of our existence within this universe, for the great wonder of the incomparability and unrepeatability of each moment of every one of our lives. Each human life emerges thanks to a fracture, a break—it plunges from nonexistence into existence—and traversing the same fracture and break, it is thrown back again: from existence it falls back into something that, for want of a better term, we are compelled to call nonexistence. These two unknowns— preceding and following existence—form the roots of suscepti- bility to metaphysics. It is not necessary to be a philosopher; this susceptibility resides in everyone; in certain situations it flares up, becoming an experience that sweeps everything else away. If for no other reason, then, it is because of the consciousness of our own mortality that we are doomed from birth to this home- sickness for the metaphysical. As Vladimir Nabokov writes in the first sentence of in his memoir *Speak, Memory:* "The cradle rocks above an abyss, and common sense tells us that our existence is but a brief crack of light between two eternities of darkness."

Light and darkness. Hegel and Dostoyevsky. Reason and the monsters. Happiness and melancholy. Faust and Mephistophe- les. Lord Chesterfield and the Demon of Frankenstein. The Whole and the Fragment. The essays in this volume were written along the lines of these and other similar dichotomies. I did this not so that one side would necessarily defeat the other, but rather so that an argument for a multiplicity could be made: namely— while not disputing the intentions of reason, and its attempts to elucidate all—to draw attention to the importance of the open- ing to metaphysics.

Dostoyevsky
Reads Hegel
in Siberia and
Bursts into Tears

MASS AND SPIRIT

*In memory of Elias Canetti on the ninetieth anniversary of
his birth*

In Venice, in an of the out-of-the-way corner of the Piaz-
zetta located at the corner of the basilica of Saint Mark, there
is a statuary group depicting the Four Tetrarchs. Carved out of
the hardest granite, the sculpture, dating from the beginning of
the fourth century, depicts Diocletian with three of his chosen
co-sovereigns. They huddle together as if ready to brave the in-
cipient end of the world. But we cannot exclude the possibility
that they might be looking at us—we who are still living—from
beyond the end of the world. It is as if they had been frozen into
stone from the gaze of an invisible Medusa. If a living person
happened to look at them, he or she would be drawn into a kind
of unknown circuitry, and from that single gaze would become
numb. For the viewer will have gazed upon the forms of human
beings who are in possession of the secret of that which is in-
human.

What strikes one the most are the similarities among the four
figures. Slightly smaller than human scale, they mutually embrace one another, their bodies clinging together, and they create the impression of being Siamese quadruplets emerged from

a single ovum. Each draws our gaze; nonetheless, they are so uniform that no matter which one we begin to look at, we see the others as well. It does not matter with what small detail we commence our examination, we always perceive, involuntarily, the *whole* of the sculpture. Their shoes and their garments are uniform, their swords, crowns, and belts are uniform, the fabric on them is draped in a similar fashion, their foreheads are wrinkled in a similar manner, their gazes are uniformly careworn. There are four of them, and yet they appear to be *one single* living being. As if they were *one* body, grasping at each other, they melt into one another; they lose themselves within each other. And yet in no way are they destroyed; they simply continue being identical to their own selves. This is the secret of the strength that radiates from within them: the Four Tetrarchs truly become identical with themselves in surmounting their own selves, in the sacrifice of their own individuality. Each of them is who he is only through the others.

If we were, in imagination, to somehow tear off any one of the figures from the group of statuary, this magnetic force of their existence within each other and for each other would become dissipated. We would stand not before a figure now on his own but in front of a mere stump of a being. Not an individual, but a cripple. All the same, this imaginary amputation would not separate these four men from each other but would instead separate them from an invisible body. And with that we would be annihilating the *secret* of their unity. Because the statue of the Four Tetrarchs is not composed of four men—somehow

brought together by circumstance—who will then at one point
separate, each one following his own path. For that to be the
case, each of them would have to be an individual personality,
and the sculpture would resemble Rodin's *Burghers of Calais*.
In this case, however, we perceive no separate personalities or
individuals. The secret of their metaphysical unity is carved into
the stone. And this unity is not a question of determination or a
decision. It is

> Beyond thy lectures, learn'd professor,
> Beyond thy telescope or spectroscope, observer keen—
>   beyond all mathematics,
> Beyond the doctor' surgery, anatomy—beyond the chemist
>   with his chemistry.[1]

The oppressive similarity of the figures and their close physical
proximity—unimaginable to anyone today, because such proximity would be unbearable—reveal to us that this unity is something both final and fateful, namely, it is also made up of a divine
(or perhaps demonic) interdependence. Even if they wanted to,
these figures could not become separate from each other. This is
not because the Roman Empire would fall apart (a fact of which,
looking at this group of statues, we are not necessarily aware), but
because *order* itself would become damaged.

   This order is something that goes beyond every human intention and conception; it cannot be planned: rather, it itself
renders all kinds of plans possible. Just like the movement of the
stars in the sky or the passage of time, it can never be susceptible

to influence. This order is cosmic; to revolt against it would be as futile as revolting against the rhythms of birth and death. The utmost it offers us is the possibility of not noticing it, of stifling within ourselves the experience of this order. And if we decide to do so, we might even believe ourselves to be freer for a while. The illusion might even arise that at last we are the masters of our own self, autonomous beings with no accounts to settle with anyone or anything. Refuting cosmic order, we try to create our own — which for all intents and purposes means that we wish to impose our own will upon the world — and we are therefore obliged to match our individual strength against the strength of all the others coming forward with their own similar desires.

And who are these others? They are the ones who are present, even though I might prefer to be left alone. And the more of them there are, the harder it is to accept them.

This is the crowd of modernity, formed by those who are broken off from the cosmic order; more precisely, it is the multitude of individuals who have refuted this cosmic order. A crowd which is made up of all those who uniformly sense the universe as aimless, accidentally thrown together. The crowd wishes to be independent of everything that is beyond the human; the crowd rejects that metaphysical state toward which it could gravitate; and in order to somehow withstand the experience of the weightlessness of its own existence, it parrots ever more convulsively the slogans of freedom, considered to be irreconcilable with any sort of concession toward the concept of any higher order.

The Four Tetrarchs are barely differentiated from each other, not because of the lack of talent of the sculptor—an artist able to carve such *careworn* faces would be capable of anything. Their similarity instead is due to the identification of that *common fate* that weighs so heavily on all human beings. In their gaze, it is not the individual but the metaphysical self that is reflected—and on their foreheads lies the seal of the invisible spirit. Cosmic order is inconceivable, and yet, due to its commanding presence, this group of four men creates a tremendous impression of *unity*; they stand in relation to each other as the four cardinal directions; they could be severed from each other only so much as the four seasons could be. Their unity is closed, like that of the cosmos; their collective existence is rendered deeply human by its trans-humanness, by its roots in the nonhuman. A deep sense of mystery flows out from within them—the secret of that which is inconceivable, that which is beyond intellect and reason; it lends to this group of statues its deeply *fatal* gravity. For the experience of cosmic order is itself unbearable. What makes the *Four Tetrarchs* such a weighty creation is its particular symbiosis of the passionate joy (of freedom) combined with the experience of helplessness, itself staggering. This weight is not physical but metaphysical. That is why the group is so dense and timeless, like a creation hailing from ancient Egypt; and that is why the viewer has the impression that the spirit flowing from it is hard like granite, that the granite itself has been transfigured. It is difficult to resist this grouping of figures; they indurate their viewers, who justifiably feel that their souls have grown heavy. We have become a *part of their mass*—just as the *Four Tetrarchs* fetters the attention of the viewer with its own immobile massiveness.

■

The term *mass* can refer at times either to *dead material* or to a multitude of *living people*. Its bifurcation into these meanings, so contradictory in nature, occurred rather late, however. Originally the term *mass* referred to a material that awaited some kind of formation. The Greek *massein* (to knead), the term for barley bread (Hungarian *árpakenyér*, German *Gerstenbrot*, Greek *maza*), and the Hebrew term for unleavened bread (*matzah* or *matzoh*) can all be traced back to the Indo-German root *mağ* (to press, to knead), as did the words for bread dough, which then spread into a range of different languages. The universe is made up of its own mass (its material), and that which we have made our own by breaking it off from this universe—nourishment—is also made up of material. And since we are identical with what we eat (see Paracelsus), we ourselves are also made up of mass. More precisely, we ourselves *are* mass, for it is impossible for us to imagine, in our life in this world, that we could exist without mass, that is, without a body.

This meaning of the word *mass* suggests something we would be hard-pressed to find in its modern, now bifurcated, usage: the homogeneity of the human being with the universe, namely, the cosmic being. Human beings have mass. Not only our body, but our entire being has mass. Our soul, our spirit has it too. And the most essential thing about this mass is not its measurability, not its size, its volume, or its density, but its *existence*. It *exists*, from the outset, like the *on* of Parmenides,[2] this fundament of the universe, which cannot be enclosed or established—the *Ungrund*, in the words of Jacob Böhme. Human beings are themselves the crystallization of this cosmic "mass," this fundament which can neither be enclosed nor bounded; our souls are nothing other than the "condensation" of the divine mass. We cannot step out of this mass-like existence, nor can we "state anything" about it, as every conjecture or declaration is made possible only by the mass. No matter what we might say about the mass, that statement would only be yet a further manifestation of the universal mass itself. And this universal mass does not recognize any difference between soul and body, between the dead and the living, between the material and the immaterial. Yet there is something divine within it—and human beings will have a connection to the divine for as long as we are able to vividly preserve within ourselves the experience of the cosmic roots of our own existence. We shall feel the reassuring mass-like nature of our own existence for as long as we maintain a healthy connection with the spirit. The bifurcation of the modern meaning of the word *mass* can be located in the disruption of this connection.

■

It is as if the only goal of modern civilization would be to maintain the loss of balance of an equilibrium previously established with the spirit. The notion that mass can be fully characterized via *measurement* emerged from humanity's desire to surpass the cosmos itself and our attempt to make ourselves master of it—namely, we wished to subjugate the spirit which sustained us. Ludwig Klages was correct when he claimed that the physicist who declared that measurability is the last criterion of reality was the victim of a misapprehension: "His [i.e., the physicist's] reality is only measurable because it had previously been replenished with a plethora of concepts alien to the essence of reality."[3] It is tempting to see the sign of freedom in this—the sign of liberation, following which humanity, so it is said, became the *lord and master* of itself. Although in order to become *masters*, we had to carry out a revolution. And in reality, the Industrial Revolution made the conviction that humans are the masters of nature, of material, of mass—namely, of the cosmos—irrevocable. We are the master of all of these, or, more precisely, the despot: because while the master is bound by internal ties to that which he rules over, the despot is bound to no one.

Material, thus deemed to be impotent, would not have become transformed into *dead material* if there had not been born, from the multitude itself of living beings, another kind of mass. The notion of a *mass of people,* in the modern sense of the word, emerged around the time of the French Revolution: it was at that time that humanity became haunted by the thought that history was something that could be made and formed, when, to use the expression of Hippolyte Taine, "dogmatists in love with themselves" desired to transform the world along the lines of political geometric axioms—namely, there was a wish to *measure* history, the same way the physicists did, as if it were dead material.[4]

In 1792, during the French Revolution, the word gained its *political* meaning, appearing in such expressions as *masse du peuple, levée en masse,* and so on.[5] When the question of the *activation* of the multitude of people came into play, this multitude suddenly became a *mass.* Despite the sensation of impotence that arises on observing the mass externally, the individuals packed into the crowd see it quite differently. They believe that they can direct, they can govern history, convinced that its egression will flow from their decisions. These decisions are outlined somehow or other, but they are in any event preceded by all-embracing, preplanned *ideas.* In other words, humans now regard themselves as the prime movers of the universe. In other words, they wish to usurp the role of the Creator.

There is something divine in the masses—unimpressionable, immeasurable, superhuman. But this is not because God has formed himself in the image of the crowd; it is because the crowd tries to take God's place. It rebels, usurping the Throne. This is even true when, in a given moment, the crowd is calm, seemingly desiring nothing. For the mere fact of the existence of the crowd is threatening, the sight of it enthralling and frightening in equal measure. An atmosphere of unpredictability emanates from even the most orderly of masses. In terms of human beings, the word truly has *revolutionary* significance: the masses appear when *universal order* has temporarily been destroyed. The mass, although it wants to form a new order, creates chaos all around itself, which compels Hegel, in his *Lectures on the Philosophy of Law* (written approximately a single generation after the French Revolution), to draw parallels between the masses and the mob (see §244). The mass feels itself to be omnipotent, but it places its "divine" power in the service of "demonic" goals. It wishes to rule over everything: the price of this desire is that it regards the living cosmos itself as a dead mass of material to be conquered. But does that death not ricochet back onto the crowd itself? The mass of people never would have formed if these same people had not seen material as finally and definitively dead. For that death was what gave birth to their mass — that particular modern variation of human beings assembled in a crowd, which, when we turn up in its midst, gives us the impression of having glimpsed the living dead, and who otherwise can seem the liveliest of all.

The problem of the mass is the problem of modernity. Humans have become alienated from their own history, as they are from their own cosmic nature. They refute the traditional order: first they refute that well-functioning system of relations, connecting them to the other members of society; then they refute that metaphysical order which renders the homelessness latent in every human life, always resulting in death, bearable; and finally they refute God, more precisely the divine; and at the very end they extinguish every spark of exultation from themselves: namely, they refute their own selves. They become members of the masses. There had always existed *multitudes*, the *densities of human beings*. These, however, never *radically* threatened the order of the world, as they themselves existed *within* this order. No matter how much unpleasantness might have been caused at times to other communities, fundamentally they never sought to derange the hierarchical order of society, they did not wish to take another's place—and even if there were rebellions, chaos, or civil strife, these always occurred for the sake of the eventual re-establishment of the original order. *The multitudes did not wish to push themselves forward at the expense of the spirit.* Every kind of order is fundamentally of a spiritual nature if we look at its roots. The spirit first and foremost is unboundedness (*Unverbindlichkeit*), says Martin Buber. We can interpret his statement to mean this: to live in the spirit means that a person, first and foremost, does not *possess* but *participates*. The person is the member of an all-encompassing order, not merely societal but cosmic. The person *trusts him- or herself entirely to it*, and, paradoxically, this trust makes him or her free.

The birth of the mass, in the modern sense (in both meanings) can be explained via the dislodging of this trust. Of course it would seem much more self-evident to mention the obvious factors—in particular, in the case of the masses of people living in huge numbers in large capital cities. Even such a factor as that, however, is a consequence of a demand lurking in the depths, for the most part imperceptible. Human beings do not congregate in masses because they are obliged to do so when taking care of everyday matters (from shopping to mass tourism); they do not become crammed together in order to derive pleasure from certain spectacles (from sports events to public executions), or in order to settle their accounts with fate (from mass brawls to mass catastrophes). No, none of these would have occurred if they had all not wanted from the beginning to be *together,* and if being a part of this mass had not satisfied some *inner need.* Modern technical civilization proves, in the most eloquent manner possible, that the problem of *mass* and *massification* is not merely signified by the sheer *numbers* of the human population (the solitary TV watcher may feel as much a part of the mass as someone taking part in a demonstration), and not merely by the *density* of those damned to coexistence; primarily it is a problem of the *spirit.* *It was necessary for the relation with the spirit to become damaged for the multitude of human beings to become transformed into a mass.* The rapid increase of the population, the growth of human density, the proliferation of megalopolises—these are not causes but consequences: for them to come about, the soul and the spirit had to "become massed together," namely, it was necessary for people to grow indifferent to their spiritual roots. In other words, there had to be an openness to the "demonic," accompanied by a closure to the "divine." Human beings would not experience the density of other human beings *as a mass* if they themselves had not become *mass-like in their own souls.* The multitude of human beings became problematic *as a mass,* became an insoluble life problem, because it could no longer come to any understanding in terms of its own "massification," its own "mass-like density." The problem of the *mass* is, in the final account, the problem of the *individual*: every decisive conflict is to be found there, from the duel between God and the devil to the conflict of openness and closure to the spirit. Lack of injury to the spirit does not depend on the mass, but upon the exertions of the individual. In the words of Jacob Taubes: "The precipice that lies between God and the World, between the Self and the Non-Self, is found within the individual himself."[6]

Each of us confronts the sight of this chasm *within* our own self. The mass comes into being when we decide to dislodge the burden of this "work" onto others, awaiting redemption from them. We seek our own face in their faces, but instead we see only facelessness: our own and the others'. They are all pursuing well-defined goals; and yet together they form an aimless human mass. Everyone is chasing something; the mass, in contrast, does not *want*, does not *seek*, but breathes with its impotent weight, like a paralyzed beast. Everyone is together; and yet it was as if we were all moving along a windswept plane, barely hanging on. Every moment spent within this mass is good only for distracting us from our original goals; we then must exert ourselves mightily so as not to forget these original intentions. And, moreover, there is no one to curse: there is no concrete, easily discernible obstacle with which we can do battle. In the midst of the mass, human beings are impeded by their own inner invisible obstacles. And they feel — justifiably — that while they are struggling to get ahead, more and more they are struggling with nothing. They are struggling with their own inner void, which has been able to make the others so faceless—has made the entire world so faceless.

■

We begin to do battle with nothingness when we come into the divine presence but are determined to turn our back on it at all costs. In his book *Crowds and Power*, Elias Canetti describes the discharge (*Entladung*) as the most important process that takes place within the crowd: the mass comes into being when every one of its members has been freed from differentiation and they all feel themselves to be *uniform*.[7] At first glance, the term *discharge* would appear to have negative overtones. In a world characterized by continual hoarding and accumulation, discharge becomes a troubling factor: the danger of impoverishment, backwardness, a precipitous fall seems to be implied. The threat of the void, of nothingness, emanates from this word.

And yet: the experience of this threatening void can, at an unexpected moment, easily be transformed into a sense of completion. For there is no state or condition in which the seed-bud of the spirit would not be concealed. And if we look at it from this angle, it is precisely this constant accumulation that leads to genuine poverty—inner impoverishment. In this case, we may regard discharge as the prerequisite for healing. For within the layers of meaning of the word *Entladung* lurks the term *Abgeschiedenheit* (seclusion), this distinctive term of the mystics and one of the preconditions of replenishment with the divine. And lurking within *Entladung* too is its sexual signification: the concept of satisfaction, ejaculation. This signifies completion as well, through the bodily process of discharge. In both these instances, discharge is a *threshold* within which, as it is crossed, we will *simultaneously lose and find our self.* It is possible to live without discharge; in the worst of cases, we will lose our self. But in order to find our own self, it is not possible not to engage in the act of discharge at least occasionally. The discovery of our own self in this case means that we come upon the roots of non-personhood within our own self: we confront our own cosmic fundament, which will bestow upon us the experience of freedom, unexpected and unhoped-for.

Mass and discharge. At first the mass encloses within itself those who have been swept into it, as into a living crypt. It offers no hope of redemption. And yet even in the most inhuman-seeming of masses, there lurks a seed from which the original, unified meaning of the *mass* may germinate. In order to be freed from that crypt, and to live, it is necessary to carry out the fatiguing work demanded by memory. Discharge must be practiced, so that one may feel, in every atom of one's body, the experience of the mass of the most distant of stars, so that in the minutest of oscillations of one's thoughts the mystery of identification with the universe may be surmised. For then one's relation with the spirit will be in place: both dead material and living people — parting from the mass in which they were contained — may once again finally take part in the experience of their own spiritual mass.

DOSTOYEVSKY READS HEGEL IN
SIBERIA AND BURSTS INTO TEARS

In the spring of 1854, after four years of forced labor, Dostoyevsky was sent as a conscript soldier to Semipalatinsk, in the southern part of Siberia. The town, somewhat larger than a village, had a population of between 5,000 and 6,000, half of whom were nomadic Kazakhs, for the most part living in yurts. The local residents hardly felt anything in common with the so-called European Russians; they referred to them as "mainlanders," observing all of them with suspicion. Their number, however, only grew: between 1825 and 1846, the number of exiles sent to Siberia increased to 159,000.

The town was surrounded by a barren sandy desert; there was not even a tree or bush in sight, only sand and thistles. The house that Dostoyevsky lived in stood in the bleakest part of this town, amid the shifting sands. The courtyard was surrounded by high fence boards, and the gate was so low that visitors, if any, had to stoop down to enter.

This is where Dostoyevsky lived, in a spacious but low-ceilinged room, in which were set a bed, a table, and a trunk; on the wall hung a tiny framed mirror. And here he made friends with the local public prosecutor, Aleksander Yegorovich Vrangel, twenty years old at the time, who ended up selflessly supporting the writer for more than ten years from the date of their initial acquaintance. Dostoyevsky related his narrative plans to Vrangel; at times he recited his favorite poems from Pushkin and crooned his favorite operatic areas. They spoke little of religious matters; even though Dostoyevsky was pious, he did not regularly attend church, and he was not overly fond of priests. But he spoke of Christ with enthusiasm. And in the meantime he worked and worked on the manuscript of *Memoirs from the House of the Dead*, allowing Vrangel a glimpse every now and then. In return, the public prosecutor got hold of some books for him. And shortly thereafter they began to study together, assiduously, day after day. In his memoirs, Vrangel does not give away the title of the textbook they were studying from. He does, however, mention the name of a single author: Hegel.[1]

The titles of the books that Vrangel might have been ordering from Germany are unknown to us, but he also subscribed to the *Ausburger Allgemeine Zeitung*. As there is some room for hypothesis, let us assume that he ordered Hegel's lectures on the philosophy of world history, presented between the fall of 1822 and the spring of 1831 at the University of Berlin—occurring in parallel with the tens of thousands of exiles continually arriving in Siberia. The lectures were published in book form for the first time in 1837, with a revised edition issued in 1840. Perhaps this was the book that Vrangel would have ordered, after having leafed through a few pages. It is possible; in his lectures Hegel makes mention of Siberia. Only briefly, it is true. And these few words, it appears, he held in reserve only so that he could justify the reason for his general lack of knowledge about Siberia. His discussion of Asia, in other words, begins with this remark: "We must first of all eliminate Siberia, the northern slope of Asia. For it lies outside the scope of our enquiry. The whole character of Siberia rules it out as a setting for historical culture and prevents it from attaining a distinct form in the world-historical process."[2]

We can well imagine Dostoyevsky's consternation as he came upon these lines while sitting next to the tallow candle. And we can easily imagine his despair as well, as he was obliged to confront the fact that "over there," in Europe—for whose ideals he had been sentenced to death but then sent into exile—no significance whatsoever was attributed to his many sufferings. For his sufferings had followed him into Siberia, into that world which was not a part of history. As seen from the European point of view, none of this could ever be redeemed. Dostoyevsky might have felt—and justifiably so—that he had not only been exiled to Siberia, he had been expelled into nonexistence itself. And from here only a miracle could redeem him, a miracle whose possibility was precluded not only by Hegel but by the entirety of the contemporary European intellectual mind as well: that mind which acknowledged the existence of God in high-sounding words but which had firmly cast aside the thought that God could issue individual commands meant for a single person (not only generalized); that mind that placed so-called natural laws in the forefront of everything, denying what Dostoyevsky later formulated in his remark that even the result

of 2 × 2 could be rebelled against; in other words, the very spirit
that affirmed the modern constitutional state, itself founded
on laws, emphasizing its own unrestricted validity—and in the
meantime forgetting that the creation of law does not strictly
necessitate law.[3]

It is very possible that it was exactly at that moment—when
Dostoyevsky became aware that he had been torn away from
the history for which he had nonetheless assumed every vilifi-
cation—that the conviction was born in him that there are dimensions to life which cannot be compartmentalized into history, and the criteria of existence within history cannot be the
only proof of existence. If someone truly feels and experiences
the weight of his own existence, then he is, so to speak, torn out
of history, and that same weight—one that is beyond history—
weighs upon him in Semipalatinsk as it does in Berlin. And
that a priori exit from history is necessary if he is to perceive the
boundaries and confines of historical existence.

It becomes necessary, however, to accept the possibility of
a *miracle*—that state at which the exclusivity of space and time
ceases. And if Hegel permits continent-sized chunks of land to become detached from history, it means that history itself does not
contain within itself divine boundlessness: there is yet something
that surrounds history which is beyond it. Namely: what is necessary will be contiguous with what is impossible, what is natural
will be contiguous with that which is beyond nature, what is law-
ful will be contiguous with the arbitrary, politics will be contiguous with theology. And yet what is beyond the borders is always

seeping through the borders, to within. Only something that has touched us from the inside can be subsequently excluded.

Perhaps it was this exile from history that ripened Dostoyevsky's faith in miracles—but this faith could have emerged from his experience of the mercilessness of the laws governing the modern world. *For history reveals its own essence to those whom it has cast out of itself.* Even though Hegel had been giving lectures on history for a decade, such a thought never occurred to him. Whereas Dostoyevsky did not need a decade of thinking to perceive this truth. He could experience, within his own flesh and blood, that no epoch of human history had ever refuted the fact of human suffering so conspicuously as the era which commenced with the Enlightenment. And the result of this was not the cessation of suffering, but merely the concealment of its own roots in suffering. Secreted and concealed suffering becomes unconcealed and evident when the confines of the spheres of influence of modern history become visible—visible, however, only to those who have been torn away (or expelled) from history. This perception, when experienced as genuine enlightenment, does not lead to a sensation of suffering but makes it possible for suffering to lead to a kind of redemption—namely, an inner balance, an inner healthiness—instead of suffocating and undermining a person from inside.

■

Perhaps it was while reading Hegel's severe judgment that Dostoyevsky wrote the following lines: "Who can say that he has sounded the depth of these lost hearts, and has read what is hidden from all the world in them? . . . No, it seems crime cannot be interpreted from preconceived conventional points of view, and the philosophy of it is a little more difficult than is supposed." These lost souls, Dostoyevsky writes, "were criminals entirely deprived of all rights of property, fragments cut off from society, with branded faces to bear witness for ever that they were outcasts."[4] A wild rebellion emanates from *The House of the Dead*: the rebellion of the outcasts, of those who no longer see any sense in returning to that place from whence they were expelled. This book is not a manifesto of political rebellion, nor is it a record of scandalized morals: it is a confrontation with the entirety of existence. It confronts that secularized concept of history of which Hegel was the chief advocate, the concept which suggests that suffering—here, in this earthly existence—might be eliminated.

Dostoyevsky speaks in the name of those who have gotten stuck outside this universal festival of joy; they were already condemned by Schiller in his "Ode to Joy" to flee weeping from the circles of the millions of happy celebrants. Dostoyevsky, while he was reading Hegel, could have justifiably sensed that Schiller's starry firmament would never loom above him. So he could do nothing but weep himself. Or he could rebel. The *House of the Dead* is the bible of rebellion. It is not held together by dialectics claiming to explain everything, but instead is bound by suffering and lamentation; the hope that emanates from it, its belief in miracles, is in direct proportion to the depths of its despair.

Of course, the verdict uttered in reference to Siberia could not have reached Hegel's reader in Semipalatinsk completely unexpectedly. The accusation is prepared so thoroughly, so circumspectly, and so logically that it might even have granted a kind of aesthetic pleasure if it had been written more beautifully and — and this is the main thing — more humanely. This is the foundation.

"Whoever looks at the world rationally will find that it in turn assumes a rational aspect, the two exist in a reciprocal relationship."[5] Or he doesn't even bother to look, Dostoyevsky could have answered, glancing into his small framed mirror hanging on the wall of his room. Nobody *looks* back at us from a mirror. We can try to bravely face ourselves: our gaze is engrossed in the eyeballs of a *stranger*, who stares fixedly into nothingness. Not only does this stranger not look outward, he does not even look inward. He is dead, numb — if we pay long attention — even haunting. We could easily end up like Narcissus as we try to discover the principle of our vitality in that which is nonliving. *We try to reach vitality via the detour of a phantom existence.* We seek the criterion of life in that which is dead. This, of course, makes life itself dead. Lifeless, numb, ghostly. And yet all we wished to do was examine vitality.

I have mentioned Hegel's famous pronouncement, uttered at the beginning of his lectures on the philosophy of world history. One of the most frequently returning concepts in these lectures is that of *rationality*. It is like a field of shoals upon which it is difficult not to founder. Moreover, it even seems as though this was Hegel's intention to begin with. He attempts to frame the concept of world history so that only one kind of person or thing is included in its procession—those who can get stuck on the shoals of rationality. If, however, someone or something can swim through the shoals unharmed, out beyond the confines of history, out to the free ocean, unconfinable by the strictures of mind, Hegel, in a puzzling manner, does not rejoice. Instead of being happy that certain individual peoples, ages, or regions have *escaped* this catastrophe, he grows somber and impatient, his style becomes grasping—at times decisively alienating—as he brusquely consigns such things or people to the curse of *oblivion*. The survivors are the losers.

The alluring metaphor of the world that gazes upon itself with rationality appears at first glance to be self-evident, almost as if it were a divine revelation. If we take a look, however, at the thoughts and presumptions amid which this thought arose, then we see that Hegel himself was forced to clutch at this life vest of rationality because of his own repressions, his superstitious fears, his most irrational terrors. It is as if he were afraid that otherwise something might be swept away. Hegel, in order to systemize (that is, to place under control) everything that surrounded his life, specifically, everything that had preceded him, *invented* a concept of history which he could then use as a kind of net to cover the entire bounty of life. Or as a kind of net for the intricate unboundedness of life. He deploys philosophy, which "approaches history as something to be manipulated, and does not leave it as it is, but forces it to conform to its preconceived notions and constructs a history a priori," as if it were a weapon.[6] The true task, however, of *invented and formulated* history is not to offer an "objective" picture of existence but to protect its *engineers and constructors* lest they become submerged in something that can neither be formulated nor planned, that is to say, something that does not obey rationality and perception.

What is history? Hegel does not give away too much in this regard. The opening statement of his series of lectures is suspiciously inane: "As to what is meant by history or world history, I need say nothing; the common conception of it is adequate." Moreover, he adds, as a form of self-reassurance: "And we are more or less agreed on what it is."[7] It is striking how unwilling Hegel is to say anything concerning the merits of the criteria of history itself, even as he is purportedly working out his philosophy of history. As if he had been compelled by superstitious dread to speak of anything, *anything but that.* Dostoyevsky, right at the beginning of the volume, could well have had the impression that the philosophy that Hegel wished to lecture about was that of the *silenced*, the *ones held in secret*, the *concealed.*

■

In order for Hegel to do this he has to close his eyes. Because what would he see if he had kept them open? A vast picture, endless variability. For all around him there whirled "everything that can occupy and interest the human mind"; "every sensation of the good, the beautiful and the great, comes into play; everywhere we see others pursuing aims which we ourselves affirm and whose fulfilment we desire, and we share their hopes and fears." But why is it forbidden to see this teeming pullulation? Because, he replies—again, with suspicious haste—because all of this is mere *contingency*. But then once again, in a subsequent addendum, he betrays himself:

> In the history of the world, we see before us the concrete image of *evil* in its most fully developed form. If we consider the mass of individual happenings, history appears as an *altar* [literally, "a *slaughterhouse*" (*Schlachtbank*)] on which individuals and entire nations are immolated; we see all that is noblest and finest destroyed. No real gain appears to have been made, and only this or that ephemeral work lingers on, already bearing the mark of decay on its brow and soon to be supplanted by another as ephemeral as itself.[8]

Dostoyevsky might have understood from this passage that the slaughterhouse (*Schlachtbank*) is that which may not be perceived. When writing about world history, one must remain silent about its most profound characteristics. In the name of rationality, one must look away from the most crucial of human experiences. One must look away from suffering, from death, from the unverifiable, namely from all that of which man is not lord and master—from everything before which he is *defenseless*. "Reason cannot stop to consider the injuries sustained by single individuals," writes Hegel, "for particular ends are submerged in the universal end."[9] Hegel wishes to sense himself as the master of all—the master is supposedly happier than the slave—although to achieve this he is compelled to restructure the entire world according to his own tastes and desires. Hegel endeavors to base his entire philosophy on the principle of rationality. And yet the most profoundly fundamental characteristics of his structure hardly cohere with the principle of rationality. Latent in this philosophy is the highly frail desire for victory, the happiness it engenders. And that watchful eye—which could have been Dostoyevsky's as well—might have been capable of discovering the secret experience of suffering, of death, of defeat and loss.

Historical rationality tries to rise into the heights from desires, instincts, fears, terrors, repressions, and denials, like a tame, snow-white, carved Roman copy of a Greek statue. And of course it cannot rise up from these elements. The seething coming from below—from the swamp—slowly and inevitably colors the marble through the hair-thin cracks. In *The Philosophy of Law*, Hegel writes that world history lies beyond the purviews of justice, morality, illegality, violence, and crime, beyond talent, the larger and smaller passions, culpability and innocence. In other words, it lies beyond everything that we designate life. Hegel uses this argument to tell us why not every nation belongs within the purview of world history. But those who do "attain its absolute right, and the nation [*Volk*] which lives at this point, and the deeds of that nation, achieve fulfillment, fortune, and fame."[10] *Fulfillment, fortune,* and *fame:* for the *Protestant* Hegel, each attribute is more alluring than the next. And in any event, they are a good deal more attractive than suffering or death. But if they manifest themselves not in an open manner but by means of the detour of repressions, then they deteriorate, become damaged. And if Hegel subordinates them to *rationality*, then, ultimately, he does so out of *fear*. He clings convulsively to happiness because he does not willingly treat the subject of unhappiness; he compulsively takes the side of those who are covered in glory because he does not wish to notice the suffering of the vanquished; and his gaze would not be fixed so persistently on the specter of success if he had not been so secretly persuaded of the impermanent nature of everything, including rationality.

■

Whoever insists on viewing the world rationally at all costs eventually falls victim to irrationality—and such people always do so more quickly and more visibly than those whose primary wish is to live *freely*. Reason is not the *master* and the *creator* of freedom but rather receives its own share from it. Freedom itself is determinative; the mind is merely one of its instruments and does not engender it. Everything that is rational or irrational finds itself within the confines; *freedom*, however—the one single divine element of humans—is beyond rationality and irrationality. I become free only through that which surpasses (transcends) me— I find myself only in that in which I lose myself once and for all.

We may attribute many designations to this state of freedom. But by no stretch of the imagination could we ever refer to it as "rational." When Hegel reduced world history, God, and the absolute spirit to a common denominator—subordinating them to the principle of rationality—he was ultimately turning his back on freedom. Rational freedom is *not* freedom. What is rational is always confined; freedom is unconfined.

In the name of God, but lacking all divine spirit: this is what characterizes the historical viewpoint built upon the principle of rationality, which in the middle of the eighteenth century super-seded the concept of world history based on Christian narratives of salvation. In the Hegelian interpretation of history, everything designated "divine" is subordinated to something under the supervision of human beings. Ultimately everything is implicitly directed to the sphere of authority of *politics*—and the manner in which Hegel seeks an explanation for the totality of the Whole is but one of the indications of that. He even seeks explanations for that which clearly has no explanation. In conformance with the continuum of modern secularization, Hegel does not seek divine unboundedness behind the political; instead he tries, at every given opportunity, to interpret divine unboundedness (namely, that which is unverifiable to the human mind) by em-ploying political criteria. For example, writing of the Teutonic tribes, Hegel notes: although they lived in communities, this was not a political condition, and therefore they too "lived outside the historical process."[11]

From the second half of the eighteenth century on, every cultural and theological question was portrayed with ever more manifest political overtones, and freedom itself was the loser. More precisely (because that which is unbounded can ultimately never be wounded), attention was directed away from freedom. Of course, behind the belief in the exclusivity of political solutions there still lurked religious and theological timbres (as Donoso Cortés wrote in the mid-nineteenth century, there is no political question behind which theological questions do not lurk). As, however, these theological considerations (concerned with divine freedom) were pushed into the background of questions of governability and supervision, faith in transcendence grew far less compelling.

It is true that in Hegel's history of philosophy—just as in contemporary Western culture—the word *God* occurs with the same frequency as the word *rationality*. But this concept of God is more like a backdrop behind which something else is crammed in—something that is anything but godlike. The chief criterion which can be derived from Hegel's philosophy of history is that people create history from their own power, on the basis of supposed rationality (which, of course, their political opponents—from the viewpoint of their own rationality—perceive as irrational), but this can be carried out only at the cost of the *exclusion* of the unverifiable, the inexplicable, the "irrational." From Hegel's time on, politics does not signify all-encompassing human endeavor but instead indicates exclusion, partitioning, sectioning—in other words, repression. As Carl Schmitt put it, the middle class wants a God, but he must be passive; it wants a ruler with no authority to rule; it demands freedom and equality but wishes to limit suffrage to the ruling class, so that by means of wealth and education it may bring its own influence to bear on legislation (as if wealth and education justified the exploitation of the poor and uneducated); it abolishes aristocracy based on family but supports the rule of a mercantilist aristocracy, which is still an aristocracy but an idiotic and commonplace one; it desires the sovereignty of neither king nor people. What—we could ask with Schmitt—does the bourgeoisie really *want?*[12]

■

If the infinite and the transcendent become lost behind the finite things, then it is no longer possible to speak of freedom. God, subjugated to rationality, is not the God of freedom, but of politics, conquest, and colonization. *This* is the secular religion of the God of the modern age. And history—looking at it from a Hegelian point of view—is the history of secularization. Dostoyevsky might have justifiably felt that Hegel was not just ushering Siberia (and himself with it) out the door; he was trying to convince, in missionary-like fashion, all humanity to accept as historical only that which the censorship of rationality admitted as such.

Hegel writes very little about Siberia. The reason for this is simple: the philosopher, right before turning to Siberia, discusses the continent of Africa, which, in his view, similarly falls outside history. Hegel carries out his own exile of Africa with so much *rapture*, almost with *poetic inspiration*, that at the end his creative spirit is perceptibly exhausted. And what he says about Africa is equally valid for Siberia. In both cases, the causes for exclusion and repudiation are the same: a recoiling from all that is inconceivable to the European mind, a fear of the incomprehensible, a dread of perceived darkness. Although most revealing is Hegel's passion as it suddenly bursts into flame. In his repudiation of Africa and Siberia, he is only denying something perceptibly relevant to his own inner self. And here he does not simply exploit his own feelings but repudiates his own shadow self—all that monstrosity, horror, and heinousness; he would not have had to deny them so vehemently had he not discovered the roots of these qualities in his own heart. The passion with which he depicts the alleged untrammeled course of atrocities taking place in Africa, describing indefatigably ever newer instances, anecdotes, horrifying stories without ever discovering the least cause for joy, beauty, or something worthy of amazement—this tells us that Hegel was not afraid of Africa (for he certainly had reason to feel quite safe in Berlin) but was at war with his own instincts. The frail philosopher, now light-years distant from any genuine experience of freedom, then cobbled together, for reasons of self-therapy, his own history of philosophy and explanation of existence. Perhaps, however, in the depths of his heart he desired nothing more than to be able to say—as both Rimbaud and Genet were to say later on—I am a Negro.

Hegel establishes that there is no possible history in Africa, but his reasoning hardly stands the test of rationality: "It is the Gold-land compressed within itself—the land of childhood, which, lying beyond the day of self-conscious history, is enveloped in the dark mantle of Night." In his view, Africa contributed nothing to erudition. What is Hegel repudiating here in one single sentence? He refutes *lustrous gold, childhood,* and the *night.* The density of gold, from which coins were not yet struck and which blinds like the sun; the night, which in this case overcomes conscious perception and whose darkness is no different from the darkness of the body's interior; and finally childhood, when desires may evolve and manifest themselves freely, as if in a state of paradise. Some of Hegel's psychologist contemporaries—for example, Gotthilf Heinrich von Schubert, to whom Freud was later to accord much recognition, or Carl Gustav Carus (whose work *Psyche* Dostoyevsky wanted to translate, with Vrangel's assistance, in Siberia)—surely would have been aware that Hegel, in his analysis of Africa, was shrinking back in dread from something. And perhaps this something was what Freud was to designate—as he precisely observed the accumulation of Hegelian repressions in society and culture—later as analysis. Shortly thereafter, perhaps in an unguarded moment, Hegel designates these African situations "paradisiacal"; but soon sober rationality prevails, and he repudiates that which man desires perhaps the most of all. It is precisely this paradisiacal state which is not perfect, he says, as the state worthy of human beings is *not* that of innocence: "Only children and animals are innocent [*unschuldig*]; man must become guilty [*muss Schuld haben*]."[13]

In the depths of this repudiation of the paradisiacal state, there lurks, for the European (i.e., rational) mind, an incomprehension toward an inaccessible mode of existence. Hegel shrinks back from paradise just as a natural scientist of the modern age would shrink back from the same thought that captivated Dostoyevsky: if God so wishes, he can make two times two equal five. Hegel mentions again and again that it is impossible for us (as modern Europeans) to place ourselves within this African nature and survive it because what is incomprehensible in his eyes does not appear to him to be a miracle but something wild, unrestrained. The bloodbaths, the inordinate (irrational) reverence paid to the dead, the presumed lack of respect for human life, sorcery, the mysterious ceremonies—all these truly could have been alarming for the European professor living at the beginning of the nineteenth century. But looking back at things from today, it is just as alarming that this professor—while alluding to the "pure" perspectives of rationality—truly does nothing other than those who already had, for a good long while, been colonizing "paradise" with weapons, calling upon those same Christian principles that Hegel, revealingly, often resorted to himself. Ultimately that which proved to be unreceptive, that which could not be appropriated, was subjugated by means of *weapons* and *rationality.*

Behind Hegel's vehement repudiation of Africa and Siberia lies his secret wish to assassinate God. Hegel became the victim of the mistaken belief that he could explain the unexplainable. And in reality he did not do that; he only managed to maim his own self while denying his own inner desire for the ancient (and divine)—a desire always oriented toward the unknown, the unconfined, and the unbounded. In leafing through the pages he wrote about Africa, on the one hand we see the Africans themselves, condemned to execution and genocide, whereas on the other we see a soul-maimed, perpetually terrified white man. He is terrified of gold, which is dense and blinding, of children, of night, terrified of the dead, and of those African heroes who, if they are offended, kill *themselves*; he is terrified of the women who are as competent in murder as Kleist's Penthesilea, who battled with African elephants; he is terrified of the executioners who sit next to African kings; he is terrified of those innumerable beings who are born and who die exactly as he does but who have chosen such radically different modes of existence; he is terrified of those whose daring is limitless, and who are capable of passionately squandering their own lives. And—judging by his impatient and irritated tone—he is terrified of his own terror as well. He is terrified of everything that he cannot comprehend with reason. And for the most part he still is terrified of God, of that freedom that cannot be surveyed, casting the human being out from its own self. It is no surprise that, reaching the end of his liquidation, he breathes a sigh of relief: "We shall therefore leave Africa at this point, and it need not be mentioned again. For it is an unhistorical continent."[14]

In 1864 the protagonist of *Notes from Underground* wrote, "In short, anything can be said about world history, anything that might occur to the most disordered imagination. There's only one thing that can't possibly be said about it—that it is rational.

You'll choke on the word."[15] It is not too hard to guess whom Dostoyevsky was thinking of here. Ever since humans lost that universal certitude—formulated by Chekhov toward the end of *Three Sisters*, to the effect that one day we will have an explanation for all the suffering we have lived through on this earth— we have lived in continual fear and terror. And ever since then, like Hegel, we have been engaged in a *construction* of history in order to console ourselves with the hope of the formation and eternal development of humanity. The convulsive *faith* placed in rationality serves to render the terror caused by the absence of God bearable. And if then someone, like Dostoyevsky or Nietzsche, points out the brittleness of this faith and reveals that what we call history is for the most part a constructed, blinkered, self-protecting mechanism, then everything falls apart: so much for rationality; the trust placed in the so-called truth of science dissipates, and there is nothing to take the place of God, who has been exiled.

It could be seen as a divine ruse that it was precisely in Siberia—this no-man's-land supposedly excluded from God's providence—where Dostoyevsky became convinced of the existence of God and the indispensability of transcendence. When, on the evening of December 24, 1849, he left Petersburg, two days after the comedy of his mock execution, his route did not only lead him out from among the houses lit up for the Christmas season; Dostoyevsky was also turning his back on Europe. And when he crossed the Ural Mountains, it was as if he were not merely stepping out of European space but moving out of European (historical) time. "The crossing of the Urals was a sad moment," he recalled in a letter written four years later:

> Mournful was the moment when we crossed the Ural. The horses and sledges sank deep in the snow. A snow-storm was raging. We got out of the sledges — it was night — and waited, standing, till they were extricated. All about us whirled the snow-storm. We were standing on the confines of Europe and Asia ; before us lay Siberia and the mysterious future — behind us, our whole past; it was very melancholy. Tears came to my eyes.

And yet from the continuation of the letter, it is possible to deduce that this enigmatic fate held something in reserve for him that perhaps at home — back in Europe — he never would have attained. His suffering and despair became excessive, leading him to the experience of unboundedness (the divine). From below, from the opposite direction — avoiding everything that he could have experienced in Europe:

> I won't even try to tell you what transformations were undergone by my soul, my faith, my mind, and my heart in those four years. It would be a long story. Still, the eternal concentration, the escape into myself from bitter reality, did bear its fruit. I now have many new needs and hopes of which I never thought in other days. But all this will be pure enigma for you, and so I'll pass to other things.

A little later he writes: "I'm content with my life."[16] He wrote both these statements in 1854, in the middle of his exile, perhaps on the evening of one of those days when he had been studying Hegel in Vrangel's company.

■

What could this enigma have been? Dostoyevsky devoted an entire book to the narration of his experiences in Siberia. He gave it the title *Memoirs from the House of the Dead,* which is peculiar, because in it he speaks only of the living, moreover, of those who were not awaiting execution. The countless faces, gleaming for a moment, do not create the impression in the reader of being those of the dead, but those of the damned. The damned, who not only had been resettled from Europe to Siberia (as a consequence of a political sentence), and who not only had even been expelled from history to a space outside history (on the basis of Hegelian rationality), but who had been exiled from the domain of salvation into hell itself. This hell is not very different from Dante's Hell—with which Osip Mandelstam consoled himself, a century later, similarly in Siberia. In his book, Dostoyevsky wrote the bible of hell—the bible that, a generation earlier in *The Marriage of Heaven and Hell,* William Blake had stated was in his possession and he would deliver it to the world, whether the world wanted it or not. And whence this drastic need for a bible? Blake's response: "Man must & will have Some Religion: if he has not the Religion of Jesus, he will have the Religion of Satan & will erect the Synagogue of Satan, calling the Prince of this World, God, and destroying all who do not worship Satan under the Name of God."[17]

We see hell in Dostoyevsky's *Memoirs from the House of the Dead*—we see exclusively hell. But it would not have been possible to depict this hell so colorfully and so variously if Dostoyevsky had not at the same time been certain of the existence of both purgatory and paradise. True, they are not mentioned even once. But the way in which Dostoyevsky paints hell as *immeasurable* shows that he was above all seeking the infinite within the finite. It cannot be debated that he was a genial psychologist; what makes his writing about the Siberian hell so troubling, however, is not that he was a good observer but that he discovered the unconfined in everything that circumscribed him. He sought the *divine* despite the fact that in this book he makes relatively infrequent use of the word. But he searched for the divine even where God's absence was the most plain. The prerequisite of the encounter with God is the precipitous fall from history, a plunge across into manifest hell.

There is redemption in hell. Moreover, in the view of Dostoyevsky, redemption cannot even be imagined without the experience of hell. He once told Vladimir Solovyov, the brother of the philosopher Vsevolod Solovyov, "Oh, it was a great happiness for me: Siberia and the forced labor! People say: horror, bitterness, people talk about the legitimacy of some other bitterness! Sheer nonsense! I only had a happy, healthy life there, I understood myself there. . . . I understood Christ. . . . I understood the Russian soul, and there I felt that I myself am Russian, that I am one of the Russian people. All my best thoughts occur to me, and now they only return and even not as clearly! Oh, if only they would take you away for forced labor as well!" And another acquaintance, Alexander Milyukov, noted that "Dostoyevsky was grateful to fate, thanks to which exile had made it possible for him to thoroughly understand the Russian man, and with that to understand his own self better." This is the redemption that Raskolnikov will experience in Siberia: his life there "is the story of a gradual renewal of a man, of his gradual regeneration, of his slow progress from one world to another, of how he learned to know a hitherto undreamed-of reality," as Dostoyevsky writes at the end of *Crime and Punishment*.[18]

This differentiates him from Hegel, who makes much more frequent use of the word *god*. Hegel does not want to know about any kind of other, unknown world—he allows only the present, known world to continue to expand. There are no chasms slashing human existence into shreds: Hegel is a believer in smooth, jolt-free, that is *moderate*, transitions. This is why he applies the dialectical method so persistently and stubbornly: dialectics, in his hands, is a tool for maintaining the given, the extant comfortable arrangements, the weapon of rationality. Kierkegaard later notes in relation to dialectics that it is "a chimera, which in Hegel is supposed to explain everything, and which is also the only thing he never has tried to explain."[19] It is no wonder that this was exactly what Hegel never explained: in his work, dialectics serves the advancement of suppression, of a conspiracy of silence. And like *every explicatory* principle, it is a tool for the dethronement of God.

Hegel does not know hell. On one hand, in comparison with Dostoyevsky, he was truly cosseted by fate. On the other he did not want to take notice of it *on principle*. The secularizing historical point of view deprives humankind of every kind of transcendence in the name of rationality. It deprives us not only of God but also of the devil—deprives us of hell, just as we are deprived of paradise. It is revealing that when Hegel discusses Africa—excluded from history—he feels the impulse to see in it the projected hell of existence. He appears to notice something in Africa which might be more fitting for the pen of Dante. But this is precisely why he exiles this continent from history. He obeys one of the fundamental laws of modern civilization: to eliminate suffering from life, accomplishing this even at the price of the most appalling suffering. Hegel does not try to comprehend this African hell within his own soul (for surely it formed as much a part of his existence as—to take just one example—the Prussian political system); instead, he turns away from it with loathing. He cannot empathize with the nature of the Africans, he states; they are alien to our consciousness—and with that he absolves himself of any further scrutiny. But this also explains why he takes hardly any notice of paradise either, which he remarkably glimpses in "hellish" Africa. Hell and paradise are prerequisites of each other; Hegel, on the other hand, simply wishes to discuss history. That is, he exhibits comprehension exclusively for a certain kind of world-state, the most telling characteristic of which is that it considers its own obligatory restrictions to be *natural* and judges every attempt to transgress boundaries (the attempt to approach the divine)—as deeply *unnatural*, indeed, as culpable. As Lev Shestov was later to write: "Our mind, having assimilated so much nonsense in childhood, has lost the ability to defend itself and accepts everything except what it was warned against from early childhood on, i.e., the miraculous, or in other words, effect without cause. Here, it is always on guard; here, it cannot be enticed by anything—neither by eloquence, inspiration, nor logic. But if the miraculous is not involved, then everything goes. What, for example, does contemporary man 'understand' by the words 'the natural development of the world?' Forget for a moment, for just a moment—provided that is possible—your schooling, and you will immediately be convinced that the development of the world is frightfully unnatural: it would be natural if there were nothing at all—neither the world nor its development."[20]

Dostoyevsky never contested the fact that Siberia was hell itself—hell with all its attendant horrors. Despite this, he blessed the fate that saw him exiled to Siberia. He suffered greatly there, but in the meantime he felt this estrangement from history to be a form of redemption from its gray rationality. At first he had to plunge downward, so that afterward he could veer even higher—like his fellow prisoners, some of whom, in a mysterious fashion, were "so 'desperate' [and] sometimes eager for punishment, eager to have [their] fate decided, because at last it becomes difficult for [them] to bear the weight of this assumed desperation."[21]

Later in his novels he would depict Europe, and with it contemporary Western culture—namely, all that had been accepted as authoritative ever since—similarly as hell. Siberia was hellish because it bore within its own self the embryo of the sacred; it was a place where horror was able to break out onto the surface *openly* and *immoderately*. Dostoyevsky saw Europe as being hellish because the self-imposed repressions of modern civilization were hellish: the repression of suffering, death, and the willingness for redemption. He also saw hell in Europe's everyday life, in its grayness, its habitude, in the average: this makes Dostoyevsky a demonic (or angelic) psychologist. "We've all become estranged from life, we're all cripples, every one of us, more or less. We've become so estranged that at times we feel some kind of revulsion for genuine 'real life,' and therefore we can't bear to be reminded of it."[22] The *colorful* Siberian hell stands in opposition to the *gray* European hell—that hell which appears in the twentieth century in the works of Kafka and Beckett, in Tarkovsky's *Stalker*, in impersonalized—because mechanized—destruction, and in self-oblivion, brought about by technology, and to all appearances definitive.

■

Luis Buñuel once noted (half jokingly) that the universality of faith had disappeared in the twentieth century because the church had so exaggerated the supposed horrors of hell that no one could take it seriously anymore. If now, at the beginning of the third millennium, we take a look back at the twentieth century, perhaps we can exempt the church from this accusation. The church did not exaggerate. Reality itself surpassed every possible imaginary depiction of hell. And then colored it gray. And this made hell even more frightening than ever before, when its proximity was indicated by tongues of flame, lakes of tar, and pitchforks. That was something you ran away from. But no one can do battle with grayness. Gray hell imperceptibly outstrips every possible imaginary picture and makes everything possible that can be imagined.

Everything — including the possibility of its own annihilation. European civilization has never judged itself to be as accomplished and highly refined as at the present moment, as the millennium approaches, giving rise to anxiety in many. And yet never has its existence been so threatened as it is now. It is as if we were approaching some kind of final, terrifying judgment. As if we were proceeding toward an apocalypse that will not be followed by apocatastasis.[23] This is the sign that God has definitively turned his gaze away from us. We all of us sense that. Never has humanity been so satisfied with its own self — like a spoiled and careless child, left to itself, allowed to do whatever it wishes. But that same child, when evening descends, having no idea of what to do with its freedom and fearful, is suddenly filled with anguish.

The evening twilight, "the eternal silence of the infinite spaces," filled Pascal with fear, the chill of a world that had lost its center caused Nietzsche to tremble; and Heidegger — perhaps as the last—put all his faith in a God, but with a bitterness that in and of itself indicates the frailty of his hope. But we have already become desensitized to the fears, the trembling, and the despair of the philosophers. What was earlier unimaginable has now come to pass. Our civilization has, it appears, definitively forgotten that its existence is deeply rooted in something over which there can be exercised no other power or influence. And yet it feels justified in its earthly (of course, first and foremost, technical) successes. It rejoices at what perhaps should lead it to tears—just like the effect of Hegel's statements on Dostoyevsky. Or at the very least, could lead to contemplation: Are we really proceeding on the best path?

This feeling of success can be so powerful that it can even divest God of his throne. The dethronement—in other words, secularization—has not taken place in a conspicuous fashion, but imperceptibly. We have murdered God with our ambition—an ambition which at the beginning might have even met with the approbation of God himself. And it is none other than our drive to find an answer for everything. When we began to seek solutions for things for which there are clearly no solutions, this ambition became transformed into hubris. In other words, it occurred when even transcendence itself turned into a practical question.

Contemporary civilization places all its trust in practical solutions, implicitly cordoning off anything that could potentially endanger its optimism. The many atrocities, however, are not merely operational disturbances; they are the reverse side of everything that modern civilization so blatantly admires. Hegel, in writing of the African *executioners*, reproached the Africans with the absence of civilization; Dostoyevsky, in connection to the same executioners, observed the refinement of civilization: "Haven't you noticed that the most refined blood shedders are almost always the most civilized gentlemen?" "The characteristics of the torturer exist in embryo in almost every man of to-day," Dostoevsky writes, reminiscing on Siberia; when, however, he notes that "the executioners have a very good time of it though. They have plenty of money, they are very well-fed and have vodka to drink," his words acquire an apocalyptic dimension, particularly when we correlate them to the experiences of the twentieth century. Walter Benjamin rightly said that "there is no document of civilization which is not at the same time a document of barbarism."[24] That adoration with which, at the end of the millennium, European civilization—still obstinately considering itself to be Christian—adulates technology can only be compared to its one-time adoration of God. In addition, following the example of Hegelian repression, it has allowed the means to become a goal, while crushing beneath itself its own adherents. We are in the midst of a world which is truly becoming devoid of all interstices, as well as one that can be surveilled in its totality, just as the Creator hoped. It bears the same godlike attributes, although it is characterized ever more by the absence of God— or rather, his non-presence.

"All depends on the next century," wrote Dostoyevsky in the nineteenth century.[25] The true victor of the twentieth century is technology: the "undivine" — namely, that worldly instrument "the divine goal" — is the only transcendence, ousting the human being from his or her own self. So cleverly has it achieved its victory that it has even endowed us with the illusion that instead of being its slave, we are instead the victor. This is the price we have paid for forgetting the cosmic character of our own being. And this forgetting, this true hell — the monotonous, gray hell — is not merely the demonic proliferation of technology. It is but a consequence, the result of the tragic wounding of the human spirit.

Buñuel saw the disappearance of traditional faith as occasioned by the exaggeratedly overembellished portrayals of hell. Really existing hell, on the other hand, is never as colorful as in fairy tales. Instead, it appears to be natural, sober, self-evident. It is something like the world of Hegel, the world to which Dostoyevsky returned after his Siberian exile. It was the only place he could go. A place bereft of every enchantment. When the entirety of existence, the cosmic whole is reduced to a world that can be technically manipulated — this is hell. It requires no devils, no tongues of flame leaping into the heights or lakes filled with boiling tar. All that it is needed is oblivion and the illusion that the confine of humanity is not constituted by the divine but by the tangible, and that the nourishment of the human spirit is not the impossible but the possible — monotonous beyond all measure, and rational.

THE GLOBE-SHAPED TOWER

The Tower of Babel at the Turn of the Millennium

"Almighty God, thou who holds all spirits in thy hands, deliver us from the Enlightenment [*Lumières*] and fatal arts of our fathers and give us back ignorance, innocence, and poverty, the sole goods that might create our happiness and which are precious in thy sight."[1] This supplication of Jean-Jacques Rousseau appeared in his *Discourse on the Sciences and Arts.* The young author, designating himself simply as "a citizen of Geneva," castigated European civilization with a hitherto unexperienced vehemence, and in doing so he was crowned with success: he was awarded first prize in the essay contest announced by the Academy of Dijon. This was in fact the first essay competition of the modern era, soon followed by others, continuing into our time.

Posterity has superbly vindicated those who were entrusted with making the decision in this very first essay contest. Following the publication of Rousseau's essay, it at once became the classical prototype for all subsequent civilizational critiques, and for two and a half centuries now it has served as a referential basis for those who oppose the idea of belief in progress, as well as those who support it. At the same time—and not incidentally—

it seems to have justified in advance the many announcements of prizes and competitions to follow. Rousseau's essay created a paradigm: from this point on, the various summons of academies, universities, and other institutions prompted those who participated to a critique of the prevailing civilizational conditions—even implicitly.

Reading the many questions, we feel as if we were listening to a great chorus. A chorus which sings flawlessly, but somehow its resonance feels out of tune, not so much to the ear as to the heart. From the accumulation of questions—sincerely well-intentioned, indisputably constructive, true, and at times excessively correct—a snare, nonetheless, seems to be delineated. For from 1750 on, it was *institutions* that were the guarantors for the received criticism, and it was precisely these *institutional operators*—the academies, universities, and scholarly societies, as well as journals—that encouraged their members to castigate the "instigators" while rendering their judgments on society, either openly or implicitly. And this is what makes the chorus sound a little out of tune. Is it a question of cultural "masochism"? Or the contrary: Would one of the preconditions of the functioning of society in the modern age be the necessity of integrating self-critique? and that the more globalized this critique, the more well-lubricated its functioning?

Perhaps this is true, but maybe not. More than two centuries have passed between Rousseau's time and ours. It is enough to merely read aloud his supplication above to see that when we compare the conditions of the age of the Enlightenment to those of the present day, then what is most conspicuous is the total lack of *naïveté* in our era compared to that of Rousseau. Or, to put it more cautiously: the naïveté of the eighteenth century was superseded by a completely different kind of naïveté. In the middle of the eighteenth century, it still seemed self-evident that anyone who had the audacity to criticize civilization might justifiably feel himself to be outside it. That is, the dialogue between the critics and the criticized appears to be hopeful. As Rousseau's supplication shows, prayer still had a chance. At the beginning of the third millennium, however, it now seems equally self-evident that *every* manifestation forms a part of the same global dialogue. Which means, in effect, that this ostensible dialogue is, in reality, a *monologue*. The eighteenth century was so variegated that the world itself seemed endless. The many different kinds of voices created the impression of an *opera*. Today, however, everything has contracted to such a degree that this dialogue is frequently rendered illusory, no matter how painful its absence may be. Instead of the rich strains of an opera, only an aria can be heard from the cacophony. The "world state," the advent of which was predicted by Ernst Jünger in 1960 in his *Der Weltstaat*,[2] is in formation—and in many respects it is reminiscent of the utopias of Thomas More or Tommaso Campanella. The eighteenth century still believed in these utopias, although the chance of their being realized was nonexistent. By contrast, in our age we no longer believe in them—but are closer to not only realizing them but even overtaking them.

My reference to utopias is not accidental. Questions oriented toward the optimal functioning of civilization always postulate the tacit acceptance of utopias on the part of those who answer them. Posing the question itself is a priori of a utopian nature, and it places its stamp upon the answer. This is so even when the answer appears to confirm the absurdity of utopias. And it is the decisive difference between our age and that of Rousseau. In the eighteenth century, trust in the gladdening fulfillment of history was still seen as being self-evident. Today, however, with the great redeeming ideologies behind us, historically speaking, it appears to be just as natural not to trust in any kind of utopia.

But isn't exactly this current state of oblivious uncertainty—gladdening and numbing us at the same time—the truly realized utopia? Did it come about when "activity with far-reaching consequences" became possible, to employ the expression of Anthony Giddens, the English sociologist—a condition he considers the true criterion of globalization, and one in which I see the evidence of the monologue that the civilization of today carries on with itself? To act with far-reaching consequences is equivalent to a self-vindication, everywhere present. A labyrinth of mirrors is in the process of being formed. Or, to employ a different metaphor: we are in the process of realizing the utopia of Babel; the tower is being constructed, but in this case it is in a spherical shape, for it is identical with the globe. Everyone is beginning to speak the same language, and across the world our sensibilities are open to conspicuously similar impressions. And so the meaning of human freedom itself must be interpreted anew. During the Enlightenment the pathos of freedom was granted strength and credibility because the age had a goal; its aspirations had an object which went beyond the given conditions and in relation to those was transcendent. Now, however, enclosed in our spherical tower, we seem to have abandoned all goals. Instead of conquering these goals as an object, it is they who have conquered us.

There are, of course considerable similarities between the age of Enlightenment and our own. The academicians of Dijon, creators of the essay contest, in posing the question of whether the restoration of the arts and sciences contributed to the purification of morals were not really bothering with questions of freedom. But the fact that they saw the fate of civilization as something that could be decided—and consequently a question which could be answered—shows that they too were proceeding from the hypothesis that civilizational fate is the function of human intelligence, free of prejudice, perception, and thought. Namely, at their disposal was an idea of freedom that more than anything else could be designated *unrestraint*. One of the most telling characteristics of secularization is the belief in the absolute rule of the *cogito*: this in and of itself is a radical diversion from the traditional basic societal and cultural stances—not only in traditional European culture, but for non-European cultures as well—in which the boundaries of the self and of thought are *not* determined by the individual human being. In such traditional cultures, these boundaries, as well as everything that lies beyond a person's own sphere of influence, are *suffered* by the person, in the original sense of that word. With the advent of secularization, the sense of human embeddedness within the cosmos—or the sense of one's being cast into the cosmos—was eliminated from civilization's range of vision. And thus the traditional concept of freedom metamorphized. To be free now meant that the human being wished unequivocally to be the master of not only his or her own self but of all of existence. *Cogito ergo sum* is the motto of secularization, as it were reversing the earlier formulation (which of course was never stated in these terms): *I am thought of, therefore I am.*

What is in play here is the much-mentioned rootlessness of the modern individual, which, however, at the time of the Enlightenment, the first academies, and their competitions, did not appear to be as problematic as it does more than two centuries on. On the contrary: never has *progress* ever seemed so guaranteed, the theory of which otherwise began to be delineated when Anne-Robert-Jacques Turgot came up with the idea of writing the history of human progress in advance. But the thought of progress never could have emerged if it had not been preceded by a delineated goal. In this way, the questions implicitly conformed to the answers. The eighteenth century was the century of *questioning* and investigation—it is no accident that so many academies were founded, one after the other, which then sought to justify their own existence by means of these essay contests, among other activities. This questioning was not born of the deep *wonder* that, according to Plato, is the true prerequisite of all philosophical questioning. Rather, it was a way of preparing a series of answers anticipated in advance. Those who were posing the questions wanted for the most part to hear their own answers echoed back from the responders.

To make the fate of civilization and culture the object of a question: this is as if we were stepping into a great laboratory. It can be dispiriting, but at the same time it is an invitation to adventure. And this is exactly what demonstrates the fundamental difference between the eighteenth century and the twenty-first. The thinkers of the Enlightenment, while increasingly placing the cognizable world within the field of investigation and intellectual contemplation, insisted that there was an exit out of this laboratory; it was their firm conviction that inherent to civilization is its own natural projection, untouched by intellect and reflection; freedom and autonomy may therefore be practiced further. They were guided by that belief, and the wording of their competition announcements was infused by the optimism that beyond the various phenomena of the world lay an underlying Meaning—a final and irrevocable Message. The influence of traditional European metaphysical thinking was palpable, though in a slightly altered fashion. The throne of God was occupied by Knowledge, and the pathos of final cognizability expelled the ultimate mystery. And yet knowledge and investigation still retained their transcendent character.

Looking back from a later perspective, particularly with regard to twentieth-century developments, we can see something deeply sympathetic and at the same time pathetic in all of this. The belief in Final Intellect and in Meaning Which Cannot Be Further Disassembled—the Enlightenment and its inheritance—creates a rather anachronistic impression today. And yet this was, in European history, the last large-scale attempt to preserve the achievements of the European metaphysical tradition. It lent the Enlightenment its characteristically transitory and Janus-like state. Enlightenment thinkers still believed in the possibilities of inquiry, whose precondition, as Nietzsche ascertained later on, was the acceptance of the existence of God. At the same time, they laid their own curious emphasis on human autonomy and not on God; with that they turned to the future. In other words, they held freedom to be a kind of unrestraint, and yet secretly, they did not sever the transcendental constraints of the human being.

Originally, the term *secularization* referred to the expropriation of church holdings. The secularization of the spirit, however, turned out to be much more complex. The spirit is what it is precisely because it cannot be expropriated: at the most the circumstances of its functioning can be hampered or corrupted. The Enlightenment thinkers, in remaining open to the metaphysical traditions, practiced religiosity in the traditional sense of the word; at the same time, given that they had seated the human being on God's throne, they simultaneously denied this very religiosity. This dichotomy is the true criterion of secularization. Secularization means the process of becoming worldly— a process that, however, is also accompanied by internal division and disunity. It becomes dominant when a culture experiences religion in an irreligious manner, living within a myth while believing in no myth at all. Secularization comes to pass when a given society has become captive to a situation, even though it is not willing or able to identify with it. The potential results of this inner discord were characterized by the poet William Blake: "Man must & will have Some Religion: if he has not the Religion of Jesus, he will have the Religion of Satan."[3]

If we are to designate the world that existed before the Enlightenment as traditional, and we designate the Enlightenment as secularized (due to the Janus-like tension within it), then I would be inclined to designate our contemporary world postsecular, or—using an intentionally absurd concept—*unipolar*. In the traditional world, *constraints* and *embeddedness* made the human being free. Secularization gave us the opportunity for *critical* thinking, but at the same time it presented us with the ambiguous endowment of the freedom of the struggle with *crisis* (an etymologically related word). The turn of the millennium— itself *unipolar*, globalized, spherically enclosed—has rendered freedom illusory, as it has attempted more and more to limit freedom to an acceptance of adaptation to circumstances that weigh upon us as a kind of doom. The fact that civilization, in our current age, continues to declare war ever more radically on every and any implicit manifestation of transcendence is a clear sign that it is managing its own Enlightenment inheritance badly.

For this reason, I feel that questions oriented toward the fate of culture and civilization, no matter how pertinent, thoughtful, or disturbing they may be, are anachronistic today. The Enlightenment was the only period in which the posing of such questions was natural. In earlier eras—and, moreover, in the earlier millennia of human history—there was no need for such comprehensive questions, embracing the whole of civilization. That constraint between human beings and the extant cosmos, nature, or God that surpassed them was seen as self-evident; these factors made it unimaginable a priori for humans to place themselves outside the universe, and to look back upon themselves as an object—the object of investigations. Neither the radical differences of the globe's cultures, nor, within Europe, the universalism of Christianity ever made an all-homogenizing viewpoint necessary or even possible. And in the eras following the Enlightenment, particularly in our own, the posing of such questions seems at least as useless as in those pre-Enlightenment eras. This is not because of the implicit existence of this transcendental constraint, but because of the complete denial of such a restraint. We can term contemporary civilization the world-empire that has attained immanence (among other things), and this has led to a radical change in the stipulations surrounding these acts of *questioning* and *answering*.

Is there a way out of this situation? Is it possible to be freed from that globe-shaped tower, which humanity, despite the divine prohibition, has once again built for itself, imitating the Tower of Babel? Moreover, instead of having got closer to God, humanity has definitively lost sight of him.

The Tower of Babel embodied the desire for immediacy. The image of the Tower manifests the most human of demands. Because of what else could this final immediacy be composed than a confrontation, a union with the transcendent, which bequeaths to us the fullest experience of freedom? And yet, at the same time its construction proved a culpable deed — although according to the mythic origins of the story, God did not raze it to the ground, and he did not scatter the human beings in all directions speaking all different kinds of tongues. European cultural tradition confirms that in not granting human beings the possibility of the *direct* experience of transcendence (for God was hidden away from human beings), he was in fact preserving transcendence for them. This enigmatic nature belongs to transcendence — its fascination originates from its unknowability. But it awakens a thirst in the human spirit for something that seems unconquerable. It is drawn by that which it cannot, externally, see.

How does our age relate to the Enlightenment? Does it carry out its volitions consistently? Or, on the contrary, does it turn away from the Enlightenment, following a path from which the thinkers of the Enlightenment would recoil? For some, the first radical steps toward building the Tower of Babel of today began not in our own age but during the Enlightenment. For example, Heiner Müller, the German playwright, has written: "The Enlightenment was an attempt to build the Tower of Babel anew. The thinkers of the Enlightenment thought that they had discovered a universal language in that of reason. In this way, through rationality, they suppressed every other language."[4] Clearly, Müller perceives only one of the faces of the two-faced Enlightenment — namely, the one that looks ahead to the future. In contrast, others, observing the heroic endeavors of the Enlightenment thinkers, come to the conclusion that what has ensued in our days is precisely the opposite of the spirit of the Enlightenment. Jean Baudrillard observes the face of the Enlightenment that looks toward the past when he claims that this heroic age of critical thinking reached an end as "this ideal and seemingly necessary relationship between the concept and reality would, at all events, be destroyed today." The title of the work from which this quotation is drawn is itself revealing: *The Perfect Crime*. Baudrillard sees the end of the twentieth century as the era of realized criminality, just as the young Georg Lukács, in his *Theory of the Novel* (1916), perceived the century's beginning to be—and he discovers the complete absence of transcendence as the greatest proof of criminality: "The aura of our world is no longer sacred. We no longer have the sacred horizon of appearances, but that of the absolute commodity."[5]

Baudrillard senses the absence of the sacred—that is, of transcendence—in our world, and he accuses globalization of estranging us from God. His colleague Paul Virilio came to a different view, based on the same phenomena and analyses: in his estimation, it is precisely the complete renunciation of transcendence which can be viewed as an undertaking that—as it were, via a detour—wishes to smuggle this lost transcendence back into human consciousness. He explicitly judges research into cyberspace as "a search for God, or an attempt to become God."[6]

Which one of them is right? It is hard to decide—just as it is hard to decide whether we should regard the civilization of our age as a panic-stricken flight from transcendence, a final and definitive *reckoning with tradition* but also with two-faced secularization, or, on the contrary, as an overture that, as it ever more conspicuously breaks with European tradition as a whole, nonetheless prepares a new heroic age, as yet unsuspected, which should, according to Ernst Jünger, be designated *titanic*. In observing the debates of the 1980s and 1990s following the collapse of East European communism, it becomes ever more obvious that a deep divide separates our age not only from the age of tradition but from the age of secularization as well. Time has definitively lost all its references to beyond-time; history has at its disposal ever fewer dimensions that are beyond-historical. The civilization of the current age ever more spectacularly tries to arrange its affairs while refuting all forms of transcendence and declaring war on time and space.

Many have claimed to discover the *end of history* in this rupture. But if history has not exactly ended, it is nonetheless certain that this rupture has placed the entirety of Western culture in a new light. For all of human history, there never existed an age which renounced transcendence as radically as our own. Every previous human culture discovered the roots of the human being in the nonhuman, and in this way made humans interested in those states that precede their birth and follow their death. Humanity felt immeasurable responsibility for something that it was possibly not even directly involved with. In contrast to this, our own civilization, as it ever more adeptly builds its own Tower of Babel—the spherical tower—registers the renunciation of transcendence as a victory. From the destruction, now seemingly inevitable, of the environment, to the clash of cultures, everything confirms this. Humanity today has reached a stage of un-bounded irresponsibility.

Divine excess—which previously in European culture was the pledge of freedom—has been transformed into human excess. And this has made freedom itself problematic. At the beginning of the third millennium, *genuine* freedom and the *illusion* of freedom have definitively changed places. In contrast with the era of the Enlightenment and the first great essay competitions, today we are inclined to see ourselves as free when our vulnerability (our entangled state, our irresponsibility) is excessive. Everything about our current civilization suggests that we are only free when the world and its circumstances have removed from us the burden of our own existence. European tradition used to teach the opposite of this. It used to teach that the hope of genuine freedom was granted when this burden once again weighed upon us. When we were confronted with not only our everyday existence but the existence which preceded our birth and that which will follow our death. Of course, at such times a person might be inclined to see him- or herself as lost—such a person might justifiably feel cut off from history and from his or her surroundings. However, as Simone Weil writes in her study "The Love of God and Affliction," these are precisely the most hope-filled moments. At such times, the universe is once again conjured back to its previous state of enigma and mystery.

Such moments and experiences, however, fall outside the horizon of the civilization of our current age. It is difficult to address them. This is not because they are closed to dialogue, but because they stand out like a xenolith from the current ocean of universal monologue. They cannot be enclosed in the spherical Tower of Babel. In order to draw closer to these moments, what is needed is hope for a precept which is beyond every institution, and which can never be enclosed by the web of words that serve them. These moments, in all their seeming anarchy, strike me as being the most constructive. They destroy while building up: like the winds or the sands, they beat away and they erode the Tower of Babel. They help to demolish so that something else might be built, something for which we still have no words but which will be in any event the guarantor of freedom.

BELIEF IN THE DEVIL

Goethe, when just eighteen years old, wrote, in one of his letters of the fall of 1767: "Wir sind unsere eigenen Teufel, wir vertreiben uns aus unserem Paradiese" (We are our own devils, we expel ourselves from paradise).[1] Only a philologist could tell us if Goethe already knew about Faust and his pact with the devil. In any event, though, he had already concluded a pact with the devil—his own. But this pact did not mean capitulation. On the contrary: the one who begins to suspect that the devil resides in his innermost being has already taken the first step toward expelling him. The young Goethe suspected that the devil did not reside in fiery hell, deep beneath the earth's surface, but that his true terrain was the soul. It is no wonder that Goethe almost immediately came upon the figure of Faust. A few years after the letter quoted above, in the early 1770s, he was already working on his *Urfaust*, the preferred theme of which was *diese Seelen Noth*—the soul's needs. And in what is this need, this Noth manifested? "Am I not homeless and a fugitive? / A monster without aim or peace, / roaring like a cataract from crag to crag, / with greedy rage toward the abyss?"[2]

In the subsequent versions as well, Faust sees himself as an *Unmensch* (monster, nonhuman). Why? Because he is unable to settle down. He yearns for certain things (family, home, fame, acceptance), and yet when the slightest possibility of them appears to quiver on the horizon, he flees. He feels homeless even on a metaphysical level, for within him two souls reside. He is a being eternally tossed back and forth between the nearer and the farther shore, deeply entangled in the ancient European problem of the sensual and the nonsensual. What makes him an Unmensch is that his soul has "split into two." This is a truly demonic situation. The word for "two" in the Indo-European languages can be traced back to the root *duon* (Greek *dúo*, Latin *duo*, German *zwei*, English *two*, and so on), as well as to its previous Indo-German auxiliary form, the root **dis-* (apart, asunder; see also Latin *dis-*, Greek *dia-*, German *zer-*, and so on). This etymology also gave rise to the various words for devil: *diabolos, diabolus, Teufel, devil, diavolo* . . . The state of being torn in two is embodied in the character of Mephistopheles. The battle is internal, taking place in the soul. The stakes are nothing less than for Faust to find a place in which he will no longer feel himself to be homeless, unhoused — *Unbehauste.* He is in need of *Heimat* (a home) so that his existence will no longer be *unheimlich* (uncanny, eerie). In this case home is not a building but a state in which the sensual and the nonsensual can meet, and where a man can feel that his life is nested in a greater coherence lying beyond societal, political, and economic — that is, human, constructed — structures, and which might best be designated by the term *cosmic.* Goethe, at the end of *Faust,* wished to plan and build a home for the spirit.

The activity of planning (*Entwerfen*) always suggests a sequence of practical solutions. The final goal, however, is the creation of a home for the spirit where this cosmic coherence can be glimpsed and experienced in its own transparency and purity. That is why Faust could only say to the moment in which transparency would be glimpsed: "Linger—You are so wonderful!"[3]

The act of design is one of the great topoi of European culture. If God is the master builder, the human being can surely be nothing else, for God created humans in his own image. Humans can do nothing else, therefore, than plan, whether they keep the world of the spirit in view and build or turn away from it and destroy—which, of course, they also understand as a form of building. In 1485, a century before Faust stepped onto the stage of European civilization, Giovanni Pico della Mirandola published a treatise titled *De dignitate hominis*. What is the goal of man?—he posed the question—and he answered with a beautiful parable. God is the cardinal master builder who planned the world, then built it, and he populated all its regions. The world was already prepared; it stood like a colossal, well-designed church building, but there was no one to love its beauty or to admire its greatness. And so God created man and said to him: All the other creatures are obligated to live constrained by laws, and they are subjugated to their own determined natures. You, however, are different, for, as he said,

> But you, constrained by no limits, may determine your nature for yourself. . . . We have made you neither of heaven

nor of earth, neither mortal nor immortal, so that you may, as the free and extraordinary shaper of yourself, fashion yourself in whatever form you prefer. It will be in your power to degenerate into the lower forms of life, which are brutish. Alternatively, you shall have the power, in accordance with the judgment of your soul, to be reborn into the higher orders, those that are divine.[4]

What is the task of man, asks Pico della Mirandola. To admire the Great Design. Man can, however, practice this in such a way that, like God, he can invent, plan, and construct his own life. But there is no one to help him with this. It is no coincidence that the God of Pico della Mirandola warns man: What you will shape your own life into, as well as whether you will be able to preserve the world in its own perfection or, on the contrary, destroy it with dogged labor all depends on you, your own will and your own decisions.

Faust also plans and invents things. And all the while he continually searches for his own self. No matter where he steps or what he does, everything around him is put into question. Behind every one of his successes lurks failure; yet the ensuing failures are all immersed in good intentions. He nurses and cultivates his own spirit in a sovereign manner, while destroying the lives of others; with the help of Mephistopheles, he produces the kinds of pseudo-solutions in the court of the Emperor that many contemporary financiers would welcome, but at the same time he is also prepared to help humanity selflessly. It is now more than two centuries since he became one of the founding myths of our culture; everything that can be designated European is present in Faust in a condensed fashion: his openness toward the spirit, as well as his temptation to deny the spirit. He is as much a *Mensch* as he is an *Unmensch*. That Great Plan, the creation of a home, hovers like a vision before him—a hope inextricable from European culture itself. At the same time, the repudiation of this home or even its destruction is not alien to him. He is haunted by immoderation, the circumvention of morals, stubbornness, and metaphysical blindness as well. He would truly stop being an Unmensch if he could only move beyond his own duality. And then he would be saving not only himself but European culture as well.

Can humanity help preserve the world in its own perfection, or do we destroy it with our persistent labors? This question of Pico della Mirandola's was never as pertinent as during the turn of the eighteenth to the nineteenth century, when Goethe's Faust stepped onto the stage for the first time. In the seventeenth century, the English referred to the devil as "Nobody" (making reference to his lack of a body, among other things). The devil began to be a bodiless being, and God soon followed suit. At the end of the eighteenth century, William Blake referred to God as "Nobodaddy."[5] God and the devil died more or less at the same time—at some point toward the end of the eighteenth century. More precisely speaking, neither of them died, but both took their leave of their traditional metaphysical theater. The Good lost all its transcendental constraints and became ever more conspicuously limited to concepts of utility, advantage, and prag-matism—that which could be attained and planned for quick success. Whereas Evil was now, understandably, anything im-peding what general belief proclaimed as advantageous and useful. The final horizon became the tangible—what could be quickly realized. Space began to shrink, and with it so did time as well. Eduard, in Goethe's *Elective Affinities*, states: "It is most disagreeable that one cannot now-a-days learn a thing once for all and have done with that. Our forefathers could keep to what they were taught when they were young; but we have, every five years, to make resolutions with them, if we do not wish to drop altogether out of fashion."[6] It is no wonder that the globe itself began to shrink.

Faust is perhaps the last emblematic figure of European cul-ture who, at the end of the eighteenth century, represented his own endangered mentality without ever losing sight of the Great Plan as envisioned by Pico della Mirandola. These were the last moments when the spirit of European culture was still not yet confined to a defensive position. Such can hardly be said of the representative figures who were to follow Faust. The ambitious protagonists of Balzac, for example, are propelled by a single goal; the three Karamazov brothers split apart a former unity in three different ways; Josef K. looks at history from a position well beyond it; Adrian Leverkühn revokes the most significant Euro-pean achievements; Imre Kertész's Gyuri Köves, the protago-nist of his novel *Fatelessness*,[7] observes what is left of Europe, orphaned like a test animal launched into outer space . . . This list of protagonists could be continued according to one's own predilections. But they have something in common: all are engaged in rearguard combat. They are the representatives of a culture who are desperately seeking to discover how they could once again render operational something that came to an end sometime around the turn of the eighteenth century—how they could once again save that civilization which, from one generation to another, ever more visibly marched to its own decline. In other words, how to invent Europe again—that wondrous great contrivance, depicted so superbly by Dante, which could have been the inspiration of Faust, even though he saw how narrow its horizons had become. The ideas and attempts to reopen the old horizons have been surprisingly numerous over the course of the past two centuries; what is not so surprising, perhaps, is that none of them has brought forth a reassuring solution. On the contrary: the greater the fervent planning, the greater the catastrophes which then follow. The twentieth century was not only the most developed century of European history, registering itself as the peak of unsurpassable progress; it was simultaneously undoubtedly European history's most horrific and brutal century.

We are managing badly with the intellectual traditions of Europe. Together, all of us. On October 17, 1930, Thomas Mann held a public lecture in Berlin—continually disrupted by the goons from the Sturmabteilung (SA)—titled "Deutsche Ansprache" (Address to the Germans); its subtitle was "Ein Apell an die Vernunft" (An Appeal to Reason). In this address, Mann called his audience's attention to two phenomena that, in his view, gave warning of the betrayal of the spirit. He designated the first *verschwärmte Bildungsbarbarei*—"fanatical culture-barbarism," with its favorite mottos *rassisch, völkisch, bündisch, heldisch* (race-, folk-, tribal, heroic) always prefixed to other words. The other phenomenon he designated *primitiv-massen-demokratische Jahrmarktsroheit*—"primitive mass-democratic fairground-coarseness," which he saw as spreading to the entire world, and which similarly precipitated the decline of culture, spirit, art, and ideas. Its most conspicuous manifestations were "the adventurous development of technology with its triumphs and catastrophes, the noise and sensation of sporting events, the frantic overpayment and adoration bestowed upon 'stars' attracting millions, boxing matches with awards in the millions and hordes of spectators."[8]

Thomas Mann could not have known in 1930 what was going to happen in Germany and in Europe. But still, he was convinced that this double manifestation of the betrayal of the spirit was laying the ground for some kind of barbarity. Eight decades have gone by since then. Today, Mann's thoughts—formulated in the 1930s—seem equally valid. There is presently no European country today where the verschwärmte Bildungsbarbarei could not gain ground, and where the rassisch and völkisch phantasmagorias could not move crowds, even amid the secured framework of existing legislation. And thanks to new media, whose existence Mann never could have anticipated, there is no European country to which this primitiv-massendemokratische Jahrmarktsroheit has not penetrated, forcing the spirit everywhere back into an ever more narrow quarantine. The barbarity that Mann envisioned has not reached an end. When Imre Kertész was awarded the Nobel Prize in 2002, he uttered, in his acceptance speech, perhaps the most disillusioned of statements: "Nothing has happened since Auschwitz that could reverse or refute Auschwitz."[9] What once counted as culture in Europe, which was so variegated, multilayered, temperate, dynamic, morally rigorous, metaphysically open—namely, intellectual and spiritual—now survives only in its own remnants. Everywhere one comes upon only fragments: in meeting with them, a person is lightly touched by something that has passed forever, and at the most has enough strength to awaken feelings of nostalgia. Nostalgia, however, is a defensive feeling, always overshadowed by a distressingly rational pragmatism, in the same way that so many beautifully preserved medieval or baroque European cities are trussed round by the highways encircling them, beyond which begins the concrete jungle interspersed with shopping centers and tower blocks.

In 1944, the Swiss philosopher Denis de Rougemont—at the same time that Thomas Mann, in his *Doktor Faust*, was battling with the devil—dedicated an entire book to the devil: *La Part du Diable* (The Devil's Part). In this work, he writes that one of the chief stratagems of the devil is to make us believe that he no longer exists. For de Rougemont, the devil in our days would take the form of a liberal intellectual "who does not believe in the Devil." And yet the devil does not cease to exist because people do not believe in him. Young Goethe was one of the last thinkers to believe in him. As I quoted at the beginning of this chapter: "We are our own devils, we expel ourselves from paradise." Goethe believed that the devil actually existed; this helped him struggle against his own devil. But also because he believed this, the fate of the Great Plan was contingent upon him. But contingent only in this way, in the past tense—because if Goethe were to be resurrected today, he too would just wave it away. Mephistopheles, however, for lack of a challenge, would be greatly disappointed that things had been made too easy for him.

HAPPINESS AND MELANCHOLY

Melancholia and happiness. Two engaging concepts: whenever either word is uttered, everyone nods. They have the effect of an oasis in the desert: they promise an end to the monotony of the everyday, or at the least an interruption. Who does not yearn after happiness; who would not agree that there is something about melancholy that beautifies the everyday? Both promise diversion, refreshment, accentuated responsiveness. A rest from the daily grind.

Words can intimate much. But when they are realized, is that really cause for unalloyed joy? Is it not more likely that— while speaking admiringly both of melancholia and of happiness—in actuality we arrange our daily lives and in fact our entire lifespan so as to avoid them altogether? We praise them loudly, but in the depths of our consciousness we are afraid of them, preferring the monotony of everyday life. We may consider ourselves to be either melancholic or happy, but this melancholy and this happiness have suspiciously little to do with what were identified as melancholia and happiness for millennia in European culture. What changed? The answer is that the metaphysical age came to an end; and with it the ambitious demands that had characterized European tradition (itself built on Judeo-Christian as well as Greek and Roman traditions), at least until the beginning of the twentieth century also died out. History lost its metaphysical bearings. And yet humanity, as Leszek Kołakowski writes, can never be freed from its homesickness for transcendence and metaphysics.[1] Because of our consciousness of our own mortality, if for no other reason, we are a priori creatures doomed to metaphysics. A person today who tried to vindicate the claims of melancholia or happiness in the classical sense would have to turn away from the entirety of the contemporary age. Namely, in our melancholia and desire for happiness, the experience of our own vulnerability to mortality and death will become perceptible. Herein is offered a kind of metaphysical initiation. Today, however, this has become one of our great taboos.

But if melancholia and happiness are nonetheless still engaging concepts, this tells us that their meaning has been modified. What has changed?

■

"Le Bonheur est une idée neuve en Europe": Happiness is a new idea in Europe.

Many mottos—rallying cries, slogans, shibboleths—were being pronounced in Europe's modern age. From the time of the French Revolution on, we can speak of the age of mottos: never before had they multiplied in such measure, to such a degree that each slogan began to serve as a kind of compass. Live by my motto, and you will never go wrong! The motto, like a phosphorescent buoy, designates an idea on the sea of thoughts; nothing simpler than to follow its lead. From the beginning, the great mottos of the eighteenth century functioned like the advertisements of today. It is difficult to call them into question. Either you completely accept them, or you turn your back on them. They are not suitable for dialogue or discussion. They are ideological formations. Even the concept of ideology itself was born at the time of the Enlightenment: Antoine Destutt de Tracy created the word *idéologie* toward the end of the eighteenth century.

It is quite possible that the idea for the word *idéologie* occurred to Destutt de Tracy when the motto of Louis de Saint-Just quoted above had been pronounced for the first time. "Le Bonheur est une idée neuve en Europe."[2] Saint-Just announced this on March 3, 1794, as part of his speech to the Convention in Paris, the title of which speaks for itself: "Rapport sur le mode d'exécution du décret contre les ennemis de la Révolution, fait au nom du comité de salut public" (Report on the Manner of Execution of the Decree Against the Enemies of the Revolution, Made on Behalf of the Committee of Public Safety).[3] Happiness was already a concept that had to be protected, especially from its enemies, the enemies of the Revolution. It was something that had to be fought for, just as believers in the Revolution, at its height, had been fighting all across Paris and France.

As the night of September 2, 1792, turned to dawn, pitched battles continued to be waged beneath the apartment windows of the writer Restif de la Bretonne. These too had erupted at one revolutionary's command; it thoroughly roused de la Bretonne's fantasy on that evening as he heard it yelled out beneath his window:

Long live death![4]

This was as much of a high-sounding motto as "Le Bonheur est une idée neuve en Europe" of Saint-Just, who, at that time, had about a year and a half left before his own execution in 1794. He issued the motto of happiness only to fall prey to other mottos issued by other revolutionaries, who were also fighting for happiness. We cannot exclude the possibility that deep down inside he agreed with this development—just as a century and a half later the victims of Stalin praised the generalissimo as they stood before the firing squad. That is to say, if happiness has crystallized into a motto, then it must be realized at all costs. Even at the cost of the unhappiness of others. Even believers in private joy may be sacrificed at the altar of collective joy. Happiness, once it becomes an ideological imperative, casts a dark shadow over those who do not comply with its ideology. The shadow cast is not that of unhappiness but the shadow of annihilation.

A few years earlier, in his "Ode to Joy," Schiller perhaps involuntarily sketched out this duality which later was to play itself out with such tragic implications. At the beginning of the "Ode," he evokes joy and happiness as a divine sanctuary, its universal starry vault looming above all mortals. Beneath the roof of this tent, everyone will find a companion, a friend, a faithful spouse. Not everyone, however, is capable of or has the desire to take part in this great ensemble of *liberté*, *fraternité*, and *égalité*. What is to be done with these people? In a rather surprising fashion, Schiller's answer to this does not conform with what one might have expected from him based on his dramas and other poetic works. He does not offer the deniers a helping hand, nor does he call for their acceptance. On the contrary—those who cannot integrate into this joyous collective can, weeping, take their leave:

> Who the noble prize achieveth,
> Good friend of a friend to be;
> Who a lovely wife attaineth,
> Join us in his jubilee!
> Yes—he too who but one being
> On this earth can call his own!
> He who ne'er was able, weeping
> Stealeth from this league alone![5]

The question remains of where these "non-adherents" could go if happiness and joy are the roof of the tent of stars covering all, a universal canopy looming above all of us. There is only one place for them to go—into the void. And here we can observe, deep within the heart of *collectivism*, the desire to exclude, for whatever strives for universality will inevitably place into parentheses, regard as null, and even wish to annihilate whatever stands on the side of *individual* well-being.

■

Happiness, once it has issued a set of postulates for people to fulfill, then acquires a moral character. In the above-mentioned speech, Saint-Just equated the love of happiness with the love of virtue, and in doing so he was perpetuating an eighteenth-century tradition beginning with Shaftesbury, who held virtue as the path to happiness. The degree to which this path could be sabotaged is amply demonstrated by the fate of Heinrich von Kleist. As a diligent student of Enlightenment doctrines, Kleist gave his first treatise on happiness, written in the spring of 1799, the title "Essay on the Sure Way to Find Happiness." Happiness, in his essay (which is rather naive in tone), is a function of conscious choice: any of us in possession of a mind and consciousness can direct our life so that the surety of our happiness will never be shattered by anything. The prerequisite for happiness is for us never to give any space to instinct, to those domains unconquerable by rationality—namely, to all that which, in the history of European culture, was for the most part associated with darkness and which, as nothing could ever illuminate it, led to deep sorrow, melancholy, and despair. How could sadness and melancholy be avoided? If we always came to the correct conclusions and did not allow ourselves to be led astray. If we are capable of that, then not only will we be happy, "we shall see through the secrets of the physical and moral world, at least up to the point where an eternal veil covers it—that much is obvious."[6]

For the young Kleist, that "eternal veil" only served to conceal the presence of God from us—not unlike Schiller's heavenly vault of stars. The thought that was to occur ten years later to the philosopher Friedrich Wilhelm Joseph Schelling (in his study on human freedom) did not, however, occur to Kleist: namely, that the fabric of this veil is woven from eternal gloom—presented in Schelling's essay as a given fact. Kleist's concept of happiness is restricted to the realms which can be perceived by consciousness and the mind; it is a function of virtue. Ultimately, he considers it a postulate applicable to everyone. In his view, happiness is something like the Kantian categorical imperative: it can be demanded of anyone at any time. And whoever does not satisfy this universally valid postulate is not only behaving irrationally but is not even worthy of membership in human society.

The command to "be happy at all costs" is so tyrannical that nobody can internally identify with it. Kleist surely could not. He must have soon come to the realization that he was incapable of actualizing what he himself considered "happiness." Two years after his "Essay," at the beginning of his so-called Kantian crisis, he wrote to his sister, Ulrike, in a letter dated February 5, 1801: "You do not know how my world appears from within," after which he complains of the indescribability of his inner state: "I always have a feeling as of dread, therefore, when I am on the point of baring my heart to someone, not because the nakedness would embarrass, but rather because I cannot show *everything*, simply *cannot*, and must fear being misunderstood because of this fragmentation." Then comes the tragic recognition: "Oh, you do not know, Ulrike, how shaken I often am to my innermost being. . . . Ah, my dear Ulrike, I am not suited to human company, it is a sad truth, but a truth nonetheless." A month and a half later, on March 22, 1801, he writes for the first time to his fiancée, Wilhelmine von Zenge, of the origin of his crisis: "I recently became familiar with the more recent so-called Kantian philosophy." Then, in order to render his despair palpable, he employs the example of green glass: "If everyone saw the world through green glasses, they would be forced to judge that everything they saw *was* green, and never could be sure whether their eyes saw things as they really are, but did not add something of their own to what they saw. And so it is with our intellect." Then he gives voice to this despairing recognition: "My one, my highest goal has sunk from sight, and I have no other."[7]

Kleist had sunk into deep despondency. He was forced to confront the bankruptcy of the rational virtue and philosophy of happiness of the Enlightenment in terms of the formation of his own personal fate. Ten years later, this sense of breakdown was to culminate in his suicide. In the meantime, however, he wrote immortal stories and dramas, the theme of which is invariably the unrealizability of happiness. Metaphorically speaking, one could say that he was incapable of sustaining his own rationally interpreted concept of happiness—it made him a writer, then caused his death. He had been banished into that void where Schiller sent all those incapable of subordinating themselves to the collective. The new idea of happiness which had been propagated by Saint-Just drove Kleist to his death. But we can hardly suppose that it made those who remained among the living too happy either.

■

Happiness is a new idea in Europe, announced Saint-Just. He was mistaken. Happiness in Europe was and is a very ancient idea. If there was something new in it, then it was that Saint-Just had pronounced for the first time that happiness had to be "purged" of melancholy, liberated from every gloom. Earlier in the history of Europe, the two—melancholy and happiness—had always stood in close relation to each other. Indeed, the first attempts to separate them occurred in the eighteenth century, with happiness raised up as a "distilled" concept, freed from all "disturbing" elements. This was the only formulation of happiness suitable for *ideological* interpretation. It was first at the time of the French Revolution that happiness became mandatory, but it was also to become so in the twentieth century, not only during the period of the two great totalitarian systems but after their demise as well, within the framework of the subsequent, our own globalizing world system—a system in which, first and foremost, one must be happy. The chief command is that of happiness (inseparable, as a rule, from hedonism); the second command, however, is the banishment of all elements which may cause disturbance to happiness, first and foremost melancholy and gloom.

In a rather curious fashion, the more ubiquitous the command "Be happy!" becomes, the more the quantity of unhappiness on the globe seems to increase. Not only because from time to time—particularly within the two great twentieth-century totalitarianisms—people were obligated to be happy by means of force but also because if something is repressed, it will surely return in intensified quantities. Melancholy, which Schelling referred to as the "gloomy veil," not only in earlier times covered the light, it opened our eyes to something which by far and away surpasses our competence: the frailty of human life which can never be abrogated. A human being receives life without ever having asked for it, and then loses it as well without being asked for his or her consent. Melancholy, of course, does not only help a person with the perception of this frailty and helplessness. It also helps us see that our lives are nested within a much larger coherence, one which could be described in many ways. It could be designated God, or Existence—it could even be called the Void—but in any event it is something which, in its own inconceivability, is much stronger than any one personal life we could call our own. If a given culture (such as our own) does everything in its power to banish melancholy, or at the least seeks to render it "harmless," then not only does it deal with melancholy in an irresponsible fashion, it also seeks to deprive human beings of the experience of transcendence surpassing their own lives, depriving them of the perception that humans, no matter how great, no matter how able, are anything but omnipotent beings. The persistent lack of transcendent experience causes unhappiness; and every attempt to stop up this lack with our command to "Be happy!"—no matter with what variations, confirming universal access to material goods—is futile. That kind of unhappiness is not the same thing as melancholy. Melancholy assists us in attaining deeper realization; in contrast, mere unhappiness, as it were, empties us, makes us apathetic, deprives us of our own inherent creative energy. Melancholy can even animate; unhappiness exclusively frustrates.

Imre Kertész once wrote an essay whose title, "The Unhappy Twentieth Century," is very revealing. In this essay, he wrote:

> Who cannot see that democracy cannot or does not wish to be equal to its own established value system: it has never engraved its inviolable laws onto a new stone tablet, no one has prescribed the ideals for which it would be worthwhile for us to live. No one draws the boundaries, so democracy itself has become so malleable, so "democratized," that there is nothing that cannot fit within its limits; it reacts with mass hysteria and symptoms of political insanity to the most trifling signs of crisis, exactly like someone suffering from paranoia in his dotage, no longer capable of applying rational replies to the simplest demands of his environs. It is always being suggested to us that our redemption is contained within economic upswings, and that the solution lies in politics, although the problems of our world are only partially economic in nature, and as far as politics is concerned—at least since the collapse of the last totalitarian empire—the world has become undefinable and informulable, simply because political concepts have become chaotic.

Kertész most emphatically does not speak of fascism or Stalinism in this passage, but of modern democratic mass societies, in which the chief reality is made up of "economicism, capitalism, and the pragmatic lack of ideals . . . an alternative world, and in any event, one without transcendence, where there is no longer any accession to the accursed or the promised land." Accursed or promised—no matter which, both are similar in opening a person's eyes to something which can be regarded in a kind of amazed devotion. And Kertész mentions happiness in this context as well. If the entirety of the twentieth century, including the beginning of the twenty-first century, is characterized by unhappiness, then happiness itself is what would be the most anachronistic of all in this modern age with its pursuit of happiness: "And so the thought of happiness is related to the thought of creation and everything, which does not include the state of static rest, the peacefulness of ruminating cattle. On the contrary: the demand of happiness presumably inflicts the gravest of inner struggles upon human beings, one in which they must measure their own selves according to a set of vast criteria, so that the divinity present within each one will, as it were, raise up the fallible person to its own self."[8]

Kertész associates the recognition of this inner divinity with happiness. But he could just as well have associated it with melancholy—as many others have done for millennia. "Ay, in the very temple of Delight / Veil'd Melancholy has her sovran shrine," wrote John Keats in "Ode on Melancholy." For melancholia indicates the intense presence of the transcendent, just as happiness does—but accompanied by other omens. While experiencing the transcendent, that which (in the language of the traditional cultures of Europe) was referred to as the "divine" materializes in the human being. At such times, it is as if God has come to life, and humanity begins to feel its own self as divine. This inner god is resurrected in such moments of happiness; it "approaches." In moments of melancholy, this god begins to dissipate, is on the verge of departure, and yet remains animate enough so that his effect nonetheless makes itself felt. When, however, the divine presence is fully alive, and neither approaches nor departs but is simply present, then the person is filled with a kind of feeling or sense in which melancholy and happiness cannot be distinguished from each other. In the terminology of European tradition this was known as either *shock* or *purification* (catharsis). These are the moments of presence. The Latin word, *praesens*, in addition to signifying the present tense of verbs, also referred to the might of the deities. In antiquity, one spoke of presence only when referring to these gods and heroes. Namely, *presence* offers a sense of the divine: in the moment when we experience our own temporally unique presence, we are torn away from the pressure of surrounding circumstances. Maps, compasses, or milestones merely betray where one is in terms of location; they do not indicate whether one is *present*. Presence is not a state which can be physically registered. Instead, it is something like an emanation, which, like a glance or a smile that has reached its goal, is capable of creating a spherically enclosed world. It is no accident that in modern industrial mass societies, presence defined as such is taken to be a disturbing factor precisely because it refutes the importance of what is considered, in modern societies, to be the most important: the force of circumstances.

Presence, understood in this way, contains two aspects: melancholy and happiness. Within both of them resides a deeply archaic, subversive character: both these aspects subtract a person from the pressure of the collective, leaving him to himself. In the case of melancholy, this is particularly manifest: the melancholic precisely falls into melancholia because he sees that no one will remove the weight of his own existence from his shoulders. And so he perceives that he is completely alone in existence. The melancholic cannot find anything to grasp on to, feeling that existence has cast him out from his own self. Anyone who is truly a melancholic will perceive the unknown face contained in all things. He will feel an eternal homesickness for the unknown region this face is turned toward.

This unknown region lies beyond every border. And in modern society, it is neither his sadness nor his bad mood which cannot be forgiven in the melancholic, but rather that in his soul he has stepped across the boundaries integrated without exception in a perfectly globalized world. In other words, one of the prerequisites for any human collectivity is that those who are part of it must bind themselves to its restraints; they must respect the borders. To step across these borders is, in every respect, antithetical to the spirit of the collective. This applies to melancholy as well. And yet if this is indeed the case, then why can melancholy be designated a kind of positive state, without which the world is truly impoverished? The reason is that when a person steps across these borders he will come upon the inconceivable fundament of his own existence. When speaking of these boundary-crossings, we might be inclined to postulate that the experience of god also comes into play: for if god wishes to appear there is certainly no border which can hold him back.

The god, however, who makes his presence felt to the crosser of boundaries does not only bring tranquility. In the course of the experience of the divine or godly, the unbounded suddenly breaks through into life; something which casts a person out from his own self. The unbounded is not to be found within the "void" beyond existence but is itself the enigma that has burst through into existence. It is a maelstrom capable of turning existence out of its own self—endlessly, in every moment. The roots of melancholy are concealed within this maelstrom. It is therefore no accident that the great melancholics were always great rebels as well. When Aristotle designated melancholics (he was the first to do so), he was referring to such men who were guilty of committing the transgression of hubris. But, he added, they were all outstanding, extraordinary people who accomplished the greatest of deeds in their own fields. And this is characteristic as well of the exemplary melancholics of the Renaissance or baroque ages who researched, more intensively than anyone else, the secret of death, so that in the end they came to regard annihilation as a greater miracle than life itself. This also goes for the melancholics of the Romantic age, who, anticipating Nietzsche, were the first to announce the death of God. This was the greatest possible revolt—one that, in an unexpected fashion, was to prove culturally fertile.

If existence is limited to what is graspable, conceivable, thinkable, imaginable, or definable, then in reality there is nothing which is boundless. At the most what can be called boundless is that which has not yet been determined. But are the ultimate statements which can be made about existence really about its limitability and its definability? And if there is really nothing beyond that final border, does this nothingness not entrench itself into unbounded existence as a kind of parasite, displacing its own lack within it? The unbounded is not the infinity of depth, height, volume, weight, or distance but rather its inexhaustibility. The experience of this inexhaustibility is melancholia. That is why it is unacceptable in an age such as our own, when the "holy trinity" of technology, economics, and politics proclaims a solution to everything, without exception.

What is the situation with happiness? What is the nature of happiness, the inner threads of which are connected to melancholy, and which is identical in name alone to the happiness of our modern age, itself a happiness made obligatory, a hedonism purged of every melancholy? If the modern age treats melancholy with suspicion, doing everything in its power to render it harmless, then it can be presumed that this applies as well to the happiness connected to melancholy. If happiness is one of the great precepts of our age ("Be happy!"), then it can be suspected that this new kind of happiness is one of the manifestations of a practical and rational lifestyle, a function of duly formed and regulated economic, political, and technical conditions. And as such, it fundamentally differs from that other kind of happiness, which—like melancholia itself—is intimately connected to the dislodging and transgression of boundaries, not only simply filling a person with a good feeling and a sense of satisfaction (which of course is hardly contingent) but also keeping alive feelings that are oriented toward transcendence, causing the human being to confront the basis of his or her own existence.

The word *happiness* is not first and foremost indefinable because it is so polysemic, rich in meaning, or mutable, but because it forces us to confront the inconceivable fundament of our own life. The proximity of happiness is haunted by the miracle, by the feast or by love. And even if we don't pronounce it, in the meantime there is still a word we must consider: *god*. It cannot be excluded that these words are the synonyms of one single word *god*. For surely there is something in them which explains why we consider them divine, godlike. This goes as much as for the word *happiness* as for the words *love* or *miracle*. Yet this is a god not of the temple but of the chasm. For the inconceivable can be sensed in these words. At such times we will be powerless before something for which there are truly no words. There is no dictionary that could precisely define the meaning of *happiness*; in order to do so, it would need to define the deep strangeness residing in this word. No matter what we say about happiness, we unerringly feel that in no way have we said everything about it; this leads to that sense of lack emanating from the anthologies, the collections, the scholarly volumes — or from the ever more popular happiness handbooks and guides to being happy — which all try to circumscribe happiness in some way. Kant ventured the thought that the cause of happiness is nothing other than the indefinability of the concept of happiness. Instead of conquering it, words and concepts make us even more distant from it.

Happiness comes over one unexpectedly, it bowls one over. It does not issue warnings. It is impossible to plan, impossible to prepare for. Indeed, we cannot even generate much knowledge about it. Anything that is capable of stirring up the human being to such a degree, and even subjugating a person with its utter strangeness, far exceeds the ability of any kind of objective recognition.

Today we usually narrow happiness down to a kind of joy or to the absence of unhappiness: if someone is not unhappy, we are inclined to state that that person is happy. Although, as far as happiness is concerned, there are many different kinds. To wit, "happiness" casts a person out from the world. That is why it is impossible to speak of a larger or smaller happiness. In the case of joy, such a comparison as possible. If I rejoice at something I am its *master.* In the state of joy, the objects do not only exist in time and space; they exist there in a well-ordered fashion — this is what causes joy. Happiness, first and foremost, holds not joy in reserve (more precisely put, not only joy) but excess. When one is in the state of being happy, one begins to enjoy one's own powerlessness in relation to the universe: a helplessness, which in this case does not indicate a kind of inability but rather the experience that one's being is identified with an impersonal universe beyond the human. "I enjoyed the innocence of unhappiness and of help-lessness," says the protagonist of Georges Bataille's *My Mother*.[9] In this case, he felt so immoderately defenseless that his condition of being deeply lost opened up new horizons before him — horizons that were not of this world.

■

In everyday life, a person on the one hand *lives* the world of re-straint, and on the other *knows* of the unbounded world, which he designates either God or Being. His consciousness deepens into something true to life, however, when he finds himself in the state of melancholia or of happiness. At such times ab-stract *knowledge* turns into concrete *experience*, what is *distant* becomes more *present* than anything else. In these two states, deeply connected and yet by no means identical, a person will discover the infinite within his own finitude. The difference is manifested in the displacement of the emphases. As has already been mentioned, in the state of melancholia, infinite (and de-finitive) annihilation makes itself felt to a person; subsequently it casts its shadow upon all that is finite, causing the world to ap-pear in a radically new perspective. Everything that until that point appeared to be exclusively important and authoritative suddenly becomes secondary, and we learn that there is noth-ing in life which cannot be undermined, which would not be transitory, the days of which would not be numbered. Cessation casts its shadow upon all beings and things. And yet to insist on this is unacceptable in such an age as our own, in which the prevailing standard is endless progress, infinite fulfillment, and excessive incorporation. Melancholy—at least in its classical manifestation—is unfit for society in the world of today; it should be shoved into the background or smothered as soon as possible. Otherwise it would muddle everything, and it would certainly disturb the lubricated functioning of the modern world.

> In my hands, in my lap
> it I must hold until I die.
> Since what I put forth,
> out into the world,
> falls,
> as if placed upon
> a wave,

wrote Rilke—one of the greatest melancholics of the twentieth century.[10]

As, however, melancholy is a state which sooner or later will be experienced by everyone, the most satisfactory mode of taming it was to finally withdraw it from the suzerainty of public speech. Melancholy—which, throughout two and a half millennia of European history was one of the most prominent manifestations of the human condition, and frequently held to be the sign of increased health—began at the beginning of the nineteenth century to fall away from the field of vision. That which was considered by Aristotle a trait of the greatest intellects was suddenly restricted to a kind of sentimental mawkishness, a kind of kitschy "sense of the beautiful," permitted only on beautiful autumn evenings, at sunset, or during lachrymose films; otherwise it was something to be smiled at. And if, here or there, melancholy has still somehow managed to stubbornly persist, and the one who has been touched by melancholy is not inclined to free himself from this state, then that person is quickly introduced to the interventions of medical science so that the "happiness" of his "normal" course of life may be restored—although in this case, one speaks not of melancholy but rather of depression, which is a straightforward state of illness and as such can be ameliorated with the help of pharmaceuticals. Medical science has thus taken on the role of the animal trainer. And yet, no one succeeded in eradicating the concept of melancholy from common use. Everyone can sense the difference quite well. In every age, depression counted as an illness, whereas the estimation of melancholia used to be more permissive. One experiences one's own depression as a burden, as an illness, in which one's biological existence is deeply affected; the melancholic, in contrast, has no knowledge of his own melancholy: the living out of a melancholic fate does not even preclude gaiety. This is indicated as well by linguistic usage, ignored by science: in depression, everything is closed off; in a state of melancholy infinite horizons open up. It is precisely this limitlessness that disturbs science, which has, for two and a half centuries now, tried to limit melancholy within the confines of depression.

The situation is the same with happiness as well — or at least with the kind of happiness which cannot be conjured up by the contemporary motto "Be happy!" It is very telling that when Saint-Just announced happiness as a new concept in Europe, just at that moment at the turn of the eighteenth century, the French psychiatrist Philippe Pinel stigmatized melancholia as a "mistaken belief," and, finding even this concept to be too broad, redesignated it monomania. The happiness that Saint-Just had in mind — the joy felt at the formulation of the world — was mandatory for all who exerted themselves for the sake of the perfection of this world. And as such this kind of happiness depends not only on our own inner state but on the appropriate political and economic formations as well. Still, it could not render null and void that other happiness, emerging from the same root as melancholia, which in no regard was a new concept in Europe. For that other happiness emerged when humanity awoke to the fact that we ourselves are but an infinitesimal point in the cosmos and shall never be its master. This is the consciousness of transcendence. In a state of happiness, a person, moreover, does not "know" about transcendence, but instead experiences, with full intensity, how transcendence sustains his or her entire being, and discovers the completion of his or her own self in that which is, strictly speaking, beyond the individual. In these moments of fulfillment, it is no longer the finite horizon that gratifies one, as in melancholy. It is as if one were made dizzy by what is beyond oneself — in that infinity which can never be immured by political, economic, or technical means. These latter always prescribe *temperate* happiness; the kind of happiness that is associated with melancholy rattles people to their bones. However—turning to Goethe again for help—we can say that "true pleasure is only present where man must faint."[11]

Over the past two centuries, melancholy has been domesticated to such a degree that instead of being perceived as a state offering deeply existential realizations, it has been reduced to a kind of mawkishness mandating nothing. As for happiness—which, beginning with Plato and the great Western mystics, and up to and including the Romantics, was always understood to be an exceptional moment tangential to transcendence itself—it has been narrowed down to the experience of mere satisfaction. This has frequently led to an uncritical acceptance of extant conditions, behind which stands the implicit compact: Do not disrupt the course of the world, and we shall leave you in peace. The economic and political implications of this are very clear. Not only in the totalitarian dictatorships but in the systems that followed them the absolutism of the economic world order has become so excessive as to seem to justify the philosopher Slavoj Žižek's assumption that sooner or later life on the earth will cease, and yet the gears of capitalism will continue to grind on. And if this is so—and nothing, for the time being, would seem to point to the contrary—then both melancholia and happiness must be placed in quarantine. Because they are opposed to the logic of capital and capitalism while affirming a different kind of life, rich in a different kind of abundance.

"FOR ALL BUT FOOLS KNOW
FEAR SOMETIMES"

Fear and Freedom

I have borrowed the title of this chapter from one of Heinrich Heine's poems.[1] I was happy to do so because I believe him, and in part so that I will not have to correlate this statement back to myself. I know fear, and I also know that I will never be able to definitively keep it at a distance from myself. I am not afraid of fear: I am aware, though, that it remains ready to jump. Yet instead of brushing it under the carpet, I believe that it is worth the effort to look fear full in the face. Personally, in the first-person singular. I emphasize this because these days we are always inclined to formulate everything in the first-person plural: everywhere we hear about how we must be afraid of this, we must be afraid of that. Fear is an eminently timely topic: it must count as one of the most frequently mentioned concepts in world politics today. It looms over humanity like a net. One hears from every direction about all the things that must be feared: terrorism, political extremism, radicalism, the radical right, or, conversely, the radical left. Not only that: one must fear the destruction of the environment and the dangers of globalization, just as one must fear global warming or the water taps running dry. And so on.

One *must* fear, I say, although I would much prefer to say that fear is appropriate. *It is appropriate* to be afraid. Because anyone who is not afraid—or, more precisely, anyone who gives voice to a lack of fear—can easily be branded indifferent, uninterested, very possibly cynical, or perhaps even insane. And of course, this will be someone who behaves incorrectly in a political sense. In short, fear today has become something like a test: be afraid, so you can prove that you are on the right side. Insulate yourself with your fear—including from those who are conspicuously unafraid. Like, for example, the suicide bombers. And be afraid—of course—of their ideologies.

But is it really possible to be afraid in this general sense, in the first-person plural? Does anyone really experience fear of something not affecting him or her directly, with no influence on his or her momentary existence? It is possible to be apprehensive but not, I think, afraid. And that explains why I feel resistant to treating fear as a political category. For is not fear an infinitely private, individual phenomenon? And when a person is overcome by fear, does that person have regard for others—have that laudatory quality of the *zoon politikon?* Isn't it exactly fear that makes an individual feel excluded from the universal? There are examples of individuals who sacrifice themselves for the sake of others in the midst of terrifying situations. I have never been in such a situation myself. But I suspect that those who are capable of such actions can perform them because they have overcome their fear: their sacrifice is the proof that they are behaving in accordance with general expectations. If they had remained in that state of fear, they would have continued to be paralyzed. In other words, fear is the work of the absolute present, and as such it is closely connected to terror, if it is not completely identical with terror. As the prisoner of the exclusive present, however, a person is torn from every connection. As a political being, a person does not fear; at the most he or she is apprehensive about something; as a natural being this is even more the case. Not only does fear isolate a person from the others, but it raises that person out of time. Fear is always of the moment, the present. It casts a person back into nature. If someone is afraid, it does not matter if he or she is living in the twenty-first century, suddenly that person will be akin to an animal. Or like one of the prehistoric Neanderthals. In such moments, a person cannot be consoled by looking back into the past—back to a time when he or she wasn't afraid—just as the person cannot be consoled by thinking of the future, when once again he or she won't be afraid. Fear exists only in the present tense. And what else is there that has no consciousness of the past or of the future? The body. In the course of being afraid—just the same as during the experience of pain—the body will be more important than anything else. In a state of fear, a person, more than anything else, reacts within the body's corporeality. Just as the Russian and Soviet theater director Vsevolod Emilevich Meyerhold once wrote, in general, people will say, "I became afraid, and then I ran away"; but in reality, something else happens: "I ran away *while* I was afraid." The body does not follow the soul but is identical to it. And in these reactions of the soul, there is equally no consciousness of the past or the future. Such momentary feelings lift a person out of time. The consciousness of time is offered not by the body or the soul but by the spirit. A person may enter universality exclusively by means of the spirit.

Fear is, in and of itself — if it can be thus isolated — the identical reaction of both body and soul. Of course, fear never disappears without a trace. But what appears following fear is already no longer a quality of the body or the soul (Greek *psyche*), but rather one of the spirit (*pneuma*). The spirit, which offers insight — even if not on a conscious level. This spiritual "supplement" thus brought forth, which a person then receives as a "gift," is more important than the components of the body and soul of fear. In addition, this gift is very close to other gifts of the soul that a person might receive — whether they be anxiety, sadness, gaiety, ecstasy, heartsickness, or even profound boredom. In every case the body and soul begin the process, going along until they reach their own limits, as it were, and they offer entry to a dominion, understandably no longer that of the soul. Fear, at least in my view, is interesting as it allows a glimpse into this other domain, which is not corporeal and not of the soul. In other words, what makes fear interesting is that which lies beyond fear. This is what I would like to speak of in this essay. Namely, of that tilting in the course of which the spirit can somehow be sensed through the body and the soul. I am not interested in the spirit in and of itself, as a kind of distillate; instead I would like to investigate how fear can fertilize the spirit, what kind of anchors it lowers into it.

"All but fools know fear sometimes . . ." Or, conversely, only those who are insane think that a person is capable of existing exclusively as a spiritual being. Or believe that they may attain a state in which they will no longer be at the mercy of either their own bodies or the tremors of the soul. Heine never believed in anything like that. I tend to think he was right.

■

I have, in the course of my life, seen many variations of fear. I have seen individuals—who I thought would never be susceptible to such states—grow pale from fear; I have seen others who suddenly began to shake from fear of something which otherwise they would never have even noticed; I have seen individuals fleeing panic-stricken while others remained in the same place with nary a problem. And so on. Everyone could furnish a long list of examples. There are infinite varieties of fear, just as what provokes it can be infinitely variegated. Nonetheless, its symptoms and its signs are relatively uniform. Allow me here, as a way of commencing this discussion, to evoke a rather—for me, at least—staggering variation on the subject of fear: I am referring to when a little child feels fear. More concretely, I am thinking of one time when I saw my small son become afraid of a large dog, a dog that was in fact infinitely dear and decidedly friendly. My little boy could not yet talk at the time, but he still manifested a kind of ancient trust toward the world. And this was the first time that I had seen him afraid. Perhaps this is why the experience of his fear was so devastating. He was not simply alarmed—I had already witnessed that in him before. This time he was decisively afraid: he did not cry, he did not drop back, he did not cling to me, but he stared; and all the while—I don't know how else to put it—fear welled out of his eyes. In a peculiar manner, his gaze at that moment made me think of the gaze of a newborn child, when it opens its eyes for the very first time. That time too, my son saw something for the very first time in this world—more precisely, something of the world, which he had never noticed before. In his gaze was reflected a dread that lay beyond any ability to address it. I couldn't say to him, Don't be afraid, the dog won't hurt you; and I kept petting the dog, in vain, to show him that there was no reason to be afraid. Nothing helped. As I gazed into his eyes, I discovered a depth within them that truly shocked me. The anchors of fear are cast deep into a place where words never penetrate. Cast into something that perhaps even preceded existence itself. As I observed the terrified expression in my boy's eyes, I was forced to realize that when an adult is afraid and reassures himself or someone else with words, the fear is by no means eliminated—it is only dissimulated and suppressed. And it is by no means certain that it has disappeared. We have a great need of words: they put distance between ourselves and the object of our fear. They cover something over, and in doing so make life more bearable—they help us when we are stuck. For a small child, however, this veil of words does not function in the same way. Let me be precise: it is not that fear itself will be unconcealed but that in the state of fear, something is uncovered that makes life unbearable. In the gaze of this small child who could not yet speak it was not a lack of consciousness manifesting itself, nor was it the lack of recognition that was so striking. It was this baldness, this state of being uncovered. And when such a child begins to fear his gaze penetrates everything, like a lead ball being dropped into a bottomless well. Something appears before that gaze, something for which there are virtually no words, for it is beyond words. He does not simply see a dog from which he wants to hide. Instead, total untrustworthiness has opened up before him, embodied by the dog. In that moment there is nothing to which he could entrust himself. This experience could be something like what the gnostics of old used to call being *cast into existence*. That is what made the child's fear so vertiginous—and the child's gaze even made me dizzy: I was able to glimpse into something that otherwise I would never wish to perceive. In Rilke's eighth Duino elegy, he writes, in relation to the regard (*Antlitz*, "countenance, face") of the animal, of the Opened (*das Offene*), which, in his view, people, including young children (*das frühe Kind*), no longer perceive. This does not refer, I think, to children who cannot yet speak. When such a tiny child begins to feel fear, then before him the Opened is revealed. But it immediately becomes a terrifying Unbounded: it is not its capaciousness which makes it terrifying, but rather its unfathomability.

We all know how grownups usually react to the fear of children: for the most part they smile, considering the child's fear unwarranted. As far as the object of fear is concerned, for the most part they are right. Although for me, this grownup smile is at least as terrifying as the fear of a small child. Because the smile chooses not to notice precisely what the child, at that moment, is experiencing: the unbounded, the unfathomable, the untrustworthy. In other words, that which can surge into life in any given moment, haunting existence everywhere as an eternal threat. "He who mocks the Infants Faith / Shall be mock'd in Age & Death," wrote William Blake in "Auguries of Innocence," alerting grownups to this particular sensitivity of children. The fear of children is a belief deprived of hope, namely of trust. This is what makes it intolerable. It is possible to smile at an adult's fear: if somebody catches sight of a mouse and suddenly jumps on the table and starts to whimper, it really is something that can't be taken seriously; an individual who sees phantoms and moans about it demands patience more than sympathy. All the same, though, that person's fear is on this side of the words; with appropriate argumentation, and strength of conviction, an adult can be guided to better perceptions. The situation is completely different with tiny children. Their fear is not on the side of the words but far beyond them, in a place where words can never penetrate. This is why I would be inclined to state that for children—although, agewise, they stand "in front of" adults—in view of their inner world, they are not at the beginning but at the completion, the end. A child is not an "unopened" adult; instead, the adult is the one who has forgotten the child who lives within. That is what the fear, glimpsed from time to time in a child's gaze, tells me. At such times it is abundantly clear that a child is a mystic. Especially if the child has not yet learned how to speak, or rather if it has not yet been enfolded in the net of words which later will be so difficult to tear apart as an adult, in order to be able to see somewhere—into that place which Rilke calls the Opened. The fear of a child does not cause me, as an adult, to feel fear, but rather I experience something that otherwise I prefer not to notice: the complete incomprehensibility and arbitrary nature of my existence. Of course, the experience of that fills me with fear, although it is a different kind of fear from that of the child. The child is afraid; I am anxious. It is for this reason that it is absurd to sit tranquilly by while the child is in a state of fear. Once again I call upon the words of William Blake:

> Can a mother sit and hear
> An infant groan, an infant fear?
> No, no! never can it be!
> Never, never can it be![2]

Two great concepts have been mentioned: fear and anxiety. No matter what psychological textbook or philosophical treatise we might care to open, the distinction drawn by most authors between these two states is the same. Notably: in the case of fear, there exists a more or less describable object to which the state of fear refers; in the case of anxiety, however, such an object will be difficult to find, or if it can be located, it will be so meaningless as to make the manifestation of anxiety seem inexplicable. I managed to open, among the volumes in my own library, almost by accident a book titled *Spirit as the Adversary of the Soul*, by Ludwig Klages (first published in 1929), in which the author paraphrases the difference between the two in the following manner: "An indisputable sense of the meaning of words forces us, in essence, to match the word 'fear' to the fear of something definite, and the word 'anxiety' to the anxiety of something in- definite." Klages formulated this distinction with extraordinary clarity. His employment of concepts, however, especially when he writes of anxiety as a state "which cannot be referred back to any concrete thing," greatly captures the thoughts of another writer.[3] I am thinking of Freud, who, somewhat earlier, drew a par- allel according to a similar logic — not between fear and anxiety, but between sadness and melancholia. Allow me to make a brief detour in that direction — it might even help us to see fear in a slightly clearer light. In his study of 1917, *Mourning and Melan- cholia*, Freud places the crucial difference between mourning and melancholia thus: the cause of sadness is always known, in contrast to melancholia, in which the cause is always unknown. "So the obvious thing is for us somehow to relate melancholia to the loss of an object that is withdrawn from consciousness, un- like mourning, in which no aspect of the loss is unconscious." Freud explained it in the following way: a person who is sad has lost "only" the world, whereas the melancholic has also lost his own "ego."[4]

I confess that I have always found Freud's distinction prob- lematic. Freud describes mourning as the most natural of phe- nomena, as a kind of state which always has a clearly definable cause, rendering it explicable, justifiable, acceptable. As such, a parallel can be drawn with fear: apparently, both would seem to have an object. And as such, both are "normal" phenomena—that is to say, not causing obstacles to the progress of life, in fact even assisting it to be trouble free. None of this, however, can be said about melancholia. According to Freud, it is the lack of an object that characterizes it, and as the ego is also wounded, we could even perceive its twin—anxiety—within it. For Freud, melancholia is an abnormal state, demanding therapeutic intervention. "In mourning, the world has become poor and empty, in melancholia, it is the ego that has become so."[5] What Freud has done, however, is execute a rigid and artificial separation which will ultimately impede him in unraveling the deep and broad spectrum of life interpretations lurking within melancholia. Namely, Freud—like instrumental medical science and its spirit of investigation exclusively rooted in the natural sciences—examines the melancholic state as a state of the self facing the world in neutrality. The world, in his analysis, is a lifeless *object*, which is suitable (or perhaps not) for a person to satisfy his or her own desires through it. Since for Freud, every occurrence taking place within the soul is first and foremost determined by instinct, when interpreting melancholia, he rigidly contrasts the self with the objective world: everything takes place in the self, whereas the world seen as outer in relation to the self withdraws into a kind of neutral intactness. This stance—even beyond the fact that its differentiation between the inner and outer world is as much an unhappy undertaking as the differentiation of body and soul—seriously hinders the comprehension of the phenomenon: it abolishes that dynamic unity, without which we can hardly speak of life understanding. And this is what I find problematic. In Freud's analysis, melancholia loses the depth and the indisputably positive signification that, in more than two millennia of European culture, it had pronounced as its own; and instead of discovering capaciousness, depth, or even—as previous thinkers had done, from Aristotle all the way to Schelling—a source of creativity in it, he regards melancholy as an illness, specifically a wounded state.

This is why I find Freud's distinction problematic. Returning, however, to the subject of fear, I also find this rigid partition between fear and anxiety, which became over the course of the twentieth century nearly a self-evident commonplace, just as questionable. By regarding fear as a state inherently possessing an object, the psychologists and the philosophers implicitly begin with the hypothesis that the human being is an inherently reactive being, who reacts first and foremost to the stimuli of the outer world regarded as neutral material. In this analysis, fear is helpful to human beings in that they can sense the presence of a dangerous object and react to it. If their reflexes are good, they can sustain themselves. Fear renders human beings capable of adequately reacting to the dangers of the outer world. Citing Klages again: fear "is founded in the interests of self-sustenance." In contrast to human beings who are afraid, anxious people, insofar as their anxiety is "gratuitous"—as there is no clear objective cause for their behavior—not only bear witness to their own state of anxiety but demonstrate their own inability to respond appropriately to the world, to their surroundings. They are not capable of finding the object of which they should be afraid, and due to the lack of such object, they begin to feel anxiety. In other words, the relation between the anxious person's own self and so-called reality becomes distorted, out of proportion. That is why anxiety—to cite Klages for the last time—is "a danger to self-sustenance."[6] I quote him because he expresses with great precision the stance the great majority of psychologists and psychiatrists share as well. In other words, they create a rigid partition between the so-called inner and outer worlds just as Freud did between mourning and melancholia. In both instances, the outer world withdraws into a kind of neutral intactness. And so the possibility of glimpsing a deeper, more dynamic life understanding is snatched away from melancholy, just as it has been from anxiety. This amply demonstrates why in the twentieth century both mourning and melancholia uniformly became distorted into states of illness: within the systematic categorization of common psychiatric illnesses, both are identified as forms of psychosis, and specifically as neurotic.

In the first decades of the nineteenth century, however, no distinct classification existed between mourning and melancholia, just as none was made between fear, dread, or anxiety. With a view toward avoiding any potential misunderstanding, allow me to clarify: I would not dispute for a moment that in reality fear always does refer to some kind of concrete object. Everyone would be able to supply a long list of what inspires fear. But in the case of fear, I do not consider the existence of an object as the determining factor. In my view, fear is not fundamentally qualified by an object, but by the quality and dynamics of the feelings that object provokes. Fear is not made enormous by having an enormous object: instead, fear depends on how I—who am afraid— react to the thing that calls forth a reaction of fear. For example, one person will be only minimally afraid of earthquakes, whereas another will be so frightened by a simple beetle that he or she might nearly faint. While watching a horror film, some will find their heartbeat increase, their face turn red, and themselves gasping for breath; they will hardly be able to control themselves; others, present at the same film, will start giggling, or even laugh out loud. But is the person who is afraid of the repulsive insect truly afraid of that insect? And is it really the horrific scenes playing out on the screen that fill the viewers with fear? On first impression, we might say yes. If however, we examine that feeling more thoroughly, it might turn out that the insect, like the horrific scene in the film, instead functions as a kind of fuse. Its presence is necessary so that an anxiety-provoking depth will open up between the postulated object and the perceiving self. This depth has existed within human beings since ancient times; the insect or the frightening cinematic scene only helps it to finally become visible. And as fear gains in strength, the person experiencing it realizes that he or she is no longer capable of traversing over this deep chasm. That precipice which opened before the self gave rise to fear, and then that same fear is projected onto the poor little insect, which in and of itself is not so scary, for surely nothing would be easier than to trample on it. And why is this precipice so frightening? Because it appears to be unbridgeable. If I were able to step across it, then I wouldn't be afraid; my fear is sustained by the fact that something impedes me from doing just that. I am not afraid of the insect: instead, it gave rise to fear within me, because when I saw the insect I became isolated from everything, and I remained completely alone.

What, then, is fear? Fear is the apprehension and experience of isolation. It is one of the most universal human experiences that the one in its grip feels isolated not only from the world but from his or her own self. It is not even possible to draw a sharp distinction between the two in the end. The essence of fear is loneliness, of being left completely alone—let us just consider that one of the most frightening things is silence, muteness.

I see, therefore, a deep affinity between fear and anxiety, even if I do not dispute the difference between them. If a person becomes isolated from the world, then inevitably that person is in a state of discord with the self, and vice versa. In his essay on fear, Montaigne wrote: "And the many people who, impatient of the perpetual alarms of fear, have hanged or drowned themselves, or dashed themselves to pieces, give us sufficiently to understand that fear is more importunate and insupportable than death itself."[7] Today we would classify such a reaction as anxiety, as in this case the relation between the object of fear and the self has become disproportionate. Montaigne, however, did not draw such a sharp boundary between anxiety and fear. Certainly he would have recognized differences of degree; but even so, he would have been able to demonstrate the deepest nucleus of anxiety residing within the most trifling of fears. If someone is afraid, then truly, within that person's line of sight will be an object soliciting a reaction of fear within him or her. But since human beings are not just natural but also spiritual creatures, they are capable of entering into a more intensive relation (for fear is one of the most intense human feelings) with the perceived object in such a way that they, as it were, lift it into their own selves—they incorporate it, they appropriate it, it becomes endogenous. And in the meantime they project their own selves onto it. In this way, it is not merely a drama of the soul that unfolds but a spiritual drama. Fear is the manifestation of the movement of the soul, a dynamic which does not recognize boundaries. Depending on the strength of this dynamic, after a certain point every boundary collapses, and the soul, as a spiritual entity, recognizes its own self. At this point it can state, justifiably, that it is anxious. I would also say that in a state of fear the soul is still not completely unbounded, that is to say, it is still not completely free; in order for it to become wholly free—namely, for it to acquire spiritual dimensions—it must, as it were, intensify fear, must strengthen fear until the fear finally transforms into anxiety, which is one of the manifestations of freedom of the spirit. Fear can be paralyzing, but within the effect of this paralysis is also the promise of freedom—and liberation from fear cannot occur by my stepping back into the world of security (where my own self and the outer world face each other with relative neutrality). But if my own Self has fallen prey to fear, then I should keep on moving forward, toward the direction of anxiety, where the movements of the spirit are confined by no kind of object whatsoever. Kierkegaard would say that in this state anxiety confronts the Void itself. For twentieth-century psychologists and psychiatrists, anxiety is a state of illness which must be terminated, cured with therapeutic intervention—just like melancholia. Until the middle of the nineteenth century, however, anxiety was seen as having an indisputably creative aspect—as offering possibilities to the deepest questions of life explanation. In this regard, fear was an important waystation along the path. But it was not the terminus.

The twentieth century primarily tried to explicate fear as an inner psychic phenomenon. But two and a half millennia of European culture teach us that such inner phenomena always ensue from the movements of the spirit. Fear is not merely an inner, that is a psychic, state; it is a spiritual state, namely a pneumatic phenomenon as well.[8] Only the soul can state that it is surrounded by objects, indeed, that it is enclosed by objects. As far as the spirit is concerned, no kind of enclosure exists. The essence of the spirit is the capacity of infinite movement, the traversal of a world made up of objects. What makes a human being a spiritual creature is that his boundary is, as it were, infinitude. More precisely: it is something which is not under the human being's power. In other words: the human being is a metaphysical creature. Modern civilization continually wishes to convince us of the opposite; nonetheless, no human being can ever fully free himself from feelings oriented toward transcendence and the metaphysical. Because of the awareness of his own mortality, the human being is doomed to metaphysical homesickness.

Fear—just like anxiety—plays a crucial role in keeping the sensitivity toward the metaphysical alive. Both shimmer deeply within the experience of human vulnerability before mortality and death. They offer a metaphysical initiation. In our times, however, this is one of the great taboos. This is why, in my own view, anxiety as such has become narrowed down to a sickly, pathological state; in terms of fear, all civilization strives to eliminate every and all kinds of fear, and, in the name of an exceedingly shortsighted altruism, to liberate humanity completely from fear. I would never for a moment dispute that pathological anxiety—from which a person truly has to be freed and requires help—does exist; but this does not at all mean that anxiety is an a priori pathological state. This applies to fear as well: of course, one person will always try to help another, if he or she is afraid. But I don't see that as a reason not to take into consideration the positive energy concealed within fear, through which means our lives can become more abundant. In other words: there is no point in throwing out the baby with the bathwater.

■

Fear is a negative manifestation of the soul; nonetheless, I would be committing the sin of one-sidedness if I did not discover within it the pledge of freedom as well. I know that many will not concur with me on this point. In his treatise "On the Sublime," Friedrich Schiller writes that in the course of feeling afraid a person is obliged to suffer a kind of violence: in this state of suffering and violence—namely in this state of fear—humanity is deprived of freedom. And Schiller is completely right. And yet if the conclusion is drawn—as has been the case for a good while now—that the fruits of civilization can be produced in such a way that there will be no negative affect, no dark side, in other words, no cause for newer fears, then such an idea demonstrates a certain narrow-mindedness. This is why I consider the twentieth-century stance peculiar that holds that humanity must be liberated from each and every fear, a stance which is widespread in our days, indeed practically obligatory. Friedrich Nietzsche characterized this goal of the modern age—to liberate all of humanity from fear—in *Beyond Good and Evil* (written in 1886) with the following words: "Anyone who probes the conscience of today's European will have to extract the very same imperative from a thousand moral folds and hiding places, the imperative of herd timidity: 'We want the day to come when there is nothing more to fear!' The day to come—the will and way to that day is now called 'progress' everywhere in Europe."[9] Behind the intent to definitively eliminate fear can be discovered a utopian idea: a world can be created in which there will never be any kind of suffering or violence. The words of Walter Benjamin come to mind: "There is no document of civilization which would not be at the same time a document of barbarity."[10] In his own way, Benjamin takes the measure of the situation as realistically as Nietzsche does. It is very telling that it is precisely the twentieth century (with all its historical dimensions) as well as the first decades of the twenty-first century that saw fear augmented to a degree never before witnessed—and all the while never was the theme of eliminating all fear in the world ever so widely discussed.

The idea of Schiller that fear and freedom exclude each other creates a further problem, in my view. It is a given fact that in a state of fear, the human being is not fully in control of his own self. This, however, can also be said about joy, pleasure, happiness—and, of course, about mourning, sadness, and melancholia. And so on. Is there any feeling in the state of which a human being would be completely master of his or her own self? I don't believe so. But of course, anyone in possession of "perfect" ice-cold rationality would be inclined to think so. (Allow me to refer here to Heine, who, in his *Pictures of Travel*, paints the portrait, with enthralling comedy, of just such a cold, sober, rational person, a professor, who has taken it into his head that he will drive all such so-called unwarranted—i.e., irrational—fears out of Heine's head. He forces the matter until finally he perishes of his own futile efforts.) And the reason why the human being is not completely master of his own self is not that he has yet to arrive at a state of freedom but that he is a metaphysical creature who with his entire being is nested within a series of connections that greatly surpass him. He has received the gift of existence without ever having been asked about it, and he will lose his life as well without having been asked for his consent. This in and of itself is sufficient reason for existence to be filled with fear; as Kierkegaard once wrote in his diary, "All existence makes me anxious, from the tiniest fly to the enigmas of the incarnation."[11] This same recognition is the pledge of freedom, however: as Kierkegaard demonstrates in *Fear and Trembling*, the precondition for ultimate freedom—which he refers to as the station of faith, namely, the enlivening of the metaphysical sense—is fear intensified to the utmost point. He mentions the parable of the sacrifice of Abraham: Abraham, with his son Isaac, had to reach a level of fear from which it would no longer be possible to grow distant from God—and it was only then that the way opened to come face to face with God.

That is why I believe that freedom and fear—even if they are not identical—do not exclude each other. In our own age, when, as I mentioned at the beginning of this essay, many strive to make political capital out of fear, this hypothesis could truly come across as anachronistic. But let us not forget: one of the greatest fundamental concepts in European culture referred precisely to the cathartic strength of fear. According to Aristotle, it was through catharsis that human beings became inured via pity and fear—as it was through this pity and fear that an opportunity arose for them to step out of the previous narrowness of their own lives. And where would they step to? In the view of the Greeks, it would be into a more capacious life, where the human order would begin to imitate that of the divine. According to Judeo-Christian culture, it was where we come into contact with God, and discover our own boundaries within our own infinity. And in Kierkegaard's view, it was there where a person would confront the Void or nothingness itself. According to Nietzsche, it was where one could return to "the womb of existence." For Heidegger, it was where existence itself would come into contact with being. And for Rilke, that step would lead into the Opened (*das Offene*), into that same Opened which, a century earlier, had been cited by Hölderin in his poem "Bread and Wine." And so on: one could enumerate all of the documents of European culture which inspire us to discover positive possibilities within fear. Namely, that within the movements of the soul (psyche), entry into the spirit (pneuma) is offered to man. If it is an inborn trait of human beings that we will always be obliged to be afraid of something for some reason or another, then one of the pledges of freedom is that we can learn to husband our fear. We can observe—even within its indisputably crushing and paralyzing effects—a liberating element as well. Namely, that fear itself is a miraculous phenomenon—for surely whoever is afraid does nothing other than be overcome with astonishment at the great enigma of existence with his entire being. At the beginning of this essay I described how I discovered a conspicuous amazement in the countenance of the tiny child who could not yet speak, as he was filled with fear and on the verge of crying. For an adult, this is a true challenge—to put the question of the child into words, without the faintest hope that there could ever be any kind of reassuring response.

THE SHADOW OF THE WHOLE

The Romantic Fragment

This world, this life, are fragments unconnected,
But I a German teacher have selected;
The scatter'd fragments he together tags,
In an intelligible combination:
And with his night-gown, and his night-cap's rags,
Stops all the holes up, and completes creation.

These lines from Heine's *Book of Songs* bear witness to their author's cheerful and unfettered mood. And yet they also bear witness to a change in the general mood toward the end of the 1820s. The system — namely, the idea of the Whole — had finally become an object of scorn: instead of a divine attribute, it was merely a disguise with which certain mortals tried to present themselves as immortal. Heine makes no secret of the emperor's being naked: he wishes to present himself as a divine Whole, but in the depths of his heart he feels an icy fear, which he then tries to conceal by means of the mask of the system and common sense.

What gives rise to this fear? Heine tells us that it is a fear of fragmentation. A fear of something which otherwise truly can be frightful. Lurking within it is the danger of disintegration and decomposition. The fragment is like a landmine: if I step on it, it will explode. And there is much else that will explode with it as well: literature will explode, just as morals will, or the system of social convention. Perhaps even the state itself. Something almost terrorist-like lies within it. It is commonly considered that the fragment managed to become an aesthetic category toward the end of the eighteenth century. The aesthetic viewpoint, however, was itself already the result of a kind of domestication: even within the depths of the fragment cult of the Jena Romantics, the fear of the fragment's destructive power can be sensed. In one of his better-known aphorisms, Friedrich Schlegel compares the fragment to a hedgehog: "The fragment, posing as a smaller work of art, must be completely separated from the surrounding world, and it must be complete in and of itself, just like a hedgehog."[1] If we are to expand on the metaphor of the hedgehog, and—just like the Romantics themselves—begin to view the entire universe as one gigantic fragment, then this hedgehog is suddenly distorted into something ghastly, like Kafka's "peculiar apparatus" in his story "The Penal Colony": it is not tree leaves that will be stuck on its points but living people.

In what is to follow, I will be speaking of not the aesthetic aspects of the Romantic fragment but of its destructive force, its threat to human life. I will be speaking of its potentiality, like an inevitable machine, to slice human existence itself—including the human body—into pieces, into fragments: in other words, of its potential to hew human existence into stumps.

Heine located fear concealed as it was by the disguise of the Whole. Under the right circumstances, the fragment will passionately consent to even its own destruction and liquidation. And, of course, it creates a disenchantment with life: it deprives life of the illusion of having some kind of overall sense. That is why we need nightcaps and nightgowns: every orifice can be plastered over with them, and life once again seems nice and round. The impression is created of life having meaning, as if its beginning and its end would coincide.

"People die because they have no strength to connect the beginning and the end," wrote the pre-Socratic philosopher Alcmaeon of Croton; this saying remains to us only in fragmentary form.[2] To put it differently: with the reins of their own lives in their hands, people lose sight of the Whole, and they will become embodiments of the fragment with their mere existence. So it is understandable that from this fragment they always long for the Whole: for immortality from within the position of mortality. The entirety of European culture can be described as the story of this yearning, from Plato to Hegel—suggesting to the poets, the thinkers, and even to the lovers that from the shadow world of the fragment they should try somehow to reach the sunlight of the Whole.

In relation to the Whole, the fragment always counted as a kind of shadow. But what would it be the shadow of, if not the Whole? And if this is so, then we can ask why the Whole casts a shadow at all. Why is it simply not content with its own self, with its own luminosity? Why is it constrained to endure something beyond its own self, which it then excludes and denies? This was one of the fundamental questions of the gnostics, and toward the end of the eighteenth century it gained a relevance it had previously lacked. And at the same time, it assisted the fragment, broken off from the Whole, in the advancement of its glorious career.

In this same era, an answer began to be passionately sought for the questions of the relations between the Creator and the creature who turns to it, between the good and fathomless evil, now independent. The career of the fragment occurring at the end of the eighteenth century cannot be separated from the inquiry into the origins of evil, which, in the Romantic era, left no one untouched. This is connected to the shattering of the universal faith in the Creator, the effects of which were felt well before the Romantic era. In the greatest Puritan epic of the mid-seventeenth century, Milton's *Paradise Lost*, Raphael says to Adam, when the latter attempts to pry into the secrets of the universe, revealing his wish to gain a glimpse into the workings of Whole,

> Heav'n is for thee too high
> To know what passes there; be lowlie wise:
> Think onely what concernes thee and thy being;
> Dream not of other Worlds, what Creatures there
> Live, in what state, condition or degree,

Contented that thus farr hath been reveal'd
Not of Earth onely but of highest Heav'n.[3]

The human being — if the beginning and the end is excluded
from the mystery of his existence — justifiably feels himself to be
a shard, broken off from the Whole, fallen into the void. Later,
Adam rebukes the Creator:

Did I request thee, Maker, from my clay
To mould me man? Did I sollicit thee
From darkness to promote me?[4]

The question would seem to be self-evident. But what is also
self-evident is that one and a half centuries later the same question became the epigraph of a novel which took up the matter of fragmentation in the most radical fashion possible. Mary
Shelley's *Frankenstein* (1818) demonstrates that fragmentation
is indeed the fundamental situation of life. The Demon created
by Frankenstein — who embodies his creator's innermost doubts
and desires, the Demon's body cobbled together from living
fragments of his own body and from body parts taken from the
slaughterhouses and the morgues with the stitches well visible —
says, in a decisive moment in the novel: "My person was hideous
and my stature gigantic. What did this mean? Who was I? What
was I? Whence did I come? What was my destination? These
questions continually recurred, but I was unable to solve them."[5]
The Demon could have also come across these questions in
Kant's *Critique of Practical Reason*. The conclusions, however,

diverge from the ones Kant drew. The Demon is the character-istic shadow of the man of the modern age, one who has lost his confidence in the Creator, who no longer registers—either be-hind himself or above himself—any kind of metaphysical con-nection to which he might entrust his existence, and thus he can no longer connect the beginning with the end. In Shelley's novel, the Demon receives life without ever having asked for it, and he loses it similarly without anyone's asking his opinion about it. For him, life is truly a single colossal fragment. An event with neither precedent nor antecedent.

■

The emancipation of the fragment in the Romantic era was marked out to create a counterbalance for the final breakdown of metaphysics. The fragment, as it were, enacted the final de-thronement of the Whole, in such a way that as it took its place, it itself became a new Whole—the negative universe. In place of the light, it established the empire of darkness, just as toward the end of Novalis's fragment-novel of 1802, *Heinrich von Ofter-dingen*, the sun is smashed into pieces. In its place, Novalis posits the empire of the evening sun, whose light shines like daylight, only its light—as in the nighttime paintings of Caspar David Friedrich—casts a deathly hue. The fragment is the instrument of creation, its nighttime aspect.

The fragment creates in such a way that with the same ges-ture it extinguishes creation. The effect (that which was created) erases the cause (the gesture of creation), and with that also precedes it. In addition to the theoreticians of the German Romantic magazine *Athenaeum* (published 1798–1800), we should refer to a contemporaneous author usually not mentioned in connection with them: the Marquis de Sade. In his novel *Justine* (1791), the libertine Bressac absolves evil by alluding to nature, refuting the common belief that every effect has its cause: "With officious faces, they try to drum it into our heads that there is no effect without cause; they continually repeat the world is not self-generated; whereas the universe is both cause and effect." The world, claims de Sade, is not a system of interrelations, but instead comprises a mass of unrelated parts which subsist in and of themselves: everything exists only for itself, and no single part can be referred back to any kind of Whole. In his later novel *Juliette*, the heroine states: "Earlier I aligned myself with nature, but in my thoughts I had already broken away from it. Perhaps we are even less dependent upon nature than upon God. And perhaps cause and effect are not even related."[6]

De Sade, just like Alfred Jarry—who conceived of the theory of pataphysics a century later—elevates the principles of discontinuity and the accidental to the level of statutory force without ever attributing any kind of unifying strength to this "law." On the contrary: this is the "law of fragments," which works against unified explanations. Everything turns ghastly at its touch. This is the law of *death*. In the universe of de Sade, the world falls apart into lethal fragments. Or every individual case obtains an absolute validity without ever ceasing to be individual (which is, in effect, the same thing). Such an existence is at once dynamic and paralyzed. On one hand, the fragment is the manifestation of temporal uniqueness, living and infinite; on the other, it is monolithic, lethally numb. It is agile, turned toward the outside, and yet at the same time looks inward, a closed substrate. It creates while at the same time it rescinds creation.

■

This double aspect of the fragment is demonstrated well if we compare two novels of the era in which fragmentation has a similar structural significance: de Sade's *120 days of Sodom* (1785) and Novalis's *Heinrich von Ofterdingen*. Both these works are written in fragmentary form, even if dissimilarly. Novalis's novel remains fragmentary primarily because of the death of the author. At the same time, the structure of the novel and its planned egress in themselves render the possibility of its ever being finished questionable. *Heinrich von Ofterdingen* creates the impression that it did not remain fragmentary because of its author's death but that its author died because it was a novel that could never be finished. *120 Days of Sodom* is in and of itself a kind of torso, even if the author placed a full stop at the end of the book. Its fragmentation is of a different category. In a certain regard, *Heinrich von Ofterdingen* is vertically infinite: Novalis sketches metaphysical dimensions which point well beyond traditional metaphysical thinking, opening the novel into an impossible direction, one which can never be fulfilled. In contrast, the novel of de Sade seems to be confined by iron bands. It is within this closure that the impossible appears, taking the form of death. The deathly impossibility finally not only undermines everything but makes the progress of the novel itself fragmentary and brittle. In Novalis's work, the strengths that create the fictional world explode, making it fragmentary; the fragmentary quality of de Sade's book is the result of implosion. *Heinrich von Ofterdingen* is a volcano; *120 Days of Sodom* is a darkly incandescent slag heap.

The fragmentary natures of the two novels are symmetrical: they reflect and complete each other. Both works in striving for completion remain gigantic torsos. The absence of the Whole — instead of the completed Whole — has left its stamp upon both. Each author wished to seize upon the universal Whole with a kind of vehemence unknown in French, German, or English epic poetry. If we wanted to find a parallel, we would have to turn to Dante's *Divine Comedy:* the negative universe that unfolds in both these novels can only be compared to Dante's universe, turned toward the positive. In this regard, the universe of Dante, as well as those of de Sade and Novalis, remains closed within itself. At the end of the *Divine Comedy* we can read:

O eternal light!
Sole in thyself that dwell'st; and of thyself
Sole understood, past, present, or to come;
Thou smiledst.[7]

The universe of de Sade is just as enclosed within its own self; as the author himself stated: the world he shows us is also an effect without a cause. On the other hand, this universe is directed not by Dante's immobile impetus but by the surrounding void, gradually seeping into the pores of the universal. The closed manor house, set among high mountains, of the banker Durcet, where the four libertines withdraw with their retinue and their victims, is something like a solitary revolving planet. It is surrounded by an unbridgeable abyss: after its residents move in, they destroy the one single bridge connecting the outside world to their hiding place. The result is a perfectly solipsistic universe. In this macrocosm, cut off from everything, complete in and of itself and yet still fragmentary, negative fulfillment must be brought to realization. Paradoxically, this will be possible only through means of fragmentation. De Sade's imagination is haunted by the idea of a fragmentary, negative universe. He wishes, with its assistance, to destroy positive Completeness, from which his libertine friends have also sought refuge here.

The negative or destructive Whole, however, is not only the destroyer of the positive Whole; it also gradually consumes its own self—as can be seen in Goya's painting (dating from not too much later, 1820–1823) *Saturn Devouring His Son*. In this painting, the murderous god, devouring his child's bones, destroys his own self as well. Christian mythology and the story of Jesus are turned against themselves. With the shattering of trust formally placed within God, the destructive aspect of the Jesus narrative becomes decisive. In Goya's work, God himself will become fragmented through the act of ripping his own child to pieces. We can observe a similar process with de Sade: the manor house of

Durcet becomes a complete, yet fragmentary universe, in which everything is the prey of death.

This is demonstrated by the novel's structure. Until the thirtieth day, the narrative proceeds in the manner of the traditional novel, following a characteristic linear progression. At the end of that day, the author suddenly makes an appearance, asks for our attention, and takes note of all his previous mistakes. From this day (December 1) on, not only will the succession of the perversions quicken in their pace, but the text itself will become confused. De Sade, in striving for completeness, explains what is going on less and less, confining himself to ever more fragmentary remarks. On the one hand, he catalogues the individual perversions precisely, soberly, almost with a clear head; on the other, he feverishly rushes ahead, his writing flustered and sketchy, leaving everything in fragments.

The fragment will thus be the lethal principle of *120 Days of Sodom*: everything must be recounted, but it is precisely because of this that nothing can truly be recounted. De Sade's text smolders, forced in between the *all* and the *void*. There is no precedent for the individual criminal acts (there is no explanation for them), just as there are no consequences (no reprisals, no punishments—everyone drops the matter with no further mention). For that reason, these enumerated and listed offenses cannot even be termed perversions, for they are utterly divorced from any kind of morally comprehensible system; they are commeasurable only with their own selves. Their single gauge is their own state of fragmentation—each of these felonies is a categorical imperative in and of itself. Written toward the end of the eighteenth century, the work of de Sade demonstrates in the clearest manner possible the destructive power of the fragment as it consumes everything. Fragments, in his oeuvre, are like the messengers of a universe that has fractured into pieces, its impossible manifestations. It is no wonder that after a certain point the fragments contained in *120 Days of Sodom* will become ever more surreal. A libertine "fucks a goat from behind while being flogged; the goat conceives and gives birth to a monster. Monster though it be, he buggers it." "A sodomite rips the intestines from a young boy and a young girl, puts the boy's into the girl, insert the girl's into the boy's body, stitches up the incisions, ties the bodies back to back to a pillar which supports them both, and watches them as they die."[8]

In de Sade's novel, the fragments are not simply the shards of the disintegrated Whole, but gestures—primarily the rescinding of creation mentioned earlier. The fragments of *120 Days of Sodom* smolder until eternity—the goal of their author is nothing less than to annihilate everything by means of these fragments, including the fragments themselves. The void can be sensed behind these fragments but also within them, as it grows and grows. De Sade's protagonists would be all too happy to destroy the universe itself. As one of his protagonists, Curval, puts it: "How many times have I not wished to seize the sun, to fray the universe, or to destroy the entire world."[9]

At this point, it is worthwhile to refer back to *Heinrich von*

Ofterdingen. The upstanding and almost frighteningly mild Heinrich is at quite a distance from the conceptions of de Sade's libertines and, as opposed to their crimes, his goodness enchants us. In his own way, however, he strives for universality just as much as the libertines do, and his way of thinking is just as exclusive as theirs. It is therefore no wonder that, like Curval, he longs for nothing more than to dismantle the empire of the sun. It is true that he has an idea of the good: "When, in the universe, will there be no more need for dread, pain, lack, and evil?" Heinrich asks Sylvester in the second half of the novel. The gnostic overtones in this question are audible, just as they are in de Sade's merciless outpourings. And his answer is as radical as that of the gnostics and de Sade: in order for evil and the need for it to disappear, the universe as it presently exists must disappear: "The world will collapse into an infinite number of worlds enclosed into ever larger worlds. Finally, every feeling will be a single feeling. That single feeling, as the one single world, will increasingly lead to all worlds."[10] The path to the fulfillment promised in the second half of the novel (titled "Fulfillment") leads across destruction, but the novel does not live up to its promise. First, the world has to fall apart into fragments so that a qualitatively new universe may come into being—one whose innermost principle will, nonetheless, be fragmentation, without precedent or aftermath, and resistant to every context. The kind of surrealism that is betrayed at the end of 120 *Days of Sodom* is in evidence as well at the end of Novalis's novel. Everything that is uncanny will be natural, the flowers and the beasts will begin to converse about human beings, the characters will fall prisoner to the seasons, time comes to an end, space will be annihilated. In other words, everything that exists will be destroyed so that place will be made for that which is nonexistent.

◾

Enthralled by the negatively determinant Whole, de Sade and Novalis turned their backs on the idea of the positive Whole they had inherited from European metaphysical tradition. One of the most pregnant expressions of this can be found in Hegel's *Phenomenology of Spirit* (1807), in which the author, in his interpretation of religion, writes: "Only the Whole has intrinsic reality, inasmuch as it has at its disposal the form of pure freedom, as opposed to all that that manifests within time."[11] Whatever exists within time is correspondingly impoverished and limited. In other words, this is finite, immediate existence, a life determined by the bounded. And what is bounded is not what it is through its own self; it is determined by something which we could never find within it.[12] Namely, that which is direct, sensory, and unique ultimately gains its form from what it lacks. Looking at things from the viewpoint of the Hegelian Whole, the fragment has become a fragment because it lacks the Whole. Hegel's concept is the consummation of two and a half millennia of metaphysical tradition that endowed the fragment with a priori negative portent. As formulated by Martin Luther nearly three centuries earlier: "Fragments, whether they be the ruins of the past or the fragments of the future, always point beyond their own selves.

They exist, and they have effect in that completion and in that tension with which they are not identical, which they do not represent, and which the one who observes them completes. The fragment compels one to an investigation of the Whole, but they themselves cannot offer this and do not allow it to be found."[13]

At the end of the eighteenth and beginning of the nineteenth century, de Sade and Novalis, as well as most of the Romantics, turned away from this traditional Whole, increasingly sustainable only by force. Why was it necessary to turn away from it? The reason was that in parallel with accelerating secularization in the eighteenth century, the protective vault cast over the idea of the Whole began to show fissures, and the divine principle that had kept the idea of the Whole alive lost its earlier relevance. In his poem *The French Revolution* (1791), William Blake wrote: "God, so long worshipp'd, departs as a lamp / Without oil."[14] In 1798, the young Hegel opined: "The feeling upon which the religion of the new age is founded is the feeling or sense that God himself is dead."[15] And in 1804, the night watchman of August Klingemann says, "Thanks be to God, for death exists, and behind it there is no eternity."[16] Human beings die from not being able to join the beginning and the end together, as quoted earlier from Alcmaeon of Croton. The experience of the Romantics, on the other hand, was that if the divine guarantee was lost, then the Whole (namely, the supposed joining up) no more protected humans from the ultimate certainty of death than did fragmentary existence. That is why they primarily tried to draw strength from the givens of sensation: dissipation, experienced as lethal, yet which was still so vivid that it could be lived until the end of life. "The world is chaos. Nothingness is the world-god yet to be born," wrote Georg Büchner in the fourth act of *Danton's Death*.[17] Christian Dietrich Grabbe wrote: "God created from nothing. We create from ruins! First we shall break ourselves into fragments, so that we may know who we are and what we are capable of!"[18]

For the Romantics, the fragment is the manifestation of nonidentity, just as it is in the traditional Christian conception. The decisive difference is that for the Romantics, this nonidentity is not the manifestation of lack, but of fulfillment. The fragment truly points to something beyond itself—namely, it is no longer identical with its own self, not because it is a shard of the past or future but because it is burdened with the idea of its own definitive fragmentary nature. It becomes complete by means of the prevailing lack within it. And this ensures a kind of internal infinity on its behalf, which can only be compared to the infinity of the positive Whole. It is precisely because of its own nonidentity that the fragment may become divine. Parallel to the accelerated secularization of the beginning of the Romantic era, the transformation of the positive *idea* (ideology) of identity into the positive *experience* of nonidentity can be observed. From this point on, the final word belongs to tragic dualism, which, according to Hans Urs von Balthasar, "heroically sees imperfectability (as the eternal return) as absolute (with Nietzsche); or else the fragment experiences in its 'failure' (Jaspers) and in its 'determination to accept death' (Heidegger), a gleam of wholeness which one sees and shares in only in renouncing it."[19]

■

Let us return to the question of the shadow. We have spoken of how the fragment can be perceived as the shadow of the Whole—more precisely, of thought within the Whole. Although if the fragment is "emancipated" and lifted out of that metaphysical interrelation which, in the course of the history of European culture, loomed above it like a vault, then the shadow as well becomes independent and autonomous, breaking off from the "body" of which it had been a function, and itself will be a source of dark light. The story of Peter Schlemihl, written by Adelbert von Chamisso in 1814, is relevant here: in this work, the shadow not only metaphorically but physically splits off from its bearer and becomes self-contained. Schlemihl splits into two, his being becomes fragmented. The body without a shadow creates the impression of an amputated stump, just as does the shadow lacking a body. In Goya's series of etchings *The Disasters of War*, created in the same decade (from 1810 to 1820), similarly amputated bodies and bodily fragments can be seen (as in Plate 39: "A heroic feat! With dead men!") as well as in the somewhat earlier series (dating from 1799) *Caprichos*, in which, in some of the plates, self-standing shadows, similar to the shadow of Schlemihl, menace threateningly (see, for example, Plate 3: "Here comes the bogeyman!" and Plate 52: "What can a tailor do!").

One year after Chamisso's story appeared, E. T. A. Hoffmann published "The Sandman." This narrative conspicuously demonstrates that the body becomes fragmentary when the soul loses its unity (its oneness), and breaks down; it disintegrates into a heap of fragments. The body of Olimpia, mechanically assembled from fragments—organic and inorganic parts—perfectly mirrors Nathanael's soul fallen similarly to pieces. And of course it resembles the body of Kunigunda from Kleist's drama "Katie of Heilbronn; or, The Trial by Fire" (1808), as well as foreshadowing the body of Frankenstein's creation in Mary Shelley's novel of 1818, in which the Demon's "yellow skin scarcely covered the work of muscles and arteries beneath."[20] The Demon, however, is himself a mirror image, Frankenstein's shadow become a separate entity, and Frankenstein's soul has fallen into pieces just as did the souls of Nathanael and Schlemihl.

In *Frankenstein*, the fragmentary nature of the human creature is woven into the question of creation itself. If the Creator (Frankenstein) is a priori a fragmentary being, then fragmentation will be the natural state for his creation. At the turn of the eighteenth century, Julien Offray de La Mettrie's theory of the human-machine was not only revived by many; it was even further elaborated: the human being is a machine from which—to quote Blake—the oil oozes out, and because of that the body creaks, rattles, and falls to pieces.

With the progress of secularization, the body becomes estranged from those broader connections of which it earlier had formed a part. The academic literature in this regard finds that the ensuing "self-determination" of the body can be connected to the French Revolution: whereas earlier, the extemporal bodies of the king and Christ formed the authoritative standard, by the end of the eighteenth century the temporal "civil" body of the individual, stepping into the political arena, had become representative.[21] To this, however, must be added that the "civil" body can be deemed not only political but also desacralized. This desacralization of the body means that it has lost its *metaphysical* dimension and has become a mere *physical body*. The body is reduced to material, to its bones, muscles, guts, flesh, blood, skin— to that which had already doomed it to disintegration, literally to falling to pieces. In the work of de Sade, Blake, Shelley, Chamisso, and Hoffmann, but even in the work of Matthew Gregory Lewis or Charles Robert Maturin, the altered role of the human body and the "local value" of civilization that had occurred by the end of the eighteenth century are rendered palpable. In *The French Revolution*, Blake thoroughly describes the variegated mutations of the body, piling up the details, the endless many tortures which await the prisoners in the seven prison towers, to such a degree that these passages resemble more than anything else the descriptions penned six years earlier by the Marquis de Sade in his 120 *Days of Sodom*. Like de Sade, Blake examines the secrets of the body by penetrating into the body in the strictest sense of the word, bringing all that had earlier lurked in the darkness into the sunlight—the body is ultimately dismembered. For both de Sade and Blake, it is not an interest in sadism that causes them to depict the body in this manner but the opposite: human existence, become fragmentary, deprived of the possibility of resurrection, gives rise in them—and, conspicuously, in many of their contemporaries—to sadistic fantasy.

In 1792, in the *Dictionnaire des arts de peinture, sculpture et gravure*, Claude-Henri Watelet writes under the heading of the *beau idéal*: "The *beau idéal* is today, in our opinion, the uniting of the greatest perfections that certain chosen individuals can in part provide. If one wants to conceive the *beau idéal* in a manner relating more to the ideas of Greek artists of the time of Pericles, it is necessary to imagine the beautiful as it would exist if Nature formed its products, and man above all, with the most exquisite selectiveness, with all its general and particular perfections."[22] Watelet makes it clear in his dictionary entry that the ideal consists of a joining together of individual parts. To express it differently: the ideal is nothing more or less than something which has been assembled from various components. It is therefore not surprising that precisely around this time, in the teachings of the academicians, so-called *écorchés* began to feature prominently: this is what the mechanician and sculptor Jean-Antoine Houdon termed his mannequins, which could be disassembled into pieces; he had prepared them under the direction of a surgeon, and they were used for the instruction of painters in the French Academy in Rome. The protagonists of the work of Blake, de Sade, Mary Shelley, or Hoffmann are unthinkable without Houdon's invention. But it even makes an appearance in Goethe's *Wilhelm Meister's Apprenticeship* (1829):

in an anatomical workshop, Wilhelm takes notice of body parts
carved and formed from wax, which the master ("artist") has prepared while taking precise consideration of the joints, bones, and
tendons. "Wilhelm now learned that such models were already
widely distributed, but without publicity. But to his greatest astonishment he learned that the current stock was to be packed
up and shipped across the sea."[23]

But it was not only Houdon who did much for the instru-
mentalization of the body and its dispersal into many parts. In
Paris, in 1774, Henri-Louis Jaquet-Droz presented three automatons which were so lifelike they were termed *androids*; his disciple Henri Maillard settled in London, and in 1800 he demonstrated his own automatons there. Even earlier, in 1772, James
Cox had opened up his own museum with fifty-six automatons
in Spring Garden.[24] Books about automatons were popular;
among the better-known was a work by Dr. W. Hooper, *Rational Recreations*, published in London in 1794. In 1770 in Paris,
Phillippe-Guillaume Curtius established a cabinet of wax pup-
pets, and prepared death masks of all the illustrious executed.
His colleague was Mme. Tussaud, who, in 1802, opened up her
own affiliated cabinet on the Strand, in London.[25] In 1798, a Bel-
gian physicist named Étienne-Gaspard Robertson opened his
magic lantern (an early form of slide projector) exhibition under
the title *Phantasmagoria*, and many viewers fainted in fright.
In 1802 in London another phantasmagoria opened under the
direction of Paul de Philipstal; the figures he introduced were

capable of changing their form and dimensions, they grew in size, contracted, dissolved, disappeared into the air, and even merged into each other.[26]

While in Jena and Berlin the poets and philosophers were preoccupied with the theory of the fragment, in other European nations the theorem of the fragmentation of the body was well on its way to being put into practice. While Grabbe and Hoffmann were fantasizing about "breaking the body into parts," the English and the French had already began to produce, one after the other, models of the body which could be disassembled and screwed back together. The human body became the object of a new kind of *anatomical interest*, just as even de Sade's protagonists were not victims of his sadistic torturers' instincts, but rather of his *spirit of anatomical inquiry*. So many écorchés: the body is built from parts. Or so many *corps morcelés*: the body disintegrates into fragments. If the body becomes desacralized, then it is merely a matter of viewpoint as to whether we see the same body as beautiful or as the harbinger of cessation, disintegration, or fragmentation. Just as *Heinrich von Ofterdingen* and 120 *Days of Sodom* are not antitheses but complete each other—so the freakish and the ideal, the fragment and the Whole, the living and the dead are not opposites but each other's fulfillment. Each is the shadow of the other, in such a way that at the same time each serves as a self-contained, unsurpassable source of light.

"ONLY THAT WHICH NEVER CEASES TO *HURT* STAYS IN THE MEMORY"

Variations on the Human Body,
Subjugated by Fantasies of Power

If I think back upon the subject of what, long ago, the body meant to me in my childhood or, more precisely, my own body, my recollections are extraordinarily variegated. The memories that have remained the most powerful are those connected with some kind of wound. I once almost sliced off my left index finger with a bread knife. Another time, while at Lake Balaton, the big toe of my right leg was split open by a large shell. And once I split my forehead open on a column. In each of these cases, I remember the spectacle of the flesh splitting apart much more vividly than the physical pain. I caught a glimpse of a place which had until then been concealed in darkness. I had seen something which in principle could never be seen, and which should always have remained hidden, for at least as long as I was alive. These were not serious injuries, and yet they were still memorable: the scars remain to this day. My body has retained the memory of these childhood injuries.

And yet, just as memorable as all these injuries are all the commands that arose in connection with my body. Wash your hands. Wash your ears. Take your hand out of your mouth. Brush your teeth thoroughly. Wash up properly after you've been to the toilet. Don't run. Don't scratch your wounds. Put your hand in front of your mouth when you yawn. Learn how to blow your nose properly. These commands are as memorable as all the physical wounds. They penetrated into my instincts. Admittedly, they didn't hurt, per se, but my body has preserved them as much as it has preserved its scars. Of course, by now the scars don't hurt anymore. Which makes me suspicious: Is it possible that at the time these commands also hurt—but differently from the cut of a knife? And if there were a particular kind of instrument for them, then could I also come upon the scars of these commands on my own body? "Only that which never ceases to *hurt* stays in the memory," writes Nietzsche.[1] And truly one could say that everything preserved in memory is connected with something that once gave pain. And the possibility of this pain continuing until today can't be excluded, even if I don't sense it, as I've grown so used to it.

Let me evoke another body. More precisely, the body of the young woman who was standing in front of me in line by the cashier. The weather was scorching, and her suntanned back was barely covered. The line was long, so I had plenty of time to observe it. And I could have taken a great deal of delight in it, indeed I could have found it erotic even, if my gaze had not continually, almost involuntarily, strayed to the tattoo beneath her neck. There was a sentence that ran from her left shoulder to the right. It was hard for me to decipher it: the letters were rounded and elaborate, and the serifs, branching out, crisscrossed each other. In addition, they weren't even in Hungarian, but in English. The letters coalesced into words, and the words coalesced into a sentence. It read, "To thine own self be true."

We were in a grocery store in the Hungarian countryside. Observing the girl's face, I suspected that she was not really aware of the precise meaning of these words; even if she knew some English, she would hardly be familiar with the word *thine*, and she certainly would never be interested in the source of the quote. The tracing of the elaborate letters showed that a primitive stencil had served as the basis for the tattoo. The windows of tattoo salons are full of such stencils. Later I had a look at it on the internet, and I saw that this was a very popular tattoo pattern. For me, however, it was an opening into a world previously unknown.

The quotation is from the third scene of the first act of Shakespeare's *Hamlet*. The sentence is pronounced by Polonius to his son, Laertes, when the latter is about to leave for Paris. Polonius depicts the dangers awaiting his son at great length and warns him to be observant of his own material situation. And then he says, "To thine own self be true." In other words: Don't live beyond your means. Only buy what the contents of your wallet will allow you to, do not take any loans. So the stakes were not at all about personal authenticity, as today, in the spirit of the Enlightenment, we would be inclined to interpret the admonition, but instead the statement contained very practical counsel: Don't spend any more money than strictly necessary. A piece of advice which the young woman, standing in front of me by the cashier, her shopping basket filled up with items, certainly had not heard. On the contrary.

I looked at the girl, I looked at her back, and I tried to imagine something I'd never actually seen: the process of tattooing. People say that today it is a pain-free procedure, and that one hardly feels a thing. For me, however, the process of tattooing is still closely associated with the pain that might have accompanied it in the old days: the pricking of needles, corrosive pigments, blood, indispensable wincing from the pain, sighs, indeed even tears. Tattooing is certainly no longer like that: "But in those days the writing needles let drop an acid fluid, which we're no longer permitted to use." I have borrowed these words from the writer who captured the process of tattooing in the most precise manner in all of literature: Franz Kafka. The mechanism that the Traveler glimpses in the penal colony is a perfectly constructed tattooing machine, each detail perfectly worked out, which engraves the sentence dealt out to the convict into his body. For example, "To thine own self be true." The sentence is programmed into the electronic inscribing mechanism in an elaborate, flourishing script which is hard to decipher; a harrow appended with long needles inscribes the sentence into the body of the condemned, who is tied up on a bed placed beneath the machine. "In the Designer are all the cogwheels that control the movements of the Harrow, and this machinery is regulated according to the inscription demanded by the sentence." What is most peculiar in this scenario is that the condemned man does not only not know the sentence, he is not even aware that he has been condemned. It is only during the process of the inscription, as the sentence is being carried out, that he will discover that he has sinned, and what his offense was. He does not perceive the sentence by hearing or absorb it by reading but apprehends it, literally, with his own body. The sentence is inscribed into his body, and the condemned "experiences it on his own body." The entire process takes twelve hours, and when the condemned man finally is fully aware of his crime, it's all over for him: "By that time the Harrow has pierced him quite through and cast him into the pit, where he pitches down upon the blood and water and the cotton wool."[2]

Gazing at the girl in the grocery store and the tattoo that could be read on her back and keeping in mind the epidemic-like spread of tattoos across the entire planet — a process to which people subject themselves voluntarily — one could truly say that we are all living in a penal colony. A penal colony where for the time being none of us suspects that we have committed a crime, and not in the least that we have been condemned. But all the while, the execution of the punishment is already well on its way — only we are still far away from the twelfth hour of Franz Kafka, a twelfth hour in which enlightenment and destruction occur simultaneously.

For we are in the midst of a judgment that is being carried out as we speak, a judgment of which we know nothing, although our bodies begin to suspect its presence. "Enlightenment comes to the most dull-witted," says the Officer in Kafka's story; later he comments, "How we all absorbed the look of transfiguration on the face of the sufferer, how we bathed our cheeks in the radiance of that justice, achieved at last and fading so quickly!"[3] During the course of enlightenment the body becomes aware of everything that happens to it; as a result of the judgment inscribed upon it, the condemned may finally feel his body to be exclusively his own. Because until then it was not his. It is true that his life would have been unimaginable without this body; nonetheless this body was subjugated to so many external commands and laws, had to fulfill so many expectations, that whoever lived within it could never really feel it to be completely his own. His true crime—of which he had no idea—might have been exactly this: that he never "bore" his own body; his body and he himself lived next to each other like two strangers wedged into each other. In Kafka's story the mind becomes enlightened during the slow annihilation of the body. With the intensification of pain, the condemned may finally begin to feel himself completely at home in his own body, although at the same time this means a farewell from life.

But then to whom does the body belong, if not to the one who lives in it?

If I had to answer in only a few words I would say: to the others. The others, who—to use the expression of Rilke—"turn the baby around,"[4] so that it will not see what Rilke called "the Opened," and who subsequently do nothing but tattoo their expectations onto this body. At the end of the eighteenth century, William Blake, observing this "turning around" of infants, burst out, "Sooner murder an infant in its cradle than nurse unacted desires." And he also said: "The tigers of wrath are wiser than the horses of instruction." Both citations are from his book of proverbs, *The Marriage of Heaven and Hell.* Blake attacked those who wished to create trained ponies out of human beings with such vehemence and stood for the liberation of the body so radically that many of his contemporaries considered him simply mentally deranged. He only began to be appreciated in the twentieth century, and then primarily by those who themselves wished to free the body from the grasp of the invisible shackles coiling around it: the surrealists as well as the Beat poets, primarily Allen Ginsberg.

"Horse of instruction." In Blake's writings, we do not find any trace of his having known the letters of Lord Chesterfield to his son. Nonetheless, I am convinced that when he wrote the Proverbs of Hell—one of the most radical texts of the past two centuries—he was directing his words to the already deceased Chesterfield. Lord Chesterfield (1694–1773) was the most famous letter writer of his day: he wrote more than four hundred letters to his illegitimate son, Philip Stanhope; their correspondence began in 1738, when the boy was six years old, and lasted until Stanhope's death in 1768. In 1774, a year after Chesterfield's death, his son's widow began publishing the letters, and from that point on the publications followed one after the other: in the eighteenth and nineteenth centuries the book was considered an indispensable addition to the bookshelf or mantelpiece in every respectable household. These letters were, in effect, the most renowned and most read of any modern guide to conduct—and the last of its kind as well in a genre. They could have also been titled "How to Create a Horse of Instruction out of a Child." The relationship of Lord Chesterfield's letters to Blake's proverbs is something like the relation between Kant's 1788 *Critique of Practical Reason* and its categorical imperative to Mozart and da Ponte's *Don Giovanni* (which had premiered one year earlier). And so a few counsels, picked out at random: When in society, observe everyone well, follow closely the manners and behavior of others, study well how they sit down, and how they stand up, how they engage in chitchat, how they hold their walking sticks, what they do with their hands, how they hold their legs. And so on, and so on. And after all this advice: "When you go into a good company . . . observe carefully their turn, their manners, their address: and conform your own to them."[5] From this volume, containing more than a thousand pages of letters—on whose basis Charles Dickens named Chesterfield one of the greatest of all English writers—the most consistent, as well as the most intimidating, picture emerges of the behavioral culture of the modern age. Chesterfield's enterprise was not without precedent: the books of Machiavelli, Baldassare Castiglione, or Baltasar Gracián similarly offered paragons and confessional guides to their readers. The difference was that whereas these guides placed emphasis on the uniqueness of the individual, his peculiar traits and, in the original sense of the word, his distinction, Chesterfield's emphasis was on the individual's adjustment, adaptation, and integration—namely, the relinquishment of individuality. Always pay close attention to the society in which you find yourself, for "this is an attention due from every individual to the majority."[6] In other words, the greatest responsibility of the individual is alignment with the majority. The ideal readers of the earlier "behavioral guides" could have been something like the subjects of Renaissance portraits, who have no essential connection to the background of the painting but stand out from their environments like statues. In contrast, the ideal readers of Chesterfield are like students in high school class graduation pictures who, seen from a certain distance, hauntingly resemble one another. The first group were the representatives of a behavioral culture that was aristocratic; in contrast, Chesterfield, although he was a lord, was a typical frontline fighter for bourgeois behavioral culture.

What is most conspicuous in these letters is how Chesterfield tries, through the dense forest of prohibitions, to drive his son toward the correct mode of life. He bombards him with a multitude of seemingly innocent counsels. Be patient, don't argue with anyone, don't whine, be reserved, don't hurt anyone, listen to the principles of others, think before you open your mouth. And in addition, he expected his son to know how to behave appropriately: be courteous, thank people respectfully, look at the person you're speaking to, conduct yourself with politeness. But don't allow yourself to become conspicuous in whatever society you happen to find yourself; let your dress be appropriate but not too blatant, so that you "avoid individuality." And the best way to avoid individuality and singularity is to imitate the manners of others—imitate their courtesies, their behaviors, their ways of interacting with each other, the ease of their conversations, their variations. And for all this, of course, one has to know how to move appropriately, for which reason Lord Chesterfield through the course of the years can never emphasize enough the significance of the dancing master. Hire a dancing master, and always the best, he writes to his son, who resides in various cities of Europe and studies with his tutor. But not so that you will know how to dance well, but so that you will learn the most appropriate way to sit down, stand up, stand in one place, use your hands, know the proper way to take off your hat and then put it on again, to hold the teacup and then put it down, to handle cutlery, to use the salt and pepper shakers at table, to walk, to stroll, or even to hurry so that you never have to run.

And with that we find ourselves at the regulation of the body. Power—the power of the majority that we have mentioned, nameless and faceless—must become thoroughly enmeshed within the entire body. Never scratch yourself in society, no matter how much something might itch. If you're speaking, articulate appropriately and don't mumble, don't grind your teeth. But if you have opened your mouth, then make sure it doesn't stink; for that reason always keep your teeth clean—wash them every morning with a sponge and lukewarm water for four or five minutes, and then after every meal as well, at least five or six times a day, so that your breath won't be malodorous. And keep not only your teeth clean but your hands as well, and of course pay attention to your nails, don't cut them too short but rather into the shape of a half-moon, and if you wash your hands, push back the skin around the nails, don't let them grow in. And in the same manner take care of your ears, don't pick them in company, and wash them once a day. Don't dig around in your mouth, and especially don't pick your nose—Lord Chesterfield admonishes his son concerning that with suspicious frequency over the course of the years. Use a handkerchief, but don't even think, when in society, of scrutinizing what you just blew or spit into it. When you're speaking don't grab another's arm, or the buttons on his clothes. In other words, remain in control of yourself. And control your facial muscles as well; never laugh, just smile, but in such a way that it won't distort into a grimace. Laughter is very easy to stop, he advises his son: "Laughter is very easily restrained by a very little reflection."[7]

Yes, Chesterfield mentions the enchanting word *reflection*. Whoever is in possession of reflection may avoid the greatest danger of them all, namely "an ill-bred body." Chesterfield emphasizes many times over that for him the chief goal is the gaining of grace: "I repeat, and I shall never cease repeating to you, *the Graces, the Graces.*"[8] An extremely peculiar concept of grace emerges from Chesterfield's letters. For him, grace is a function of a kind of absolute reflection, and as such is the exact opposite of Kleist's definition of grace. Kleist wrote: "The more that reflection becomes darker and weaker in the organic world, so does the grace within it emerge all the more living and radiant."[9] For Chesterfield, grace emerges as a result of reflection. Looking at his store of examples, grace means the integration of conduct deemed acceptable by the majority. For him grace occurs when a person's gaze is continually trained upon others, the result of which is that the will of the anonymous, faceless majority extirpates from the individual that which is singular and individual within him and, as it were, stretches him across the torture rack—just as the condemned man was tied down in Kafka's story so that the inscribing machine could engrave into his body the command and judgment which seemed to be eternal but were in fact mundane. "I repeat, and I repeat again, and I shall never cease repeating to you," he writes while dispensing yet another piece of advice, then adds: "Air, manners, grace, style, elegancy, and all those ornaments must now be the only objects of your attention." To repeat until the end of time—to engrave it into the brain, so that at last the body and the soul will become a well-functioning mechanism. "We are complicated machines," he writes, "and though we have one main spring, that gives motion to the whole, we have an infinity of little wheels, which, in their turns, retard, precipitate, and sometimes stop that motion." To employ the expression of Julien de La Mettrie, this machine is a human machine—*l'homme machine*—an expression Chesterfield, as the personal acquaintance of Voltaire, Fontenelle, and Montesquieu, might have heard. The human being is a machine, which nonetheless has to be carefully watched, because it can easily break down. Not because of some illness, but because individuality might get the upper hand, from the horse of instruction the enraged tiger will burst out, endangering the majority, to wit, the well-oiled functioning of society. Supervision, eternal surveillance, perfect transparency and pellucidity, just as a generation later Lord Chesterfield's compatriot Jeremy Bentham was to conceive of it. Bentham dreamed of the ideal prison in which the guard never loses sight of the prisoners. Chesterfield would have been delighted to lock his own son in a prison, in which, of course, the prison guard would be none other than himself. Writing from London, he threatens his son—who was fifteen years old at the time—with something like that when he is resident in Leipzig with his tutor: "I give you fair warning, that at Leipsig I shall have a hundred invisible spies about you; and shall be exactly informed of everything that you do, and almost everything that you say." A few months later he repeats, "Be assured that I have many eyes upon you."[10]

This striving for perfection, however, frequently has the opposite effect. For Lord Chesterfield, inner and outer discipline were meant to become indistinguishable: the final goal was for his son to make all the external expectations and commands his own, to interiorize them, and, finally, to fully integrate them into his own instincts. What at the beginning seems like a form of punishment—for in the end Chesterfield does little else but train his son; disinheriting him would be a blessing in disguise—at the end creates the best of impressions. Through endless repetition, the enunciated advice becomes distorted into a series of commands, and as they proliferate day after day, the person subjected to them finally becomes something like a pit pony: he could hardly imagine that life could be anything different from what it is. The final goal of this kind of psychic terror is that at the end of it all the greatest desire of the human being is to become a sacrifice. Of course, when we read these letters today, we merely smile and brush them aside. In fact, we don't even read them anymore; that's how banal we find them. Virginia Woolf was the last person who made the effort to read them, in the 1930s, and subsequently penned a luminous essay about them—full of reservations, even a kind of scorn. But why don't we read these letters anymore? The reason is that we have already learned all of Chesterfield's prescriptions by heart—we, as it were, anticipate them. We no longer pick our noses in front of other people, we put our hands in front of our mouths when yawning, we know how to deal with our bodily fluids, and so on. What had to be learned in the eighteenth century—even at the price of blood, sweat, and tears—seems more than two centuries later to be perfectly self-evident. Even our most private instincts wait in readiness in order to conform to public expectations. So ready are we to obey Chesterfield's commands, it is as if he had hypnotized us. His letters are brilliant examples of mnemonics. And the technique of mnemonics appears to be the most natural of all, although—as Nietzsche writes—"Indeed there was nothing more fearful and uncanny in the whole prehistory of man than his *mnemotechnics*. 'If something is to stay in the memory it must be burned in: only that which never ceases to *hurt* stays in the memory'—this is a main clause of the oldest (unhappily also the most enduring) psychology on earth. . . . Man could never do without blood, torture, and sacrifices when he felt the need to create a memory for himself."[11] Kafka knew this; the girl standing in line at the cash register had already forgotten it, and had voluntarily bent her neck underneath the tattooing machine. She had even paid for it.

Philip Stanhope, Lord Chesterfield's illegitimate son, was unwilling to stick his neck underneath that mechanism. "There are some additional qualifications necessary . . . such as the absolute command of your temper" — this, according to Chesterfield, was the chief consideration; his son, however, did not want to hear it. To no avail the supervision, to no avail the spies, Stanhope resisted. An acquaintance of Chesterfield's met up with the young man in Germany and, returning to London, gave an account of his behavior. "He told me that, that in the company you were frequently most *provokingly* inattentive, absent, and *distrait*; that you came into a room, and presented yourself very awkwardly; that at table you constantly threw down knives, forks, napkins, bread &c. and that you neglected your person and dress, and to such a degree unpardonable at any age, and much more so at your years."[12] For the father, the ideal was the body governed to the fullest measure; the son, however (at least for the time), behaved like a savage — his instincts overriding any societal-cultural commands. (And we can also note parenthetically that these instincts did not emerge from the void, but themselves are complex cultural formations.)

The body must learn how to behave and so has to be bound hand and foot with invisible preventive measures. Around the visible and palpable physical body there weighs down, like a set of iron rings, a second body — invisible, societal. This second body — held up as an ideal as well as a functional body according to the mechanisms of social control — was at that point (the turn of the eighteenth century) proving to be extraordinarily frail, just as it it was becoming a moral imperative; what Chesterfield designated the "well-bred body." It was this "well-bred body," so to speak, that provoked the "ill-bred body" — and consider, right at that time, the way the human body becomes deformed and unrecognizable in the works of the Marquis de Sade, how Olimpia's body falls to pieces in Hoffmann's story "The Sandman," Kunigunda's fate in Kleist's *Katie of Heilbronn; or, The Trial by Fire*, or the deformation that results from the desire to create the perfect body in Mary Shelley's *Frankenstein*. And of course we must recall William Blake's numerous depictions of human beings, in connection with which his English-Swiss painter friend Henry Fuseli commented: "Blake is the master of emancipated anatomy."[13] In 1796, John Gabriel Stedman's *Narrative of A Five Years' Expedition Against the Revolted Negroes of Surinam* was published in two volumes, for which Blake created the illustrations (between 1792 and 1794). The etchings that Blake prepared for Stedman's account are veritable studies in just how far one can go in the propositions of torture, ruination, and perversion.

It is very easy to picture how, while Chesterfield was trying to train his son's body to perfection, figures like those subsequently created by de Sade, Hoffmann, Mary Shelley, or William Blake might have welled up in his fantasies as deterrent examples. Earlier, such images would have been difficult to envisage. In order for the physical being of the body to be foregrounded to such a degree, for its physical being to become its exclusive quality, the body had to be withdrawn from its earlier, natural metaphysical context. The academic literature dealing with history of the body in European culture tends to connect this phenomenon to the French Revolution: whereas earlier the king, with respect to Jesus Christ, had been the emblem of the extemporal body, by the end of the eighteenth century the individual body, just then stepping into the political arena, became anchored in time and became the standard.[14] The "civil" body was ever more increasingly confined to its own mere physical being. This process, however, had already begun well before the Revolution, as is manifested by Chesterfield's letters, in which the admonitions and warnings directed at the body bear witness to the desire to transform the body into an automaton.

The duality between the "well bred" and "ill-bred" body at the turn of the eighteenth century, is, in my view, paradoxically demonstrated most palpably in a twentieth-century creation, the film *The Marquise of O*, based on Kleist's story and directed by Eric Rohmer (1976). The main character, the Marquise, from the beginning of the story until the end, is deeply captivated by Count F. When he appears for the first time—he saves the Marquise from ravaging Russian soldiers—"he seemed an angel sent from heaven." Later, however, when it emerges that it was he who had raped the Marquise after she had fainted, he becomes a devil in her eyes. As it is stated in the last line of the story: "She would not have seen a devil in him then if she had not seen an angel in him at their first meeting."[15] The Count, who in the beginning seemed to be "well bred," in reality was very "ill-bred."

In relation to this film, Rohmer did not refer to himself as an auteur, but rather as a *metteur-en-scène*;[16] although the fact that he not only brought the story to the screen but interpreted it as a co-author is best demonstrated in the way the Count's duality is present in the figure of the Marquise as well. And for this he made use of images from the visual arts at the turn of the eighteenth century.[17] Among these images, two particularly stand out. The Marquise, after the Russians have seized the citadel, along with her aristocratic parents moves into a decidedly bourgeois house, where not only her lifestyle and clothes become middle-class, but the arrangement of the home and the furnishings do as well, from the furniture to the upholstery and the curtains, even the articles of daily use. The pastel palette that Rohmer employs in these scenes almost exclusively moves between various shades of light and a warmish brown, as well as gold and creamy yellow. Everything is restrained, including the behavior of the protagonists—in part so that later the father will all the more conspicuously lose his self-control. In this new residence, the Marquise, after realizing she is pregnant, begins to spend more and more time resting on a kind of divan, which the French used to call a *chaise longue* before it became known as a *récamier*, following the portrait of Jacques-Louis David which depicted Madame Récamier (1800). And in reality, the Marquise of Rohmer's film is seen sitting quite a few times in the pose of Madame Récamier, on a similar divan, in similar clothing. The original painting is the emblem of perfect restraint and self-control; radiating out from it is the orderliness of the body and the self-discipline which Chesterfield expected from his son.

Madame Récamier hailed from a bourgeois family: at the time of David's portrait, she was twenty-three years old, the daughter of a notary and the wife of a banker. Benjamin Constant considered her the most beautiful woman of the age, and she captured the hearts of many men; one year before the painting of the (unfinished) portrait, Napoleon's younger brother Lucien Bonaparte fell in love with her and wrote her passionate love letters; later Prince Augustus of Prussia implored her to divorce and become his wife (a novel of the era, *Athénaïs*, written by Madame de Genlis in 1807, was based upon this passionate romance). The young woman, however, turned out to be unapproachable while at the same time presumably doing all she could to whip up men's passions. In the portrait by David, we see a woman who is perfectly in charge of the situation. As she turns toward the viewer, she invites him, and yet at the same time remains secluded (just as later on, the great Odalisque of Ingres will do, even while nude); her naked upper arms and feet draw one's gaze, her garments, however, decisively issue the command to stop—the white hue of her garment suggests virginal purity, as does their tailoring. This kind of garment followed the fashion of the era for Greek-style clothes (à la grecque); in the 1790s women for the most part wore such antiquating garments consisting of loose white gowns, and they were generally accepted as a norm. Because of the transparency of the fabric, however, women who dressed in such a fashion were accused of exhibitionism; the exposed neck and upper arms, as well as the translucency of the fabric, made them appear quasi-nude. In 1799 — a year before the portrait of Madame Récamier was created — a letter appeared on the pages of the *Journal des Dames et des Modes* concerning women who dressed à la grecque and à la romaine: "Women have chosen the costume of Psyche, Venus and her nymphs. Dressed in an enchanting manner, they attract and hold our regard. Their breasts whose movements give birth to our desires, whose delicious forms are hardly concealed by a light fabric . . . in order better to draw their voluptuous contours, everything in this new fashion provokes voluptuousness; and yet women complain of the little decency that is preserved near them."[18] This could also apply to Madame Récamier. In appearance, everything about her is restrained, measured, and suggestive of order; and yet Chesterfield would hardly wish such a bride for his son. The vicomte de Chateaubriand, however, in his comments about Madame Récamier, quotes a passage from one of the despairingly passionate letters of Lucien Bonaparte: "I soon saw the tranquil front of indifference seated between us" — and as he too was in love with her, he certainly as well suffered from that tranquil brow.[19] Behind that indifferent surface, there could have been much turmoil. Eric Rohmer sensed the turmoil behind the constraint and moderation of the David painting clearly; his "Madame Récamier" (the Marquise of O) in the moments of her deepest despair and spiritual exhaustion begins to resemble Madame Récamier. And in addition, he throws an integrated, chaotic net of sexuality over her, which results in a particular interpretation of David's painting: behind the "well bred body," there can be glimpsed the uncontrollable world of passions, desires, fantasies.

It is this second world that Rohmer shows us. After Count F saves the Marquise, and before she is raped by him, she is given an infusion of opium, to relax her. This time she is resting upon a couch, and in her delirium, daydreaming, she half falls off, as it were exposing herself before the men who are waiting to find her. The disheveled silk negligee nearly slides off the Marquise, and grabbing its material, she seems to be presumptively calling upon the men observing her to rape her. As to whether it happens or not, Rohmer is naturally silent; although the mise-en-scène suggests that the Marquise is at least as much responsible for becoming pregnant as Count F. The mise-en-scène of the film also relies upon a somewhat more recent work of art: the painting by Henry Fuseli titled *Nightmare* (1781). Many parallels can be drawn between the paintings of David and Fuseli: the wide bed, occupying nearly the entire painting, the recumbent female figure, the white garments, in both cases disheveled, the relative lack of furnishings, the dark background. In the painting by Fuseli (known as Füssli at birth), the sexual overtones can be misunderstood. In European culture, the horse is the traditional iconic emblem of unrestrained sexuality; the demon, however, is the embodiment of the kind of tightening in the chest that sufferers from anxiety regularly experience. The woman falling off the bed is not awake, nor is she asleep; the disordered, crumpled bedspread signifies that she is at daggers drawn with her own sexuality: she is enslaved by it as much as she is terrified by it. She is the prisoner of erotic tension; this is also demonstrated in the way her waist rises from the bed, her thighs tightened. Her upper body is prostrate; her lower body tense. Only art historians can say whether David was familiar with this painting—but even if he wasn't (which is likely), his portrait of Madame Récamier can still be considered to be in dialogue with Fuseli's painting. For it would not take too much for the dark background behind Madame Récamier to become populated by Fuseli's specters (or, for that matter, the monsters of Goya's etching *The Sleep of Reason Produces Monsters*); and the woman's body will no longer be obedient to self-discipline. For the figure of Madame Récamier is also not without its own tension: her upper body, leaning on her left elbow, is inclined at an angle that cannot be sustained for long, and the two pillows can hardly be helping.

The later iconographic developments in Fuseli's paintings are also worthy of mention. In the 1790s, right around the time of the glory days of Madame Récamier, in Paris Philippe Pinel became the supervising physician in the Hospice Salpêtrière, and he began to treat his mentally ill patients, previously held amid brutal conditions, humanely, in the spirit of the Enlightenment—he termed this new approach *traitement moral*, and he freed many from the literal fetters in which until then they had been confined. In 1795, the historical painter Tony Robert-Fleury depicted these chains being removed from a female patient. The position of the woman lying in the background—

around her waist can still be seen an iron fetter—is very similar to the pose of the woman in the Fuseli picture. And here, in the same hospital, ninety years later, its most famous physician, Jean-Martin Charcot, presented his patients suffering from hysteria to the general public, their body language often hauntingly evoking Fuseli's painting as well.[20] It is well known that Freud, who worked for a while in Salpêtrière, considered Charcot to be a true master—and what could be more natural than the fact that a reproduction of Fuseli's painting hangs even today in Freud's study in Vienna at Bergstrasse 19? He received it as a present from his biographer Ernest Jones, who chose the same image as a frontispiece for his volume *On the Nightmare* (1931).

Let us return to Eric Rohmer's film. The figure of the Marquise of O oscillates between the two extremes of the female figures of David and Fuseli: between the extremes of bodily subjugation and bodily discipline, perfect self-control and hysteria. The dialectic of the Enlightenment is demonstrated in the two visual quotations: the clear and the sunlit, the nocturnal and the dark, which—and Kleist's story is a demonstration of this—do not exclude each other but presume each other. Just as, in another work of the same era, Mary Shelley's *Frankenstein*, the desire for knowledge and sober deliberation becomes the prerequisite for ghastly, anxiety-producing dread, the *Umheimliche*. It cannot be excluded that the Fuseli-inspired scene in Rohmer's film might have served as the basis for another visual quotation from Fuseli, this time in the film *Gothic*, directed by Ken Russell (1986). In this work, which takes place on the banks of Lake Geneva, the protagonists are Lord Byron, Percy Bysshe Shelley, the physician John Polidori, Byron's lover Claire Clairmont, and Mary Wollstonecraft Godwin, Shelley's wife-to-be. As is well known, Mary Godwin wrote *Frankenstein* here when she was eighteen years old. Supposedly the basis of the story was a nightmare— and Russell associates this nightmare with the painting of Fuseli. The Fuseli parallel is justified, for one of the novel's key scenes, in which the monster murders Victor Frankenstein's new bride, is hauntingly reminiscent of Fuseli's picture: "She was there, lifeless and inanimate, thrown across the bed, her head hanging down and her pale and distorted features half covered by her hair . . . with a sensation of horror not to be described, I saw at the open window a figure the most hideous and abhorred. A grin was on the face of the monster; he seemed to jeer, as with his fiendish finger he pointed towards the corpse of my wife."[21] (The mother of Mary Shelley, Mary Wollstonecraft, had been Fuseli's lover for a while, a fact of which her daughter only became aware later on; she also assisted her father in having her mother's love letters returned to the family from Fuseli's estate.)[22]

The fantasies of power directed at the body in the modern age reached their most extreme form in *Frankenstein*. In this work, the body evades every metaphysical connection and becomes a mere physical being in the strictest sense of the word. The Demon is the victim of metaphysical lack. The Demon himself is all too aware what it means when nothing remains to a person but his body. Catching a glimpse of himself, he curses his own creation, as he considers himself to be—in the French-

Romanian philosopher Emil Cioran's expression—a fault of creation: "My person was hideous and my stature gigantic. What did this mean? Who was I? What was I? Whence did I come? What was my destination? These questions continually recurred, but I was unable to solve them."[23]

Frankenstein's creation is the living memorial of the "fearful and uncanny" mnemotechnics mentioned by Nietzsche. In the strictest sense of the word, that which must be remembered throughout one's entire life is engraved onto the body: if the world is divested of its metaphysical dimensions, nothing is easier than for the body to become the prey of fantasies of power. These fantasies, as in the case of Lord Chesterfield, may spring from the best of all possible intentions; nonetheless, they frequently elicit the opposite response. The Hungarian philosopher Béla Hamvas wrote, in connection with these truisms: "In the imagination of man, nothing is as capable of stirring up the whirlpool of wickedness lurking within than the truism. This occurs because an oration or a Sunday sermon awakens in man the deepest layers of villainy, indeed, it incites them."[24] Chesterfield, as well, lectured, preached, raised his son morally in the spirit of Pinel's *traitement moral*. But it is quite possible that his son, while he read his father's warnings, in his soul became something like Frankenstein's creation: covered with scars, with wounds that could never be healed, with dark impulses. But before we would rush to judgment: as the inheritors of the Enlightenment, who among us could say with a tranquil heart that he or she is free of these scars, these wounds, and these impulses?

SLEEP AND THE DREAM

We are such stuff
As dreams are made on, and our little life
Is rounded with a sleep.
   William Shakespeare, *The Tempest*

Sleep

I once read about someone who had a mirror installed above his bed for use at night. He wanted to see himself while he slept.

The thought is not as absurd as might appear to be at first glance. There is probably not one of us who has not tried at some point or another to catch hold of that exact moment when we fall asleep or to observe ourselves while in the state of sleep. In any event, I myself have attempted both these things many times. More than once I experimented with how I might be able to track the exact process of falling asleep: to accompany myself, as it were, following from behind, watching my own self slowly growing sleepy as I left a state of wakefulness. To watch it slowly lose its contours and turn into something about which I have almost no knowledge. The one thing I can say about this entity is that it certainly cannot refer to itself as "I." The rest is just a kind of obscure feeling, something that would have a kind of floating, trembling, spongy substance, protruding and then holding back on itself. There were many times when I wished to lie in wait for it.

To observe something in a state of alertness, the essence of which is the absence of alertness. To observe as I slip out of my own self, and I leave myself behind, something which more than anything else creates the impression of a shell or envelope, although it appears to be the most palpable proof of the existence of my state of watchfulness. What exactly is going on? When falling asleep, I begin perceptibly to feel one with my body to a degree which is quite rare during wakefulness. And yet I can hardly claim with a clear conscience that the body has become absolute. But I would not say that in leaving my diurnal self behind the soul has somehow made its way back to itself, even though there is much to support this. For when I am falling asleep, already in a kind of half-slumber, I still can sense within myself a kind of impression, as if the soul were beginning to "arrive home"—presuming we are not restricting soul, whatever it may be, to the concept of consciousness. On the contrary, when falling asleep, the significance of the soul seems to be dwarfed in relation to something else. But in relation to what?

As I fall asleep, I leave my body and my soul behind, all the while palpably returning back to my body and my soul. But what is actually going on here? It is not my body that has changed, or my soul, but rather my relation to both. By day, when I'm awake, I usually observe my body from without, and although I am only capable of imagining myself as a physical body, I don't identify myself with it. In a similar way, I don't fully identify with my soul either. If I'm awake, for the most part I think of it, as it were, as someone (or something), which cannot exist without me, and yet is not completely identical to me. I would almost speak of it in the third-person singular. This is Descartes's final inheritance; not even I can avoid his influence. In the moment when I began to speak about the body *or* about the soul, I unwittingly behave as if it were possible to distinguish between them. And in doing so I imperceptibly differentiate myself from them. I create a differentiation between the soul and the body. And as I am the victim of an illusion, in the depths of my heart (my soul), I cannot either identify with what I refer to as body or as soul.

As I fall asleep, the force of this inheritance abates. Neither my body nor my soul undergoes any changes, but the misconception that there can be a body without a soul, and a soul without a body, becomes threadbare. And then I finally become identical with them: I will be fully one with my body and my soul. In falling asleep, instead of that diurnal illusion, the validity of that experience — that one cannot be pictured without the other; they cannot even be separated from one another — comes into force. I have become one with both my body and my soul to such a degree that I cannot even speak about either body or soul. For during sleep it is not possible to speak, nor is it possible to give an account of these experiences. This is one of the peculiar traps of the civilization of the modern age — I can only experience what is most natural with no pangs of remorse when I am unconscious of it.

From where do I draw the knowledge of the kinds of new experiences I have during sleep? For this, the mirror hung above the bed may be of use—namely, that state of half-slumber, what I experience while falling asleep, when I am no longer capable of speaking or saying anything, or of carrying out any of my wishes, but I am still awake enough to perceive what is happening with me and within me.

Of course, during wakeful states, there are situations, periods, and states of being when this duality ceases as well. These states include joy, happiness, convulsions, catastrophes, ecstasy, repulsion, satisfaction, laughter—one could extend the list. At such times I will feel myself to be almost in an incommunicable state. Not due to the poverty of language, but because I have entered a condition beyond language. In such moments, I am not only unified with my body and my soul, but both of them have located each other. I find myself to be in a particular, dreamlike state. I am not the master of the situation. While asleep I am incapable of inciting myself to accomplish any deed; while within the state of joy, satisfaction, or repulsion, I cannot bring myself to be preoccupied with anything other than that state. I am at the mercy of the situation. But what grows above me and knocks me down does not destroy me. On the contrary: it is precisely this new state that grants contours to my existence. It designates boundaries I cannot reject. In such situations it emerges that my identity stems from an unknown strength. From something infinitely unknown to me. Within me there is a kind of cosmic distance. And yet it is hidden within my innermost being; it is concealed there. It is a part of my own identity, I know nothing about it, but it will never leave me.

During the state of sleep, this unknown strength asserts itself. Indeed, what happens to us from one night to the next can be termed a miracle. And it is just as much of a miracle that that which occupies a full third of our lives retreats in daytime, as we wake up. At least during the past centuries of the development of the modern age, we have definitively eliminated any inquisitiveness about this miracle from the sphere of our interests. Not only are there no reassuring answers as to why we need sleep or why the state of wakefulness is not enough, there are also no answers as to why, while sleeping, amid the greatest tranquillity, we are laid siege to by dreams. And there are no answers about what is happening above our heads, precisely within our heads while we sleep, at the period when we are the least preoccupied with our heads.

While we sleep we are initiated into a kind of secret; we acquire a kind of enigmatic knowledge, of which, however, we can give no account because all the while we are asleep. And while we are awake, then we do nothing but forget about this secret — continuously, even when, mustering together all our knowledge, we try to reflect upon it. The question arises: Does this mean that wakefulness is the state of forgetting, of dispersion, and sleep is the state of knowledge, of collectedness?

I would not go that far, and yet I would still presume to state that during sleep some kind of harmony comes into being and the fatal legacy of Descartes — the bifurcation of body and soul — loses its validity. When I am awake, I am preoccupied with my body or my soul, although I could not care less about who exactly is "preoccupied" with them. When I become drowsy, this "preoccupation" slowly begins to diminish; my interest toward the body or the soul begins to die out. But this lessening does not mean that I have become voided. On the contrary — something is beginning to grow within me. The more sleepy I am, the more insistent it becomes. And by the time I have fallen asleep, this something has completely replenished me. What this unknown laying claim to me is, I don't know. I don't even know if it is something that arrives from the outside and then conquers me, or if it enters from within, from somewhere where it was hiding, and for as long as I was awake left me in peace. For this is just as much of a mystery today as it has been for millennia.

The Dream

El sueño de la razón produce monstruos. The sleep of reason produces monsters. The title of Goya's etching, from 1797–1798, is more enigmatic than what is depicted in the etching itself. And what we see there is connected to the iconographic traditions with strong threads. A man has laid his head on his crossed arms on top of a table (or a stone bench), his legs crossed; it seems he is sleeping. Behind his back, many animals can be seen: a cat, owls, bats. We can almost hear their wings rustling. The theme is hardly new. In European visual arts, ever since the time of Giotto, there have been numerous renditions of sleeping persons with their dreams depicted behind (or above) them. Giotto painted the dreams of Pope Innocent III; El Greco painted the dreams of Philip II, and Jusepe de Ribera those of Jacob. In every case we see the dreamer and above him the projected dream, whose reality is given as that of the sleeping person. These narrative paintings are imbued with the spirit of Greek tradition, according to which one does not *have* a dream, one *sees* a dream. At the end of the eighteenth century, with the conquest by secularization, this trope became favored not only among painters but among caricaturists as well. Around the same time as Goya, in 1797 George Woodward of England prepared an engraving titled "A Monkish Vision," which depicts a rotund priest in the middle of a nap, while in the background lounge lascivious women and floridly laid tables. This depiction—as in the case of Goya's etching as well—presages the procedures of the twentieth-century comic strip, in which the reader is told what the figures are thinking by small insertions of text above their heads.

The theme of Goya's etching is, accordingly, not new. What is new about it is its title—more precisely, the ambiguity of the title. For it can be interpreted in two ways: in one reading it gives us to understand that the monsters come forth when reason is asleep and no longer supervises its environs. Or it can be interpreted to mean that the monsters, which otherwise peacefully hide away in the darkness, come forth when reason has been made vertiginous by its own pride, considering that it can solve everything on its own. This is what William Blake might have been thinking when he wrote, nine years before Goya created his etching, "Thought alone can make monsters, but the affections cannot."[1] The monsters accordingly break out as reason's compensation, or, contrarily, when reason itself falls asleep, it dreams them, or, to use a more modern term, it projects them.

The interpretation one accepts will depend on one's own appraisal of the historical circumstances, and within those, the Enlightenment's. During the nineteenth century, Goya's etching was interpreted within an Enlightenment context (the expression of the triumph of reason); at the time of Freud's study "Das Unheimliche" (The Uncanny), however, an opposing analysis began to emerge. Each interpretation accords a central significance to light: in the first case, it is the "luminescence" of reason; in the second, it is the act of "bringing something into the light." Either reason unveils something or reason itself must be unveiled. Goya's own stance toward these matters allows for both explanations. His strong connections to his contemporary Spanish thinkers of the Enlightenment are well known; but so too is his passionate interest in the "irrational."

The interpretation of this title is, therefore, open, and instead of offering a point of reference to the viewer, it forces one to make a choice. Goya was probably aware of this ambiguity. Considering his attraction to sensitive situations, including political ones, it can be presumed that he deliberately chose a title with which he could justify himself in either sense.

The openness of the title also allows for a third explanation. This, however, is "programmed" a priori into its indeterminacy. For no matter how we explain it, in either case the question of the

unclear and troubled relation between reason and intellect—
and the unknown which cannot be delimited by either reason or
intellect—is raised. These are characteristic problems of the Enlightenment. A title like this would never have occurred to anyone before Goya. For Giotto, El Greco, or Ribera, dreams had an
unequivocally transcendent dimension. Heraclitus maintained
that for those who are awake there is a common world, whereas
those who are sleep live in their own world with its own peculiar entrance; the sleeper, nonetheless, steps into a kind of world
which offers trust along with all its unknowns. The precondition
of this trust is the existence of a kind of power to which people
can entrust themselves. Even the most nightmarish of dreams,
which, according to surviving accounts, the great mystics suffered, can be viewed in the light of certain divine connections to
which the sleeper can entrust himself upon awakening.

With Goya, this situation has radically changed. The ambiguity of the title of his etching signifies the shattering of this
trust. That which earlier had been "external" (demons, monsters,
devils, but equally angels, as well as helpful spirits), with secularization's ascendance became "internal," bereft of its transcendental connections, and thus transformed into inner thoughts.
The place of holistic explications was taken over by those of psychology. And, of course, the enigma of torturous dreams remains
as unsolved as it had been previously. The situation—as the soul
became separated from its transcendental roots—became ever
more problematic. If the soul and reason can rely only on their
own selves, then one may be filled with pride and the conscious-

ness of one's omnipotence, just as, in the case of misfortune, one is filled with despair, or even torturous self-hatred. Instead of the "external" unknown, humanity now was confronted with an "internal" unknown—either appearing up ahead like a heavenly ladder, a replacement for the divine guarantee, or yawning open like an abyss.

Goya's etching is not first and foremost about reason, nor is it about monsters; it is about that ambiguity with which European culture was faced at the end of the eighteenth century. When the young Hegel worked on his *Phenomenology of Spirit,* for a while he believed that he had gone insane. In writing about reason, his mode of thought had become unbridled. He must have felt like Goya's sleeping figure, for he too was threatened by demons and monsters. He might have been frightened by the recognition that what creates the greatest uncertainty in a human being is also what grants him his greatest strength: the mind. It is, accordingly, a secondary concern as to whether the monsters are occurring within the confines of one's mind or they appear externally to it. The decisive issue is that mind, while creating a sense of unboundedness, is itself hardly unbounded. If, however, it does have boundaries, these are not designated by mind but by something which is beyond its limitations. In the twentieth century, Georges Bataille designated the experience of the unknown beyond these boundaries the divine: "God isn't humanity's limit-point, though humanity's limit-point is divine. Or put it this way—humanity is divine when experiencing limits."[2] I believe Goya was more cautious. As he became entangled in the question of boundaries of the mind, he did not trust himself to the "divine." He was much too committed to the Enlightenment for that. He did not undertake to find a home for himself within "intoxication" or the "divine" while turning his back on reason. With Goya, it is not the human and the divine that meet up on that border, but rather that which inspires trust—and dread. According to the visual evidence furnished by *El sueño de la razón produce monstruos*, it is during sleep that a human being locates himself on this boundary. This boundary is the inner unknown. The true enigma which must be faced during sleep is not the army of monsters, not even the omnipotence or, conversely, the limitations of the mind, but the inner unknown creating an impression of infinity and all the while doing nothing but delimiting man and forcing him to confront his own boundaries. The man in Goya's etching, seated, his head resting on the stone bench, is not filled with the experience of the freedom of infinity—as is the case for the sleepers of Giotto, El Greco, or de Ribera—but rather with its confusion.

The man we see in Goya's etching dreams of this confusion. If, in earlier decades, the dream prepared the awakener for great acts and decisive resolutions, then the figure in Goya's etching is already subjugated to a completely different kind of inspiration. It is possible that upon awakening he would grab pen or brush in order do battle with these monsters. But it is just as likely that he would proceed like Gregor Samsa, who "woke one morning from troubled dreams, [and] found himself transformed in his bed into some sort of monstrous insect."[3]

A NATURAL SCIENTIST IN REVERSE

How did he get there, and where is that wanderer going? —
Having clambered up, he now stands on the peak of a cliff, mo-
tionless, like a cliff himself, as if he had turned to stone, rigidly
gazing at the sea of fog at his feet in Caspar David Friedrich's
painting *Wanderer Above the Sea of Fog*. His exterior appearance
leaves us in no doubt that he is not from there; he did not acquire his straight walking stick in some nearby forest but instead
had a master prepare it in a faraway city, just as his clothes were
tailored by the city tailor, his boots sewn by a city cobbler, and
his hair pomaded by a city hairdresser. He has come from somewhere far away. And he will leave, for his appearance makes it
clear that he is used to a different kind of comfort than can be
granted to him on this barren cliff. No Saint Jerome is he, nor
Saint Anthony of Padua, come to create eternal order. Certainly
those two saints would not be so amazed by the landscape extending before them, nor would they lose themselves to such a
degree in its beauty. For them, the beauty of the landscape was
"natural." For our wanderer, however, we can presume that he is
so filled with ardent admiration because this is not in the least
"natural" for him.

The "whence" and the "whither" are not visible, but an even

more palpable alienation can be felt in this painting for all that. It is covered by a double fog: the first is the fog that we cannot see, including the past and the future of the stranger who is observing the landscape; the second is the visible fog which covers the land extending before the wanderer. The first is the fog of prosaic life—in the words of Achim von Arnim, "the indifferent sea of the fog of public duties"—which compelled the wanderer to leave, perhaps even to escape.[1] The latter fog is not metaphorical but a "natural phenomenon," although it visibly corresponds so well to the wanderer's spiritual state it could be referred to as a spiritual phenomenon as well. It helps him reach that state, just as Hölderlin was assisted by the hills near Neckar:

> On those peaks the winds from the sky
> Relieved me from pains of bondage.[2]

The wanderer climbed up a cliff rising into the heights from all sides. And he himself rises up from nature, which fully surrounds him. The painting, however, leaves us in no doubt that he did not come to this place to stand out in relation to his environment. Instead, he wished to become a part of nature, to become submerged in something he could not find anywhere else. Or he wished to come across something he would never be able to locate in the city, where his tailor, his cobbler, and his barber reside. His unmoving posture and the tense observation emanating from it do not betray submersion so much as they do the desire for such. "Desire and its object": that could have been the title of this painting as well. Which signifies the deep tension present in the entire work.

In what is this tension manifested? In part, the wanderer is surrounded by nature, first and foremost by fog, and, thoroughly engrossed, he observes the captivating force of this fog: he studies its indeterminacy as it connects everything, transforming everything into one, where every kind of individualism is dissolved into universality. The fact that he climbed up to that cliff edge where there was nothing to be seen but fog is evidence that within his soul he no longer had any desire to observe anything else. He would be more than happy to dissolve into this universality. But he is not capable of doing so: the desire which emanates from his figure and his posture is precisely what separates him from the object of that same desire. The fog surrounds him, but he is shut out by the fog.

Friedrich's painting is shot through with longing. But the painter, despite his own intentions, has also represented longing's snare. On one hand, an indisputable religious aura infuses the picture: the wanderer stands before or above the sea of fog as if it were an altar. He creates the impression of someone who has found the meaning of his life in nature; an experience which earlier had been referred to as divine fulfillment. In this, the painting is also a self-portrait, for Caspar David Friedrich himself, on one occasion, following a powerful experience of nature, decided to receive Holy Communion.[3] His colleague Carl Gustav Carus wrote in a letter of such a moment, glimpsed once from a mountain top: "Within you a silent devotion is awoken. You lose yourself in endless space. Your entire being is transfigured and purified, and your own self disappears—*you are nothing, God is all.*"[4]

On the other hand, however, the figure standing out so sharply from the fog, with his bearing, sharply resistant to his surroundings, his city garb, and above all, his prominent position in the picture, indicates that the absolute desire to renounce his own self is ultimately inseparable from the self manifesting that desire. Moreover, the greater is the desire for self-surrender, the ever stronger is the self. Paradoxically, its contours are the most defined when its greatest desire is to lose these contours altogether. In terms of Friedrich's painting, the greater the fog into which the self would wish to submerge, the more resolute will be that seed of the self desiring to become submerged. This is true even if the self is able to delude itself into believing the opposite.

This is a problem which is relevant not only for Friedrich's painting but for the general longing of the Romantics to retreat from prosaic life and find in nature that universal meaning and connection which civilization was supposedly no longer able to provide. This attitude toward nature is inseparable from a completely different, almost opposing interpretation of nature—one characteristic of the natural sciences. Nature, during the course of the eighteenth century, became ever more manifestly the *object* of rational and scientific thought, the result of which was the ever more regardless exploitation of nature with the aid of technology. (In 1703, a new word appeared in Europe in the German

language: *Naturwissenschaft,* "natural sciences," which Nietzsche later analyzed as the volition for power over nature.) For the
Romantics—in, as it were, counterreaction—an ever increasing
desire arose to discover within nature the *subject* of the universe,
the manifestation of aesthetic harmony, a perfection that could
not be circumscribed by reason, a kind of mystical identity. Writing of the darker aspects of natural science ten years before Friedrich's painting, his Dresden-based acquaintance Gotthilf Heinrich von Schubert was determined to force open natural science's
prevailing conceptual framework and introduce the term *cult of
nature* as opposed to *natural science.* Others with similar intentions viewed the study of nature as a clearly onto-theological consideration, regardless of whether they were writers, such as Novalis or Jean Paul; philosophers, such as Schelling or Franz von
Baader; natural scientists, such as Heinrich Steffens or Lorenz
Oken; or painters, such as Philipp Otto Runge.

Highly specific parallels were formed during the Romantic
era. It was as self-evident for the idea of nature to be evoked by a
thinker who wished to validate the pure autonomous laws of reason, subsequently treating this nature as an object, as it was for
the adherent of a certain kind of holistic viewpoint who wished
to find within it a universal subject to do so. Anyone who wished
to find the proof of existence of God turned to nature, and so did
anyone who wished to deny the existence of God. Nature was the
embodiment of universal intelligence, just as it was the manifestation of the lack of all intelligence and universal indifference. It
is sufficient to cite the way the motif of the forest is imbued with

such highly differentiated meanings in the work of on the one hand Novalis, Clemens Brentano, and the Brothers Grimm, and on the other the Marquis de Sade.

All of the above — if we examine the infinite trust placed by the Romantics in nature — leads to a certain amount of suspicion. Are the precipices separating the rationalists and Romantics (to oversimplify somewhat), that is, the natural scientists (in the strict sense of the word) and those who insisted on a holistic viewpoint truly so unbridgeable? If we look at the wanderer in Friedrich's painting, he appears to be giving himself over to nature, and yet at the same time he is decisively isolated from it. And this indicates to us that the Romantic "deification" of nature, its enlargement into a metaphysical category results in a tendency leading toward the *violation* of nature just as much as the openly technicist viewpoint does. For there too in the background lurks the intention to call to account, to seek proof and persuasion, the *desire* for nature to become the likeness of humanity, to be the mirror of our soul. In a word, the desire for nature to be pliable to their conceptions of it — even if, in certain cases, these conceptions differ from those of the natural scientists.

The Romantics' desire was directed toward a kind of nature suffused with intelligence, which embraces, in a spherical manner, every individual who turns to it for solace. This concept of nature hardly differs from a perfectly rounded work of art. But — to consider Friedrich's wanderer again — it is not nature that becomes aesthetic; rather, the demands of aesthetics crush and overwhelm nature. This alerts us yet again to the desire for exploitation and violation. In the words of Jean Baudrillard: "Aesthetics restores mastery over the order of the world to a subject, restores a form of sublimation of the total illusion of the world, which would otherwise annihilate us."[5] The wanderer in Friedrich's painting has been enchanted by an illusion. It is not as if, in the course of his wanderings, he had unexpectedly met up with some kind of sorcery. On the contrary: he is the one who puts a spell on the world around him with his own gaze. He is the one who, with his gaze, so to speak annihilates nature by projecting the image of his own desires onto it.

In an era in which the gaze of "disenchantment" gained ever more ground, the act of "enchantment" attained a kind of metaphysical consolation. It provided a counterbalance, as it were, to the ever more irresistible march of secularization. Gotthilf Heinrich von Schubert writes that the final goal of the human being should be to once again wholly integrate into nature, so that "the chief goal of life, its chief designation, should be for the individual and all his efforts to sacrifice himself to the universal, on the altar of the sacred works of the good and the just."[6] Schubert, calling upon nature, announces a kind of self-renunciation — which corresponds to the capitulation taking place before the sea of fog visible in Friedrich's painting. This self-renunciation can be observed in many of his German contemporaries. If the purpose is, to use Schelling's expression, for "nature to be invisible spirit, and the spirit invisible nature";[7] or, to employ the expression of another acquaintance of Friedrich's, the natural scientist Lorenz Oken, for nature to be "the absolute awakened onto consciousness of self," then this means that man, nature, and God are co-extensive with each other. So that man becomes divine if, giving himself fully over to nature, he ceases to be his own self. In the words of Oken: "Every disappearance of the Finite is a retrogression into the Eternal; for it must return whence it came. It has arisen out of nothing, is itself the existing nothing; it therefore must retrograde again into the nothing."[8]

Let us look again at Friedrich's painting. Not only do we see the wanderer standing above the sea of fog, we also see the reverse side of the thoughts of Schubert, Oken, or Schelling—all the things that they did not say out loud, but that, with the passing of two centuries, have become ever more evident. Namely, that in the hope of self-renunciation, a self, with its own decisive contours, can be recognized. The desire of the individual for perfect dissolution is a specific, but in any event decisive, manifestation on the part of the same individual. Novalis termed the miner in *Heinrich von Ofterdingen* an "inverted astrologer," or "an astrologer in reverse." Employing this analogy, we can refer to Friedrich's wanderer as a "natural scientist in reverse." He forges virtue from his own frustration, and at the same time he projects his own conceptions and thoughts onto nature, violating it as much as the scientists do. He is only less sincere: whereas the natural scientist openly treats nature as an object, the wanderer stylizes it as a subject, with which he can apparently become united, as a lover with his mistress.

The political and societal roots and causes of this kind of self-renunciation in German Romanticism are so self-evident that it is almost redundant to mention them. The German Romantics dug themselves a huge trap, investing this question with such expectations and demands that they would have been difficult to fulfill under any circumstances. Friedrich's wanderer stands in front of the sea of fog extending before him like someone wishing to dive into it in the next moment so as to become eternally submerged. But the picture suggests the opposite as well. The wanderer is never going to dive headfirst into that fog, but will turn around, return to his city, and in order to disguise his own frustration begin to write rapturous interpretations of the absolute spirit embodied by that sea of fog, just as Henrich Heine would later caustically describe in connection with Ludwig Börne:

> When will harmony be achieved again, when will the world be healed from the one-sided striving for spiritualization, this mad error from which both the soul and the body sickened? A great cure lies in the political movement and in art. Napoleon and Goethe had a splendid effect. The former by forcing the nations to take on all kinds of healthy movement; the latter by making us receptive again to Greek art and creating solid works to which we can cling as though to marble images of the gods, *in order not to perish in the absolute spirit's sea of fog.*[9]

KLEIST DIES AND DIES AND DIES

As the epitaph of Marcel Duchamp's gravestone reads, "D'ailleurs, c'est toujours les autres qui meurent" (Besides, it's always other people who die). This can also be interpreted in two ways, either specifically that it is always other people who die or—and the other interpretation is just as interesting—that the longer we live the more deaths we see, with one exception: our own. This is what no one has ever been able to see. We always see only the deaths of others. And that is something that we can ponder, consider, even inveigh against. Is the function of the deaths of others to foster that which sustains life, and which appears to be inviolable, our integration into that enormous system of principles, into the dreadfully complicated web of cause and effect? There is only one thing capable of ripping it apart: our own death. This, however, we do not see—and that is why we do not perceive how the web of cause and effect of existence comes undone. All we can do is imagine it.

But (as with everything) there are exceptions here too. There are deaths, or, more properly, instances of death, following which the web begins to come unwoven, even temporarily. At such times death falls out of the order of cause and effect to such a degree that it nearly loses its designation of "death." These instances of death detach, as it were, from those to whom they pertained; they become unbound, moving freely through life, attaching themselves to us for a while, evoking fate—not only the fate of those to whom they belonged but our own as well. In thinking of these deaths, we are confronted with our own fate; we acknowledge the possibility of our own death within them. These deaths are like pictures that are forever operative, solid forms unthreatened by life: they split off from the deceased, and in the end are livelier than any living human being. In the history of European culture one meets with such figures—think of the deaths of Socrates, Empedocles, Jesus, Seneca. The death of Heinrich von Kleist is also such a death. Kleist's death split off from the man of flesh and blood; it grew into an emblem, a stylized form. In a strange fashion, his death remained more intimately human than any other death, more real than anyone else's actual death. Kleist, like a rocket, launched his own death into the heaven of culture, where it has circled ever since, an eternal image, a form that can never be ruined. He succeeded where others failed: his death, while he lived it to the end, became separated from his own self in such a way that others could also discover the possibility of their own death in his. In doing so, he rendered a service to the living, even if it would be difficult to precisely describe in what this service lay. But the excitement that was provoked in everyone who learned of his death demonstrates that his gesture cut everyone to the quick. There is something of the sacrificial victim in his death, even if it is unclear why or for whom or what he sacrificed. "She [his half-sister,

Ulrike von Kleist] has not, I believe, comprehended the art of self-sacrifice, of leaving no stone unturned in pursuit of what one loves: this is the highest blessing conceivable on earth, and, yes, in heaven too, if it is indeed true that one finds joy and happiness there," Kleist wrote two days before his death.[1] He, though, did understand sacrifice. And as with every sacrifice, in his too there was something to be gained — even if it was something for the survivors. Kleist himself could hardly ponder this. "How difficult it is to prevail on a man to venture boldly on making a sacrifice for an after-advantage!"[2] These are the words of Goethe, from his novel *Elective Affinities*.

With Goethe's novel we are already approaching our goal — the hour of Kleist's death.

■

There is no death in the history of literature which has been so circumspectly and exhaustively documented as the double suicide of Heinrich von Kleist and Henriette Vogel on the banks of the Kleiner Wannsee near Berlin on November 21, 1811. There is only one other death (belonging to the modern age) that can rival the sustained attention elicited by Kleist and Vogel's double suicide: the suicide of Werther, which had taken place thirty-nine years earlier, a few days before Christmas in 1772. We, the successors, are more familiar with the circumstances than those who were directly affected. We can follow the hours before the death minute by minute, we can read what they had set down on paper before the triggers were drawn, we can picture every one of their garments, we even know what they ate, thanks to the autopsy report, which, in the case of Kleist, digressed in great detail upon the contents of his stomach and intestines, we can reconstruct in what position the two victims lay after the pistols went off, and it is hardly a mystery to imagine how and from where the blood and the cerebrum (otherwise invisible) would spurt outward, soiling the skin, the clothes, and the immediate surroundings.

In a word, we know everything—even what they were reading in the moments before they died, and what was absorbed into their brains before the shots of lead. But before we turn to that, let us pause for a moment.

Kleist and Werther—by what right should we mention them together? One of them certifiably lived, whereas we know of the existence of the second only from a novel. Kleist was real and killed himself with a pistol of Italian make (a *Lazarino Comminazzo*). Werther's weapon was imaginary—borrowed from Albert, another character in the novel. Next to the place of Kleist's death is a gravestone that anyone can visit (on the grounds of the nearby Berlin Waterworks, however, a sign reads, "Forbidden to enter. Danger!"); in contrast, the location of Werther's grave under the heavenly vault remains as an eternal mystery. And so the sentence penned above becomes problematic. Is it appropriate to bring up a literary-historical example in relation to Kleist's death? In the case of the deaths of Kleist's protagonists Kohlhaas or Penthesilea, the context of literary history is appropriate, just as indisputable as in the case of Werther. But Kleist?

The testimony of witnesses or the anatomical report hardly belongs to the genre of literary history, nor do the police archives or the royal order forbidding the glorification of suicide. There is much, however, to suggest that the literary-historical perspective is not inappropriate here. Whoever might be curious about these legal and judicial documents should page through the literary-historical reference books which treat the deaths of their author in the same amount of detail as the deaths of Kohlhaas or Penthesilea. But what is even more thought-provoking is that the news reports and documentation ultimately rendered Kleist's life as fictional as one of his characters—let's say Kohlhaas. I am not thinking of the "death of the author," as hypothesized by the French structuralists. Instead, I consider that this documentation inevitably stylized the author's life into a narrative. And it is very difficult to draw a sharp boundary between the history and fiction. In the year of his death, Kleist wrote a sketch, "Unlikely, but True," in which the double meaning of the word *Geschichte* (history, story) is at play: it can signify fiction as much as a "fact" in a piece of historiography. And we can also quote from his novella *Michael Kohlhaas*: "And since probability is not always on the side of truth . . . at the same time, . . . those who wish to question it must accord full liberty to do so."[3] In other words: the "author" of a literary work can do nothing to prevent himself from becoming as much of a fictive hero, following his death, as the fictional characters created by him. Although the reverse is also true. The death of Michael Kohlhaas or, in certain instances, that of Werther can become as "real" as the death of Kleist. It does not matter that they are literary figures: the work which has given them a home cannot designate boundaries in which their existence would be contained. And despite the argumentations of the various literary-historical and theoretical schools to the effect that a work may be read exclusively as a self-contained autonomous system, there are always fictional protagonists who step out from the cover of that book containing them with ease, freely moving between reality and fiction.

But let us return to our reading. More precisely, to those books which Werther, Kleist, and Henriette Vogel were reading before their deaths. Perhaps this will help us to perceive the relationship between fact and fiction in a more nuanced fashion.

Kleist was immersed in the works of Goethe. Purportedly, before the double suicide with Vogel, they both were reading *Elective Affinities*. If this was the case, presumably they were perusing together a book that the reading public — according to Goethe's own confession — had taken to itself like the shirt of Nessus; its presumed "lack of morality," however, would hardly have scandalized Kleist and his soulmate Henriette Vogel. They certainly would have agreed with Walter Benjamin, who wrote of this novel a century later: "Marriage here is not an ethical problem, yet neither is it a social problem. It is not a form of bourgeois conduct. In its dissolution, everything human turns into appearance, and the mythical alone remains as essence."[4] Vogel and Kleist may have spent their last hours under the spell of mythical powers. A few days before their deaths, Kleist wrote to his cousin, Marie von Kleist: "Everything else on earth, the whole and its parts, I have completely subdued in my heart."[5] On the day before the double suicide, they referred to themselves as "two happy balloonists," who, like Eduard and Ottilie in *Elective Affinities*, finally have broken free from the world's sphere of affinity.

They must have been thinking of Werther when reading this novel. On November 21, 1811, on the morning of the suicide, Henriette Vogel wrote a letter to the ministry war counselor Ernst Friedrich Peguilhen, a friend of the Vogel family, which could have been written by Werther. Among other things, she writes, "My very honored friend! Your friendship, which you have always held so faithfully for me, has been given to withstand a wonderful test, since the two of us, namely Kleist (whom you know) and I find ourselves here at Stimming, on the road to Postdam, in a helpless circumstance, in that we lie there s h o t d e a d, and now it is up to the mercy of a well-wishing friend to place our frail husks into the safe castle of the earth. Try, dear Peguilhen, to arrive here this evening and arrange everything so that my good Vogel [her husband] would be as little frightened as possible."[6] Her contemporaries saw proof of cynicism in these lines. But it would be enough for us to think of *The Sorrows of Young Werther.* In his last notes to Wilhelm, as well as to Lotte, Werther enters into his own death in a similar manner (although with somewhat more self-pity), finding decided *pleasure* in mentally performing and embellishing the thought of his grave and the state of his body after his suicide. Following Kleist's death, among his contemporaries the painter Friedrich Meier took notice of the parallels with Werther: "You must then read *Werther* once more, to learn how one should pass judgment on the same"—he wrote to an acquaintance a few weeks after the suicide.[7] But he was not the only one who had been put in mind of Werther. After the double suicide, one author published a study identifying Werther as the cause of Kleist's "poisonous sufferings," and the author, of course not neglecting to mention the "immoral *Elective Affinities*," finally drew the following conclusion: "The adulation for these works and their poetic sensibility bereft of all morality can thus result in insanity and suicide."[8]

For the most part, the contemporaries of Kleist and Vogel explained their deed in terms of a pathological adulation for poetry. In doing so, they wished to kill two birds with one stone: not only were they casting judgment upon Kleist and Vogel; they were also administering a blow to the "newest aesthetic school." And yet even the most ill-willed commentators got something right: Vogel and Kleist faced their own authentic deaths while also bearing in mind a literary archetype. They looked ahead to their own nonliterary death through a literary filter. More precisely: while they were preparing for their own exceptional and temporally unique deaths, they were seeking models and archetypes to guide them. They did so not to dull their pain or subdue their fear, but because they had to select a certain form of conduct. Of course this by no means detracts from the "value" of their suicide. But there is no way to take the most radical step—the one that will finally take you out of the world forever—without deciding on some form of conduct for your exit. Suicide is one variation of a dialogue carried on with the world, even if its goal is the final suspension of this dialogue. Indeed, that goal makes it even more one. And perhaps the world still has the right to the final word. Kleist's farewell letters have no parallel in the history of world literature: even two centuries later, their individuality and immediacy are scorching. And they certainly can be read as *literary* works. Not because their author intended them as such but because we do not know how to read them as non-literature. The desire for *immediacy* which emanates from these letters, their perfected form, renders them *transmissible*; what in principle is incommunicable yet knows how to speak through the form.

And this form is nothing other than a certain mode of conduct. Behavior or conduct is unimaginable without some kind of imitation. And what kind of imitation is this? An imitation of death. For every mortal, there is one single death which one "dies," and yet this single "dying" is the imitation of the innumerable deaths that came before, as well as a precursor of the infinite number of deaths that are to follow. For surely in the end there exists only one single death; this is the theme of every dying, compelling everyone to its imitation; it also ensures that even the ultimate formlessness of "dying" will have a form—the form of death, which makes a mockery of the consciousness of any kind of "exceptionalness" for the person condemned to death.

The scrupulous preparations of Kleist and Vogel, their careful planning, arranging everything in advance, including what would happen with their possessions—all of this is reminiscent of Werther's preparations. It is certain that they did not want to imitate Werther—but what is equally certain is that they could not *not* imitate Werther. They would have been pleased to know that their burial would occur at 10 p.m., in the very spot they had selected so carefully for the suicide—presumably by torchlight, in the presence of only a few people, and with no clergy to accompany them on their last journey. (A church service was held twelve days later.) Werther was also buried at night—at 11 p.m.; his funeral was accompanied by only a few people as well; and there were no clergy to bid him a final farewell.

But Kleist was not the only reader; Werther was a reader as well. He too was looking for models and prototypes. When he shot himself, *Emilia Galotti* by Gotthold Ephraim Lessing lay open on his reading stand. This is the drama in which Lessing unveils feudalistic despotism, which afflicted Werther as well. And just as in *Werther*, it concludes with a death. True, not with suicide. Even so, the fact that in the play, Odoardo, the father, in his final despair murders his own daughter instead of the man who seduced her amounts to suicide—for he has definitively murdered all hope for his own life. Despite all the subversive intentions inherent in this play, *Emilia Galotti* is not about rebellion, but the inability to rebel; the death of Emilia is the final seal confirming the helpless writhing between hopelessness, desire, and obligation, sensual joy and honor. This is the least that Werther could take away from it. And if he was reading attentively, then he would have become aware that Lessing's female protagonist was also an avid reader. She incites her father, who shrinks back from killing her, with these words: "In former days there was a father, who, to save his daughter from disgrace and infamy, plunged the first deadly weapon which he saw into his daughter's heart—and thereby gave her life, a second time.—But all such deeds are past.—Such fathers are not to be found in these degenerate days."[9]

In the story told by Livy, this former father referred to lived in Rome, and, as a plebeian, he stabbed his own daughter, Virginia, so that she would not be raped by the aristocrat Appius Claudius. Emilia Galotti rereads Livy so as to find an archetype for her own death. She prepares for the wedding, she flees her seducer, she struggles against temptation—and in the meantime she armors herself with reading. That is, she dies in such a way that with her death she has also created a prototype. That which is exceptional and temporally unique is raised to the level of legal force; that which is inconceivable is turned into an object of interpretation; and that which cannot be addressed becomes stylized into the subject of conversation. Death is thus deprived of its individuality and its exceptionalness, as it is in the case of another famous suicide, Othello, who in the moment of his death similarly evokes an earlier heroic gesture:

> And say, besides, that in Aleppo once,
> Where a malignant and a turbaned Turk
> Beat a Venetian, and traduced the state,
> I took by the throat the circumcisèd dog,
> And smote him—thus.
> (*He stabs himself.*) [*Othello,* 5.2]

Othello, Emilia Galotti, and Werther die, so to speak, in opening up their deaths to the world. All three retreat into their own deaths, and yet with the same gesture they step out of them. Death, instead of absorbing everything into itself as if into a black hole and destroying it, becomes the basis of a new life. A new life, which is then requalified as an object of interpretation. It ascends before others as a prototype, becoming a basis of reference, mobilizing the living. It can even fill those who come after it with enthusiasm. But what else could this be other than the evasion and defeat of death itself?

Death as an interpreted text. Let us not forget: not only was Werther reading, but others read him. For example, those suicides who, instead of approaching the novel via the methodologies of the New Critics or hermeneutics or the deconstructionists, simply confused it with life. They imitated a fictive protagonist, and in doing so they confused not only the relation between fiction and reality but that between the concepts of "original" and the "copy" as well. Werther ended up appearing in the police files as well as in the news reports of the time; as for the suicides, they ended up in the later literary historical accounts and the textual scholarship surrounding Goethe's work. The deaths of Kleist and Vogel were ennobled as narrative, treated in newer works of art— films and narratives; in Hungary, they even formed the basis of an operatic work (*Kleist Dies*, by András Jeles and László Melis). And of course, following the same logic, they were imitated ("reread"): the story ("the fable of the mutual death of Kleist and Vogel") served as the basis for even more suicides, themselves not lacking in literary character. For example, Johannes R. Becher, who would later become the poet laureate of Communist East Germany, in 1910 planned a double suicide, based on Kleist's, with a cigarette seller seven years older than himself, Franziska Fuß. The girl died, he survived, and a year later, on the hundredth anniversary of Kleist's death, he composed a hymn to Kleist, later followed by more Kleist poems.

It is not only worth mentioning Becher, but also a writer of greater renown, Yukio Mishima, in whose mutual suicide with two companions in 1970 the deaths of Kleist and Vogel can be perceived. I don't know if Mishima ever read Kleist. It is likely that he did; manifold Japanese translations of *Michael Kohlhaas* are available, and apart from Hungary, the only country to publish the complete works of Kleist in translation—including his correspondence—is Japan. (The third most complete Kleist publication, the French edition, does not contain his letters.) And in the same way, something of Mishima's character can be found in the protagonists of Kleist. Kohlhaas's obstinacy and resolve, Penthesilea's inflexibility (in *Penthesilea*), the basic "all or nothing" stance of Alkmene (in *Amphitryon*), the single-minded sense of purpose of Count F (in *The Marquise of O*), Katie's endless humility (in *Katie of Heilbronn; or, The Ordeal of Fire*)—these figures are all are so many samurai or kamikaze pilots. And even more important than the immediate impact is the topos of *common suicide* which connects the deaths that took place in Tokyo with the ones that took place next to the Wannsee, and which vaults above these individual death instances *as an in-*

terpreted text. For it is possible that Mishima never read Kleist, but Chikamatsu Monzaemon (1653–1725) could not have been unknown to him. Chikamatsu wrote no fewer than eleven plays about double suicide, enacted onstage as the deepest confirmation of mutual faithfulness. One of the authorities on his plays, Junzo Kawada, even goes so far to say that although found in every culture of the world, double suicide is first and foremost a Japanese phenomenon that helps us comprehend the relationship of the Japanese to death. Chikamatsu's plays were not performed in Europe, especially not in early-nineteenth-century Berlin in the Königliches Nationaltheater of Kleist's greatest adversary, August Wilhelm Iffland. Still, it is hard to chase away the thought that Kleist might have been aware of these plays of "self-redemption." Perhaps his dreams assisted him in obtaining a knowledge of them—dreams during which Katie of Heilbronn or Prince Homburg walks more securely on this earth than when either was awake. Or perhaps it was those abilities by which Michael Kohlhaas's wife was able to appear on earth even after her death in order to ease the fate of her still surviving husband.

Kleist and Mishima, Werther and Emilia Galotti, Johannes R. Becher and Othello, Livy and Chikumatsu . . . We could list others as well: Novalis and Keats, Thomas Chatterton and Georg Trakl, along with the great figures of "amorous death," from Pyramus and Thisbe, Tristan and Isolde, up to and including Pelléas and Mélisande—for all of them behave as if their attention were exclusively riveted on each other while stealthily also observing everyone around them, as they diligently perfect and perform the prototypes, imitating the fates of others. They love, fatally—and in the meantime, they study, they read. In the most literal sense of the word, they drown in immediacy and in what is usually termed "elemental experience"; at the same time they are extraordinarily circumspect, taking pains to ensure that what is "exceptional" and "temporally unique" will manifest itself as authoritative and exemplary. They present excessiveness as a norm—for the simple reason that death, if elevated to narrative, a work of art, fiction, parable, a prototype, a case in literary history, inevitably becomes requalified as a cultural phenomenon. They are sustained by the fiction of death as a narratable event. This is a fiction in the face of which even death is impotent. And it is thanks to this fiction that these deaths became emblematic, and that they came to belong to the history of European culture just as inseparably as those works and those deeds which preceded the deceased.

The death of Werther was "fictional," that of Kleist was "real." The difference, though, is relative. Both are symbolic deaths in the sense that Jean Baudrillard uses the term *symbolic*: as something that dissolves the rigid differentiation between the real and imaginary. In the present case, it allows us to see much more than death in the death of Kleist; we take notice not exclusively of his exit but of his entrance as well—his entrance among the living, with whom, during his life, Kleist was never able to realize such strong connections as came to be established following his suicide.

■

It bears repeating: the death of Kleist is the most thoroughly documented event of his entire life. The French-Romanian philosopher Emil Cioran justifiably states that it is impossible to read even one line of Kleist without thinking of how he put an end to his own life. His suicide preceded, as it were, his life's work. Perhaps it was this reflection that prompted the author of my favorite Kleist biography, Hans Dieter Zimmermann, to begin his biography with the death of his protagonist; and Kleist's existential interpreter, Günther Blöcker, was writing in the same spirit when he wrote that Kleist's death was "his final poem."

The circumstances of the suicide can be quickly summarized. In Berlin, Kleist was a frequent visitor to the Vogel family, and he regularly played music with Vogel's highly educated young wife, Henriette. On one occasion, when Henriette had sung very beautifully, he spoke to her with enthusiasm: "So beautiful I could be shot dead!"[10]

Not long afterward the young woman asked him whether he would indeed perform the greatest service which one could ask of a friend. Kleist replied in the affirmative, and Henriette, who was terminally ill, spoke: "Fine! So kill me. My sufferings have reached such a degree that I am no longer capable of withstanding life." Henriette Vogel "seduced" Kleist; although she would not have been successful if Kleist had not been prepared, within his own soul, for this step. For Vogel was not the first companion with whom he wished to die; the list of names reads as follows:

Carl von Pannwitz, Henriette von Schlieben, Ernst von Pfuel, Rühle von Lilienstern, Marie von Kleist . . . as well as all the others we don't know about. It was as if for Kleist, a desire for a shared death was the greatest sign of devotion.

On the afternoon of November 20, 1811, Kleist and Vogel rented a carriage and had themselves driven to the Neuer Krug hostelry situated on the Kleiner Wannsee between Berlin and Potsdam. They took two rooms and ordered coffee. Subsequently, they went for a stroll, then spent the evening in the guesthouse. They did not go to sleep: the entire night they wrote, they read, they spoke, and they paced back and forth. The next morning at dawn (at 4 a.m., then at 7 a.m.) they had coffee brought to them. Later they came downstairs, Henriette ordering a cup of meat broth, and when the innkeeper asked if they would be having lunch, Kleist answered in the negative, adding, as it were murmuring to himself, "Tonight we'll be dining on something much better than that." Once again they set off for a stroll, in the best of moods; later, on the way down to the lake, Kleist ordered several rounds of rum, and once again they drank coffee. At noon they sent a few letters to Berlin with a messenger, afterward inquiring several times of the innkeeper as to whether the letters had arrived at their destination. In the afternoon, Vogel once again ordered meat broth, and once again they set off for a stroll holding a shawl-covered basket, in which, as it was later to turn out, the pistols were kept. They ordered yet another cup of coffee to drink by the lakeshore, then they asked the wife of a day laborer, Riebisch, for a pencil. After the woman had satisfied their requests and turned back to the guesthouse, she heard, from a distance, the sound of a pistol shot. She had hardly gone fifty steps when she heard another shot. The woman ran back to the lake, where she saw the two bodies. Kleist had first shot Henriette in the heart; he then reloaded the pistol and shot himself in the head. They died exactly like the pair of lovers Gustav and Toni in Kleist's story "The Engagement in Santo Domingo," written eight months before the double suicide. That evening, Henriette's husband and Peguilhen arrived at the scene; in the meantime, they had received the letters. The next day the bodies were taken to an outbuilding of the guesthouse, where the postmortem took place. On November 22, at 10 p.m., they were buried on the spot where they had committed suicide.

On November 26, and again on November 28, Peguilhen published obituaries in two different newspapers in which, among other statements, the following could be read: "I beg the public to suspend judgment, and not to curse these two unfortunate beings who were themselves the embodiment of love and purity. This was an act which does not occur in every season, and this was about two people who cannot be measured by the usual standard." On November 27, Frederick William III of Prussia summoned Karl August von Hardenberg, the state chancellor of Prussia; he ordered him to prohibit the publication of any such other laudatory obituaries as Peguilhen's, an order Hardenberg obeyed. The double suicide had already thoroughly churned up the public mood; not only did the Prussian and other German papers report on it, but the foreign press as well, from London to

Riga and Paris to Vienna. In accordance, however, with the order of the Prussian king, for months afterward the only reports that could be read about it were unequivocally critical in spirit, not infrequently slanderously so. The critic Friedrich Weisser, who until the end of his life never passed up the opportunity to disparage Kleist, recalled him in the following way: "Heinrich von Kleist, as a writer, has brought a great disgrace upon this family name, eternally sacred to Germans." One thing is, however, undeniable: whether we see Kleist's suicide as proof of moral bankruptcy or interpret it as an extraordinary act, the equal of which we encounter only rarely in history, Kleist, by means of his own death, gained a kind of notoriety he had never been able to attain during his lifetime through his work. With only slight exaggeration we could even say that it was through his death that he became Kleist. Death helped him achieve what he had never been able to gain in life—what life had perforce denied him. "The existence of things can only enclose the death that it brings to me, it is itself projected in my death that encloses it," he might have said, in the words of Georges Bataille.[11] Afterward, this death continued to live its own life, as it were, separate from Kleist's, gaining a symbolic force which vividly affects people to this day.

What is the reason for this?

■

Nietzsche once wrote, in relation to Kleist as well as to Hölderlin, that neither of them "could bear the climate of so-called German erudition."[12] Suicide (and with Hölderlin, insanity) did not, however, come cheaply; Kleist had to struggle for a long time with the ideal of art that his age offered, and for a long time he cherished the illusion that there was a place reserved for him among the bourgeoisie. Initially, as an adherent of the Enlightenment, he trusted greatly in the redemptive strength of erudition—until he began writing himself. One of his first compositions, *Essay on the Sure Way to Find Happiness and to Enjoy It Even in the Greatest Tribulations* (1799), would become truly revealing in light of his later suicide; here he gives the game away. In this essay, he gives voice to the hope he has placed in the happy-making "middle path," the basis of which, he suggests, is erudition and having a life plan, and which will assist us in finding our own purpose. He is well aware that this middle path is indispensable, and yet at the same time, due to some mysterious cause, he loathes the thought of it, "because a natural vehement instinct within seduces one elsewhere."[13] The reconciliation of *knowledge* with *vehement instinct* never occurs. On the contrary: the precipice between the two grows ever deeper with time. And when it becomes unbridgeable, Kleist begins to write plays and novellas.

Behind the contradiction of "knowledge" and "instinct," however, lie other contradictions. One of them is the contradiction between the communal being who accepts a bourgeois mode of life—the *zoon politikon*—and the individual who lives to the extreme his own temporal uniqueness, exceptionalness, and ineffability. Another is the contradiction between the belief placed in the expediency and orderliness of existence, and the confusion and chaos that appear in its wake. In the course of the crisis occurring in early 1801—which has been termed, in the literature on Kleist, his "Kantian" crisis—his belief in the great connections of existence collapsed. He wrote to his sister Ulrike: "The thought that we here on earth may know nothing, nothing at all of Truth, and that what we call truth has quite another name after death, and that therefore all attempts to win possession that goes with us to our grave are quite vain and fruitless: this thought has shattered me in the innermost sanctum of my soul.—My *single*, my *highest* goal has sunk from sight and I have no other."[14] Here more is going on than the question of whether Kleist could stand the climate of German "erudition" or not. The belief in the great interrelatedness of existence was not only a particularity of the Enlightenment (which, in Germany, manifested itself in the political arena to a lesser extent, receiving instead special emphasis in education); all European tradition is built upon this belief, including Platonism and Christianity. Kleist was filled with deep despair by the shattering of this tradition.

This explains in part the marked interest he displayed toward death. That "death-wish" or "death-instinct," remarked upon by nearly every Kleist interpreter, did not merely signify the desire for the final exit or annihilation. (Although of course it indicates that as well.) Instead, for Kleist death would be a kind of positive reference point: the one irrefutable truth, the single incontrovertible certainty which rises like a cliff out of a creation that has lost its purpose. Death is "the eternal refrain of life," goes Kleist's famous, off-quoted pronunciation (from July 1807): the truth of this statement recalibrates everything and creates fatal connections—if these were already missing from life.

Death is the ultimate proof of the uncertainty of life: this is a logical absurdity, meaning offered by meaninglessness. In order to respond affirmatively, however, Kleist attempted to mold two radically divergent, seemingly irreconcilable traditions into one. On one hand, he tried to write like Goethe: that is, the idea of certitude was his constant goal—he wished to hold the Whole of the world in his grasp. He was, in point of fact, striving for the same thing as his contemporary Hegel: to arrive at the fulfillment of the universe. He desired totality. On the other hand, however, following his so-called Kantian crisis it gradually became clear to him that the price of thinking in terms of these totalities—of the Great Whole—was that the part, as well as the individual, ultimately fell by the wayside, reduced to fragments, collapsed, finally losing any sort of definitive character. The great dream of Kleist was for the singular to be granted its own right, and for the momentary to be made conclusive. He tried to grasp the Whole so that at the same time the part—the single, the personal, the individual, the unrepeatable, the ineffable—would also remain eternal. He wanted to reconcile order and the extraordinary without any resulting damage. In other words, he tried to create an alloy of the classical and the Romantic without committing himself to either one of them.

It is no wonder that he could not keep this up for long. He wanted to unite fire and water—to transform death into a life-giving truth—whereas wherever he looked in life, he sensed only uncertainty, ruin, or even destruction. Perhaps it is this that granted his death such symbolic strength. What in his private life might appear to be an indisputable failure, on a symbolic level stands before us as a specific gesture. He did not permit death to become merely a partial element of the great order of life; he did not resign himself to the idea of it merging into totality. There is a great difference between someone who dies of life and someone who says yes to death. Kleist did the latter. As opposed to the *fear* of death, he was sustained by the *passion* of death.

■

Ernst Jünger argued that though it was indisputable that everyone must die, little thought had been given to why one was *able* to die. The symbolic power of Kleist's death perhaps stems from his *aptitude* for dying, witnessed in his affirmative response to death. While he was uncertain as to the question of the great interconnectedness he had envisioned, he also refuted the impersonal death that had become prevalent in the European culture of the modern age. He did not suffer death but actively practiced it, and in doing so rendered it radiantly *personal* and *individual*. This explains why the most thoroughly documented segment of his life was precisely his death. There is as well the secondary circumstance that he was relatively young. Many of his contemporaries died at a similarly young, or even younger, age: Novalis (28 years old), Wilhelm Heinrich Wackenroder (25), Theodor Körner (21), Wilhelm Hauff (24), Georg Büchner (23),

Christian Dietrich Grabbe (34), Wilhelm Waiblinger (25), Karo-
line von Günderode (26), August von Platen (39), to say nothing
of the British writers (Chatterton, Burns, Shelley, Keats, Byron,
the Brontë sisters). And yet none of their deaths stirred the imagination of their contemporaries and their successors as much as
that of Kleist. The spectacular *organization* of this double suicide
undoubtedly plays a role. But the planning of it itself indicates
something: Kleist ran straight into death and died in such a way
that at the same time he symbolically vanquished death.

The death of Kleist towers before us as a great emblem. It
was not he who became the prisoner of death, but rather death
that became subjugated to him. With his death, he confirmed
that there is always, within us, a hidden reserve over which death
shall never be the master—even if this hidden reserve comes to
light only with the help of death. In European culture, the most
emblematic death events all bear witness to this reserve. And this
is always something variable. In the case of Empedocles, it was
the belief in self-redemption. For Socrates, it was the conviction
that even in death a person may remain a member of the collective—his most personal gesture serving as a standard-bearer. For
Jesus, it was the certitude that no one is ever completely identical with his own self. For Seneca or Boethius, it was the ability
to regard death as a part of life, and in doing so to alert us to the
cosmic vistas contained within life. For Werther, it is the passion
which transforms the negativity of resignation into a positive gesture of sacrifice. In the case of the great amorous deaths (Tristan
and Isolde, Pelléas and Mélisande), it is the certainty that the

self can reach fulfillment only through the detour of strangeness, through the loss of self.

And Kleist? The seventeenth-century English baroque doctor-philosopher Thomas Browne wrote: "There is therefore but one comfort left, that though it be in the power of the weakest arme to take away life, it is not in the strongest to deprive us of death."[15] For Kleist, we can modify this in the following way: death can deprive us of everything, but there is something which it can never take away from us—the ability to die.

Kleist helped uncover that ability in us. As with the other emblematic deaths, he sought a remedy in that in which, it would appear, one can hope the least: human frailty. He said yes to it. And perhaps this requires the greatest of strength. For that, of course, it is not enough for a human being to liquidate death. But it is enough to cast down the lead plummet, and—quoting one of Kleist's farewell letters, written on the day before his death—live out one's remaining hours "like a happy balloonist."

THE FATAL THEATER OF ANTONIN ARTAUD

The lecture by Antonin Artaud titled "Theater and the Plague" was advertised as to be held at the Sorbonne on April 6, 1933, at 9 o'clock in the evening. By that time many years had passed since Artaud had turned his back on the Parisian theaters, some of which were — in addition to being the best in their field — deeply engaged with his work; and he was far beyond the failure of his Alfred Jarry Theater, founded in 1926. Two years previously, however, at the Paris Colonial Exhibition in the Bois de Vincennes, Artaud had viewed, on several occasions, the performances of the Balinese theater, after which he began to think evermore decisively in terms of what would eventually become the Theater of Cruelty: his own attempt to even scores not only with the tradition of European dramatic arts but with Western culture as a whole.

His lecture "Theater and the Plague" was to smooth the route to this new theater. Three days before he gave it, he wrote to his friend Anaïs Nin: "In these recent days I have been possessed in the strict sense of the word by a lecture, which I will give on Thursday about Theater and the Plague — I am haunted and occupied by it. This is a harsh and alarming theme, in the course of which the affinities it will impose on behalf of the spirit will incite a process contradictory to customary thought."[1] In coming upon the analogy of the plague, Artaud had found a genuine cultural criterion. Just as plague is not merely one illness among many but a particular kind of state which casts a new light on life, the kind of theater Artaud desired to create was not merely a new form or a new function of style but a particular instrument for the purification and liberation of life. As he had expressed in an earlier lecture at the Sorbonne, in December 1931, this theater is first and foremost metaphysical. It does not create; it destroys forms, so that it can lead people into the unfathomable and to the enigmatic center of existence. In his lecture on the connection between theater and the plague, Artaud writes: "The plague takes dormant images, latent disorder and suddenly carries them to the point of the most extreme gestures. Theater also takes gestures and develops them to the limit. Just like the plague, it reforges the links between what does and does not exist, between the virtual nature of the possible and the material nature of existence."[2]

In Artaud's view, this theater will lead a person to the ultimate point of perception. But this point can be perceived only if the spectator becomes a part of the experience, as one who becomes entangled in the unfathomable secrets of existence; the spectator must also become mysterious. This is what occurred to Artaud when he stepped into the blinding, harsh light of the lecture hall on April 6. His theme was the relation of plague and theater; his goal was for his large audience to become acquainted with the more elevated forms of sensation. But when he reached

the point of demonstrating the affinities between plague and theater in the mutual stirrings of the desire for immortality and the
fear of death, he began to lose the thread. In the words of an eye-
witness, Anaïs Nin:

> But then, imperceptibly almost, he let go of the thread we
> were following and began to act out dying by plague. No one
> quite knew when it began. To illustrate his conference [lec-
> ture], he was acting out an agony. *"La Peste"* in French is so
> much more terrible than "The Plague" in English. But no
> word could describe what Artaud acted on the platform of
> the Sorbonne. He forgot about his conference, the theatre,
> his ideas, Dr. Allendy sitting there, the public, the young stu-
> dents, his wife, professors, and directors.
>
> His face was contorted with anguish, one could see
> the perspiration dampening his hair. His eyes dilated, his
> muscles became cramped, his fingers struggled to retain
> their flexibility. He made one feel the parched and burning
> throat, the pains, the fever, the fire in the guts. He was in
> agony. He was screaming. He was delirious. He was enacting
> his own death, his own crucifixion.
>
> At first people gasped. And then they began to laugh.
> Everyone was laughing. They hissed. Then one by one, they
> began to leave, noisily, talking, protesting. They banged the
> door as they left. The only ones who did not move were Al-
> lendy, his wife, the Lalous, Marguerite. More protestations.
> More jeering. But Artaud went on, until the last gasp. And
> stayed on the floor. Then when the hall had emptied of all

but his small group of friends, he walked straight up to me and kissed my hand.[3]

The Parisians spoke of scandal. Artaud, though, was satisfied. He felt that he had done exactly what was required for a lecture on this theme. He had not *spoken* about the plague, he had *performed* it; he did not regard his theme as such in the traditional sense, in which he could maintain a stance of objective "outsider"; rather, he identified with it. In this way, the performance became a *happening*: André Breton, with whom during the early years of the surrealist movement he had worked, commenced a lecture given on November 17, 1922, in Barcelona, with these words: "In general, I consider that a critical study is quite out of place in the present circumstances, and that the smallest theatrical effect would serve my purpose better."[4] "I went farther than ever before," Artaud wrote five days after the Sorbonne event to Jean Paulhan, but even before this he had termed "a concrete and absolute success" his lecture containing a "poetic-clinical" description of the plague: "There is a truth that I would like the public to be aware of; one of which it was unconsciously sensible, and that is no doubt what causes this abnormal hostility during such lectures. It is certain that my mere presence calls forth indignation, creating an abnormal irritation in some, as before some kind of monstrosity, an abject natural phenomenon . . . *the entirety of my subject,* a disturbing spectacle which troubles people who are unprepared and insufficiently prepared for a certain constriction of thought."[5]

■

The scandalous reception of Artaud's lecture bears witness to just how radical his new concept of art was. Artaud himself very well could have registered it as one of the manifestations of his own Theater of Cruelty. Life and art had come into close proximity with each other, intensely and dangerously. Artaud was in fact the most consistent twentieth-century representative of that thoroughgoing, originally Romantic standpoint according to which authentic art of the highest order is homogeneous with life itself. Of course there were, on this terrain, predecessors to Artaud. It was Rimbaud who had first stated, in *Une saison en enfer*, that the "cultured" man of Europe had grown immeasurably distant from real life, and that in order to return to it, he needed to embrace a path of a radically rejuvenated art. Moreover, this art would itself be one of the manifestations of authentic life. In Rimbaud's view, one's conduct in life was the only thing that could be opposed to that general disintegration characteristic of European culture of the new age. "Rimbaud taught us a new way of existing, of behaving in the midst of life," Artaud wrote in *Fragments d'un journal d'enfer*; his statement, to the effect that "We can do anything in the mind, we can speak in any tone of voice, *even one that is unsuitable*," can be correlated not only to his memorable Sorbonne lecture but also to numerous artistic tendencies in the twentieth century (including the words of Kandinsky, who announced in 1912: "Everything is permitted").[6]

■

It is difficult to trace Artaud's Sorbonne lecture back to concepts of art. At the same time, we would be unjust if we were to discern in Artaud's peculiar appearances only the portents of illness or insanity. Instead, we should see them as manifestations in the course of which Artaud attempted a kind of *incommunicable communication*. And this will always include the danger of being labeled insanity, drunkenness, or a dream. In reading Artaud, one often has the sense that in the figure of Artaud nothingness itself has gained form, and that through his pen and his mouth chaos begins to swell out. This pertains as much to his dramatic sketches, theatrical manifestoes, and acoustical and meaningless verses and texts as it does to the letters he wrote from the psychiatric institute. "The situation that Artaud found himself in was one that did not tolerate any artistic expression . . . and would have offered, at the most, a solution of a religious character, the transition to another order of reality; and precisely this solution was what he frantically—or should we even say insanely—sought for his entire life in writing, a means clearly unsuited for such an end."[7]

Here Nicola Chiaromonte is writing of the unresolvability of a problem. This problem is in all likelihood by definition unresolvable. The only "resolution" is almost certainly death. The first reading of Artaud bears witness to a life program that could never be resolved. If we immerse ourselves in the texts, however, death begins to emanate from every line, every sentence. This too is a kind of resolution. Artaud was able to remain faithful to the "authentic life" delineated by both himself and Rimbaud only if he was faithless to factual life—including art, understood in the traditional sense.

■

According to the descriptions in the extensive specialized literature on Artaud, the chief impetus in his life was his alienation from his own self, which finally led to schizophrenia. In 1901, when the artist was only five years old, he came down with meningitis, resulting in irreversible damage to his nervous system. When he was six, he began to be afflicted with the functional neuralgia that haunted him for the rest of his life, to which, from the beginning, his schizophrenic symptoms were connected. When Artaud was eighteen, he fell into acute depression; a year later he had become addicted to the narcotics that he had been using as tranquilizers; and with this addiction began his tribulations—lasting until his death—in various sanatoria and psychiatric institutes. The renowned psychiatrist Édouard Toulouse, who was intensely involved with the arts, saw art therapy as being expedient in this case. It is not without interest that in 1920, when Artaud was twenty-three years old, a psychiatrist introduced him (also with a view to his recovery) to the famous theatrical director Aurélien Lugné-Poë, who had in the year of Artaud's birth (1896) directed the premiere of Alfred Jarry's *King Ubu* (later, Artaud would name his own theater after Jarry). Although Artaud had been drawn to the theater even earlier, Lugné-Poë helped him with his first steps, giving Artaud a nonspeaking role in one of his own productions. In 1921 Artaud became acquainted with Firmin Gémier, the first creator of the role of Père Ubu; Gémier subsequently introduced him to the leading figure of contemporary French experimental theater, Charles Dullin. The influence of Dullin—who originally wanted to be a priest—on Artaud was significant. Dullin was an adherent of both Edward Gordon Craig and Adolphe Appia, who both turned away from traditionally logocentric theatrical arts and emphasized the nonverbal element of theater; he tried to coax forth personal responsiveness from his actors. The sympathy and enthusiasm between them, however, could not cover over the differences which separated Artaud not only from Dullin, but from the whole of French theater, and Artaud quickly broke with Dullin as well.

Artaud received his last theatrical contract only two years after his first appearance onstage, from Georges Pitoëff. During this yearlong period of work, Artaud definitively turned away from French theatrical life: after three years of performing, he announced that he was disappointed in the profession of acting. His main argument was that the actor in the European theater, by virtue of his craft, creates a rupture between experience and expression. Artaud rejected not only the theatrical arts of his own day but the entire tradition of bourgeois theater, the catechism of which, Diderot's *Paradox of the Actor*, had emphasized the bifurcation of experience and expression.

And yet it was not only theater, in Artaud's relatively early declaration of uninterest in it, that separated experience and expression. He accused all of Western culture with disassociating the subject and the object, as well as overemphasizing syllogistic modes of thought, to the neglect of all other points. In this respect, Artaud was the disciple of Nietzsche (whom he termed unhappy): in his last book, published in December 1947 titled *Van Gogh: le suicidé de la société,* like both Nietzsche and Heidegger he repudiates the culture that began with Socrates, although his conviction had solidified in him a good deal earlier, in the mid-1920s. Artaud traced the crisis of European culture in the twentieth century back to its own foundations and repudiated the whole: his engagement with mysticism and cultures lying outside Europe had commenced in the early 1930s. His membership in the surrealist movement in 1924 was also a sign of his rejection of rationalist tradition; he was, momentarily, a leading figure among the surrealists. Artaud, however, found even surrealism excessively rationalist, and he repudiated it. In this spirit he then established, in 1926, the Alfred Jarry Theater, which, however, due to financial difficulties, was disbanded three years later. He discovered the absolute antithesis of Western theatrical practice in the performances of the Bali Island theater he viewed in 1931 in Paris; these performances inspired his lectures at the Sorbonne; in 1932, he published the first manifesto of the Theater of Cruelty. With the premiere of his adaption of Shelley's tragedy *The Cenci* (1935), he intended to promulgate an entirely new theatrics; as he expressed it, "There isn't anything that won't be attacked among the antique notions of Society, Order, Justice, Religion, family and Country."[8] In hopes of definitively breaking with Western culture, in 1936 he sailed to Mexico, where he

spent the happiest days of his life amid the indigenous Tarahumara; he was initiated into the peyote cult, an experience he recounted later in numerous articles and letters. From this point
on, there was no way back: the last station of his estrangement
from Western culture was the psychiatric clinic, from which he
was released only after being hospitalized for seven years, shortly
before his death in 1948.

Artaud, pronounced by psychiatrists as sick, held the true
cause of his own inner torture to be the disease of Western culture. When he turned his back on European bourgeois theater,
he did not view the separation of experience and expression as
simply a theatrical or dramatic problem, but as a problem relevant
to all Western culture. Whereas Dullin, Lugné-Poë, Pitoëff, and
the other reformers of French theater saw *re-theatricalization* as
their goal, Artaud sought to extricate theater itself from the realm
of art. He was convinced that an aesthetic revolution could never
bring an end to the crisis. Only a metaphysical theater, at once
concrete and abstract, could accomplish this: "The theater must
become a kind of experimental demonstration of the profound
identification of the concrete and the abstract," he wrote, keeping in mind the final and mysterious identification of the experience and its expression.[9]

Artaud was not one for compromise: these two attitudes
to life—one refuting every burden, the other undertaking the
weight of existence—crystallize in two different theatrical experiences between which there is no point of contact. "A theatre
that subordinates *mise en scène* and production—that is, every-

thing that is specifically theatrical—to the script is a theatre for idiots, madmen, perverts, grammarians, grocers, anti-poets, and positivists, in short, a theatre for Westerners," he writes of prevalent theatrical practice in Europe, the fundamental impetus of which is, according to him, an oblivion of life blotting out everything. A theater opposed to this (according to Artaud's changing designations: Absolute, Alchemist, the Metaphysical Theater, the Theater of Cruelty, and the Theater of Tomorrow), however, will find the path back toward "efficacity that is immediate and pernicious—in short, [toward] Danger," making its own "that spirit of profound anarchy which is at the root of all poetry."[10] Only through the practice of anarchy can the genuine and original anarchy of existence be revealed. In this instance, the identification of experience and expression means, for Artaud, that the more anarchic a person can be, the more authentically that person lives.

Poetry, says Artaud, is anarchic, "insofar as it calls into question all relationships between objects and all relationships between forms and their meanings."[11] By this logic, true poetry is anarchy itself. The viewpoints of the surrealists—although he broke off with them—can be recognized in Artaud's views. In André Breton's opinion, the most effective surrealist action of all would be to begin shooting blindly in the streets; in 1926, Georges Ribemont-Dessaignes announced: "We are in a time of bankruptcy. . . . There is no remedy. The remedy would be a sheet of flaming gasoline. . . . There is a means to remedy the absence of remedy. It is to incite the masses to destructive fanaticism, to savagery, to incomprehension of all that is 'noble.' When the artist can no longer go out without having his cheek covered in spittle and losing an eye, that will be the beginning of a fresh and happy era. For men will never have had purer and more enormous pleasure." And he nails down the thought which was too daring even for the surrealists, and because of which, along with Artaud, he was excluded from their ranks: "It is pointless to move away from a negative position, since we can deduce nothing that we did not conceive in the first place."[12]

The Theater of Cruelty as envisioned by Artaud was an instrument for somehow articulating this absolute denial, following which a new, radically different existence could take shape. When, among the numerous potential names for his dreamed-of theater, he decided upon the designation *cruelty*, he was employing the word in its metaphysical sense. He was not employing it in the sense of sadism, physical brutality, bloodshed, or massacre, but rather to indicate a new kind of approach. As he wrote to Jean Paulhan: "In cruelty, one exercises a kind of superior determinism to which the supplicating executioner is himself submitted, and which, when appropriate, he must be *determined* to support. Cruelty is above all lucid, a kind of rigid direction, submission to necessity." Artaud recognized flawed existence in cruelty. When the murderer kills his victim, at first glance only the killer seems to be cruel. And yet if we recognize in the act of murder the inevitable determinism (cruelty) of existence itself, then not only the victim but the murderer himself is at the mercy of this necessity. "It is cruelty that cements matter together, cruelty that molds the features of the created world. God is always on the outer face, but the face within is always evil. Evil which eventually [will] be reduced, but at the supreme instant when everything that was formed will be on the point of returning to chaos."[13]

The recognition of cruelty is at the same time a recognition of necessity, signifying clear-sightedness, a lack of illusions. For Artaud, the crisis of modern culture manifested in people's inability to create a living and breathing connection with their own fate. The culture itself had fallen into decline because people were afraid to take on cruelty. The one-time surrealist and adept traverser of psychotherapy's labyrinths had discovered, behind the inhibitions and the suppressions, a domain which, though full of cruelty, nonetheless offered a home. The tragedy of Artaud and the great paradox of his theory of art is that he was capable of finding a home for himself only on a kind of unfathomable precipice; in the face of everyday life and traditional artistic creations, he tried to gain acceptance for a kind of world which offered no home at all, just as it offered no chance for artistic creation in the strict sense of the word.

The most fundamental objectives of the Theater of Cruelty were the acquisition of a life deemed authentic and the elimination of alienation—and not only in the sociological sense. When Artaud collected his essays about the new theater, he titled the volume *The Theater and Its Double*, reasoning that "if theater is the double of life, life is the double of true theater, but this has nothing to do with the conceptions of art according to Oscar Wilde." The obscure meaning of the word *double* becomes clear if we examine it in its relation to cruelty understood in a metaphysical sense. Artaud named art the double of life for the first time in 1922, referring to the ancient magi of the East, in whose language the double signifies that immaterial body which is the reproduction of the likeness of the individual: "We have a spirit so made that it spends its life looking for itself, seeking not even the words but *mental state, palpable or felt,* which corresponds to its spirit. In becoming conscious, it duplicates itself, and once the state exists, the words always come. The difficulty is to fix the state, to maintain it, to *prolong* it."[14] The term *double* simultaneously refers to the state of disunity and to its cessation; at the same time there is an absolutely individual reference to this expression (Artaud's metaphor for schizophrenia), as well as a cosmic significance (in which the influences of occultism can be easily seen).

It is no coincidence that it is in *The Theater and Its Double* that Artaud explicated the two essential metaphors of theater through the help of the concepts of the *plague* and *alchemy.* Both concepts call our attention to metamorphosis and transformation, processes in the course of which the material (the body) truly redeems the possibilities that reside within it and in doing so becomes liberated from all the evil holding it prisoner. Artaud refers to Saint Augustine, with whom he is in agreement—and who similarly compared theater to the plague, in that both phenomena are capable of evoking mysterious transformations. "Like the plague, theatre is collectively made to drain abscesses," writes Artaud.[15] According to this analysis, the Theater of Cruelty provides an exorcism function as well: it chases out the demons who impede human beings from living an authentic life.

"The theatre

    is the state

    the place

    the point

where we can get hold of man's anatomy and through it heal and dominate life," wrote Artaud, in tormented prose, at the end of his life.[16] This theater understandably has a different goal from that of traditional bourgeois theater: it does not wish to solve societal or psychological problems but endeavors to transmit metaphysical truths.

                        ■

The fundamental dilemmas of Artaud's life and his concepts of art are demonstrated in his thinking about theater. And this theater was unsuitable for formation into any kind of institution. Artaud's realized plans (for example, the Alfred Jarry Theater, 1926), his productions (*The Cenci*, 1935), and his theatrical projects (for example, *Le jet de sang* from 1925) cannot be regarded as being of theatrical-historical importance. This is not accidental: the theories of theater that he created go so far beyond every possible theatrical manifestation that any sort of realization could only be regarded as a mockery of his hypotheses. The Artaudian theater is not an artistic form, but a metaphysical gesture. When, in his dramatic sketch *The Conquest of Mexico*, he gives the following instructions: "Montezuma cuts the living space, rips it open like the sex of a woman in order to cause the invisible to spring forth," he has issued an unrealizable task to the director-to-be. This is not merely a surrealistic image; it tells us that the goal of this theater—just as in the ancient myths—must be to transform all existence: "Theatre's true purpose is to create Myths, to express life from an immense, universal aspect and to deduce imagery from this life where we would like to discover ourselves."[17]

Artaud did not turn his back on theater as such, merely on European theater. His thoughts, no matter how poetic and enigmatic they might appear, do refer to extant theatrical forms. His experience of the Cambodian as well as the Balinese theater (in 1922 and 1931) exercised a profound influence on him; and while it is most likely true, as the creator of "poor theater" Jerzy Grotowski was to subsequently claim, that Artaud completely misunderstood these theaters, their influence nonetheless prompted him to turn his back on European theater once and for all.[18] "And I do not know any theatre that would *naturalistically* dare to pin down the horrors of the soul as prey to the ghosts of the Other World in this way," he wrote of the Balinese theater, in the course of which "from these strange gestures of hands that flutter like insects in the green evening, there emanates a kind of horrible obsession, a kind of inexhaustible mental ratiocination, like a

mind desperately trying to find its way in the maze of its unconscious."[19] The great advantage of the Eastern (designated alter-
nately by Artaud as ancient, later as primitive) theatrical arts for
him lies in the way they refuse to become bogged down with isolated phenomena, but instead lead their viewers into the process
of the origin of things. For Artaud, the Eastern theater "shares in
the intense poetry of nature and preserves its magical relationship with all the objective stages of universal mesmerism." He
also stated that "in Oriental theater with its metaphysical tendencies, as compared with Western theater with its psychological tendencies, forms assume their meaning and significance on
all possible levels. Or if you like, their pulsating results are not
inferred merely on one level but on all mental levels at once."[20]

In every regard, Artaud preferred the Eastern theater to the Western. The theater of the East was mystical, Western theater was
realistic; Eastern theater regards gestures and signs as having decisive significance, whereas ours prefers words and dialogue; the
Eastern theater evokes ritual and transcendence, whereas the
final horizon of Western theater is ethics and morals. Both in
painting and in the theatrical arts, from the turn of the twentieth century on, interest toward cultures outside Europe grew
ever stronger; but no other European artist refuted European
tradition as radically as Artaud. In *The Theater and Its Double*,
he rejects fixed dramatic form, just as André Breton, in his first
surrealist manifesto, rejected the genre of the novel: for Artaud,

linear narratives, strung along the chain of cause and effect, were unsuitable for rendering palpable the turmoil and chaos of the age. This was not only because the authentic drama of life could not be confined within the framework of a story, but because European drama a priori is built upon words, and consequently upon intellect. To Artaud's way of thinking, the most fundamental problem of our age is that an unbridgeable precipice has arisen between the things and the words, as well as the thoughts. Just as did other radical theatrical innovators (Mallarmé, Meyerhold, Craig), Artaud refutes a theater which relies upon words, and instead of the poetry of words he directs our attention to a different kind of poetics: "I maintain that this physical language, aimed at the senses and independent of speech, must first satisfy the senses. There must be poetry for the senses just as there is for speech, but this physical, tangible language I am referring to is really only theatrical insofar as the thoughts it expresses escape spoken language."[21]

Artaud, however, does not refute words universally: instead he refutes the point of view that attributes exclusive significance to words. For him the *intended purpose* of words needed to change; only then would it be possible to emancipate a complex idiomatic form in the theatrical arts. Theater is originally a spatial art; words, therefore, have a reason to exist on the stage only if they can be transformed into the elements of a "spatial language": "Yet to change the purpose of theatre dialogue is to use it in an actual spatial sense, uniting it with everything in theatre that is spatial and significant in the tangible field. This means handling it as something concrete, disturbing things, first spatially, then in an infinitely more secret and mysterious field permitting more scope. And it is not very hard to identify this extensive yet secretive field without a formal anarchy on the one hand and also constant, formal creation on the other." Of course, Artaud's realization is hardly new; and yet we must bear in mind that since the seventeenth century no other theatrical creator had tried so consistently to return to the theatrical arts the ancient prerogatives belonging to them; this lends Artaud's thoughts regarding "total theater" enormous significance. The idea that words were placing thoughts in fetters to an ever greater degree was a commonplace in the first half of the twentieth century; Artaud, however, with the brilliance of creative geniuses, restores the authentic truth to this truism: "To spoken language I am adding another language and trying to restore its old magical efficacity, its power of enchantment, which is integral to words, whose mysterious potential has been forgotten."[22]

The problem, therefore, is not with words, but with that dualist culture which has misused them. Artaud raises the same question as Plato does in the *Cratylus*: Cratylus considers that there is an organic and internal relationship between words and things, whereas according to Hermogenes and Socrates this connection is extrinsic: man creates words according to his own liking that, just like a drill or spinning wheel, are mere *instruments*, and their goal is not the representation of magic, but instruction. Artaud, although he did not specifically refer to this Platonic dialogue, agrees with Cratylus, just as, in a slightly different context, did

Nietzsche, or (contemporaneous with Artaud) Heidegger. Indeed, Artaud might have propounded Heidegger's statement in regard to language: "The question which comes first and functions as the standard, proposition structure or thing-structure remains to this hour undecided. It even remains doubtful whether in this form the question is at all decidable. Actually, the sentence structure does not provide the standard for the pattern of thing-structure, nor is the latter simply mirrored in the former. Both sentence and thing-structure derive, in their typical form and their possible mutual relationship, from a common and more original source."[23]

Artaud, without any kind of philosophical training but simply by proceeding upon the path of his own poetic sensibilities, arrived at the same conclusion as Heidegger. Heidegger regarded the relation to "the earth" as a precondition for the creation of art and a guarantee of authenticity; for Artaud, it was the relation to "the body." Just as with Heidegger, for Artaud the true goal is to cross over from the extant world into existence itself; for this he perceives theater—as the genre in which the body is the most determinant factor—as the most appropriate instrument. Namely, Artaud does not speak of existence but of life, which he interprets in saying: "Moreover when we say the word *life*, we understand this is not life recognized by externals, or facts, but the kind of frail moving source forms never attain. And if there is one truly infernal and damned thing left today, it is our artistic dallying with forms, instead of being like those tortured at the stake, signaling through the flames." What is needed is an "active culture," as this alone is capable of realizing the theater, as long as the words do not treat things as mere "external appearance," but as something which leads us behind the forms. Language must be expressed as "the intellectual apprehensions of the flesh"; if not, it remains a dead language: "Each word, once it falls from the body, offering to be understood or received, exhibiting itself, becomes a stolen word."[24]

■

Artaud's goal was not a new theatrical language or the creation of a new style. When one of his acquaintances asked Artaud, in connection to the Theater of Cruelty, if the intention was to create a new *théâtre d'art*, he replied: "I found it rather funny that you ask me . . . because it seems to me that the definition itself ('Theater of Cruelty') eliminates this danger: an art theater can be nothing more than an incidental theater! A theater that seeks to destroy everything in order to come to the essential, to reach the essentials again through specific theatrical means, cannot, by definition, be an art theater."[25] With regard to his stated goals, even his most famous production, *The Cenci*, was a failure; one critic, however, drew attention to Artaud's performance (he played the main protagonist): "Crying his text as if he were declaiming it at a public gathering, hacking his delivery in a monotone style, M. Antonin Artaud is a deplorable actor. And yet, with absurd violence, his eyes bewildered, and his passion scarcely pretended, he carries with him beyond good and bad into a desert where we swelter for the thirst for blood." This was Artaud's intention: with this production, he stated, "I want to return to that idea of a universal life beyond good and evil, which used to give the Mysteries of Eleusis such strength."[26]

With his reference to the Mysteries, Artaud signals unambiguously the goal of his Total Theater. "In Oriental theatre with its metaphysical inclinations, as against Western theatre and its psychological inclinations, this whole complex of gestures, signs, postures and sound which make up a stage production language, this language which develops all its physical and poetic effects on all conscious levels and in all senses, must lead to thought adopting deep attitudes which might be called active metaphysics."[27] With regard to "pure" theater, Artaud was not inclined to compromise. In 1922 he had already set his own theater "of the purest human desires" against the "theater of the boulevards," and he never relented in this demand. In 1923 he also attacked Dullin, who, in his view, accorded too much significance to literary theatrical texts. In 1929, after the breakup of the Alfred Jarry Theater, he also broke off with Roger Vitrac, cofounder of the Alfred Jarry Theater, in the name of his belief in a pure metaphysical theater: "If you want to make a theatre to defend certain ideas, political or otherwise, I will not follow you in that direction. In the theatre only that which is theatrical interests me, to use the theatre to launch any revolutionary idea (except the domain of the spirit) seems to me the basest and most repugnant opportunism."[28]

It was the task of the Theater of Cruelty to arouse the consciousness of fluidity and the immutable for the enactment of total theatrical performance. If narratives of financial affairs, anxiety over money, troubles with love, careerism, and amorous embroilments comprised the main thematic lines of the bourgeois entertainment theater prevalent in Artaud's time, then in Artaud's view the true problem did not really lie in this choice of themes as much as it did in that viewpoint which necessarily limited the mystery of existence to a set of tangible, inexplicable, and resolvable problems. The goal of authentic theatrical performance was to render palpable the "hovering quick of life":[29] namely, no kind of fixation should ever be undertaken.

■

Artaud always shrank from any kind of fixed formation; he felt form itself to be a kind of constraint which immobilizes the authentic movements of the soul or diverts it toward false paths. When in 1922 the editor of the *Nouvelle Revue Française*, Jacques Rivière, refused to publish Artaud's poems because of their formlessness—or, in Rivière's words, because they were excessively personal—Artaud responded in a letter in which he asked, Is the absolutely personal not suitable to be regarded as a work of art? Their exchange of letters, which shortly afterward saw publication, reflected two differing concepts of art. Artaud confronted the European ideal, built out of self-contained forms, with a concept of art that was perfectly open, nearly homogeneous with life itself and hardly distinguishable from it. This is the opinion of a man who was disappointed in European culture. As he was later to express it in his pamphlet *No More Masterpieces*, the cause for the rift between art and the masses was to be found in art itself: increasingly art was passing over human elemental accumulated experience. This thought of anti-art does not originate with Artaud. In Russia, Nikolai Evreinov had already, in the second decade of the twentieth century, announced that art and life were identical; according to the futurists, the entire life work of Henrik Ibsen did not offer as much excitement as the sight of seats reflected in the window of a tram; Duchamp and the dadaists, however, saw the dispute as decided in advance. Artaud himself wrote, in 1925: "Where others present their works, I claim to do no more than show my mind. . . . I cannot conceive of work that is detached from life."[30]

This is an unguarded sequence of thought. The opposition Artaud posits between form and life is easy to refute, for Artaud at the very beginning completes a logical somersault: he equates form with a kind of objectivity, and yet he envisions life as being beyond objectivity—that is, he does not think about how form itself is one of the elemental manifestations of life. One can no more expect logic from Artaud's disjointed and vexed train of thought than from a poem or a musical work. In the case of Artaud, his "illogic" is nearly anarchically extreme, as he lived his own alienation as extremely as he could. He recognized, in his own illness, the errors of the cosmos.

The one single authentic theater which met the criteria of his theory was his own life. When he wrote of an art which went beyond form, Artaud was demonstrating his own tribulations to the world. This kind of theater could never have been given any kind of institutional form. Nonetheless, the influence of his theory was vast, so much so that Susan Sontag posited that the history of theater could be divided into two epochs: before and after Artaud. His desire to radically break down the strictures of restricted form coincided with the goals of most of the avant-garde movements of the twentieth century. Jean-Paul Sartre hypothesized that Artaud was truly the ideologue of the *happening*, in which not only the melding of art and life into one was present but also Artaud's desire to transform the elemental materials of everyday life into art. (In 1952, as part of the first well-known Happening—which took place at Black Mountain College in North Carolina—John Cage read aloud from Artaud's texts, among others.) One of Artaud's key concepts was that of *actuality*—in *The Theater and Its Double* alone, he uses the word at least thirty-three times. Yet he was thinking not of political or historical actuality but rather of the actualization of thoughts—the contemporaneity of life.

The paradox of the Theater of Cruelty resides precisely in how it envisions a kind of art that does not want to be art. Since Artaud makes no distinction between art and mere thought, or between poetry and the crudest facts of everyday life, he is only willing to accept the idea of genuine art as occurring beyond the realm of fixed form. Art is homogeneous with life, and so it is worthwhile to cite once again Artaud's definition of life: "When we say the word *life*, we understand this is not life recognized by externals, or facts, but the kind of frail moving source forms never attain." Life is eternal movement, the most authentic manifestation of which is the explosive deed or action. This is why, for

Artaud, theater has such a heightened significance: it is the art of action, which fulfills an authentic (and ancient) function, as long as it does not assume any kind of fixed and unmoving form. "Culture is not in books, and paintings, and statues, dances—culture is in the nerves and in the fluidity of nerves," he wrote to Jean Paulhan in 1935. The task of theater, as well as of the art of action, is precisely to uncover this fluidity of the nerves and submerge the viewer in this whirlpool: "True theatre has always seemed to me the exercise of a dangerous and terrible act where the idea of theatre and spectacle is done away with as well as the idea of all science, all religion and all art. The act I'm talking about aims for a true organic and physical transformation of the human body. Why? Because theatre is not that scenic parade where one develops virtually and symbolically—a myth; theatre is rather this crucible of fire and real meat where by an anatomical trampling of bone, limbs and syllables bodies are renewed and the mythical act of making a body presents itself physically and plainly."[31]

These thoughts—considered from the perspective of traditional European theater and art theory—are hard to follow. Whereas traditional European theater points to life in advance as a kind of object which it then stages as a theatrical production, Artaud unpacks this "object." He was convinced that authentic theater came into being when a person returned to the "mother's lap" of existence, to that place, according to Nietzsche, where the path led through the mysteries. "We must learn to be mystical again," wrote Artaud, in the spirit of Nietzsche; and for him, the goal similarly was "to rediscover the secret life of theatre just as Rimbaud managed to discover the secret life of poetry."[32]

This enigmatic existence unfolds by means of a kind of sorcery; Artaud, who also explored the occult sciences, held the route that led to this mystery to be the revelation of the *mana* dormant in every form. The *mana*, however, "cannot be released by meditation on forms for their own sake, but only arise from a magical identity with these forms."[33] It is understandable that in Artaud's concept of theater, *trance* has a heightened role: in his view, the Balinese theater or the rites of the indigenous Tarahumara of Mexico represent that state in which a person loses the everyday self in order to come upon a self of a much higher order, which is one and the same with the immeasurability of existence.

Artaud's entire life was consumed in the struggle with this vast immeasurability. Barely a week before his death, he wrote in a letter:

> From now on will devote myself
> exclusively
> to the theatre
> as I conceive it,
> a theatre of blood,
> a theatre which with each performance will have done
> something
> bodily
> to the one who performs as well as to the one who comes to
>   see others perform,

> but actually
> the actors are not performing,
> they are doing.
> The Theatre is in reality the *genesis* of creation.[34]

In the theater that Artaud dreamed of, the viewer penetrates as far as the final borders of his or her own existence, from
which everything appears from an opposing perspective. It turns
out that the absolute theater does not simply deny existence but
creates it anew from nothingness; in contrast to the bourgeois
theater, which cannot bear any consciousness of nothingness,
it represents a *negative act*. In this theater, existence is always
turned out of itself, and in accordance with the prophecy of the
English director Edward Gordon Craig, who believed that authentic desire pointed beyond theater,[35] the Theater of Cruelty
ultimately confronts the viewer with death, so that he might seek
there a new life, more promising than the one he has lived until
now. This is what occurred at Artaud's lecture at the Sorbonne on
April 6, 1933. And it was much more than a "university lecture": it
was a theatrical performance, an authentic instance of the Theater of Cruelty. His friends, among them Anaïs Nin, could well
feel that, in respect to Artaud, they were faced not only with a
dramatic creator but with a human being who, while still in the
midst of this life, sought to cultivate a deep inner connection
with that which lies beyond it.

A CAPACITY FOR AMAZEMENT

Canetti's Crowds and Power *Fifty Years Later*

Elias Canetti's book is strictly speaking not a novel, although there is something very novel-like in its texture. It has a decisive dramaturgy as well, although this is not a dramaturgy with a linear development adhering to the rules of well-formed drama, based on the precepts of rational logic. I would refer to it as a dramaturgy of dreams. In the late Strindberg dramas the scenes follow each other as loosely as do the chapters in Canetti's book. This loosened texture, however, does not lack a strict internal coherence. The number of chapters in *Crowds and Power* indicates the number of directions in which the reader may look. There is no common focus to which all would be subordinated. And yet neither book nor author can be reproached with a lack of unity. In searching for works of a similar nature, I would refer to the experiments of the avant-garde or the writings of Karl Kraus. But, as mentioned, *Crowds and Power* is neither a novel nor a drama nor a belletristic work.

I would, with certain reservations, term it a scholarly work. Canetti, in the first chapters, already makes it clear—with a scholar's sober logic—that the sciences have their limits, although these of course are not self-designated by science. Based on my experiences in the university system, I can state that if Canetti's work were to be proposed as the subject of a doctoral or habilitation thesis at certain universities, but without the imprimatur of his name, the negative response would be unanimous. His citation apparatus, for example, is, to put it mildly, unusual. And Canetti's choice of literature leaves much to be desired: he neglects Gustave Le Bon's groundbreaking monograph on the psychology of the crowd (*La psychologie des foules*, 1895), just as he does Freud's examinations in *Massenpsychologie und Ich-Analyse* (1921) and the analyses of Max Weber on the nature of power. Instead he refers again and again to books that appear to be either obscure, peripheral, or obsolete, as for example *Specimens of Bushmen Folklore* (Bleek and Lloyd, 1911), about which he wrote: "I have often thought that this is the most important book I know."[1]

But *Crowds and Power* can certainly not be termed a reader's diary, although the books that captivated the author during the nearly three decades of its composition can easily be reconstructed from it. The reader frequently has the impression that Canetti, under the influence of his own experience of reading, is revealing his own sources of thought. Very often, in reading a glittering and zealous train of thought, Canetti's joy in the book that elicited such enthusiasm is palpable.

It is not a novel, not a scholarly work, and not a reader's diary. So then what is it? Canetti himself said that *Crowds and Power* was his own "life's work" (*Lebenswerk*). He imposed a burden

on it greater than is usual for one single book. And it is understandable that in 1960, when *Crowds and Power* appeared after
nearly three decades of labor, the author was seized by disillu-
sionment and dread. As if with this publication an entire life,
printed and enclosed between hard covers, had turned to stone.
He felt somewhat that this *book*, as a physical object, had sucked
all the life out of him, its author, eliminating his living pulse. He
voiced this fear more than once in his notes. I would therefore
say—in remaining faithful to the spirit of his work—that Canetti,
having seen the printed book, might have felt just as the Austra-
lian aboriginal people did when they saw photographs of themselves for the first time: they were seized with abject terror. They
saw themselves as real, as extant, and yet as lifeless.

So what is this book? It has the impress of throbbing, vivid
life. More than anything else, this throbbing vitality was important for Canetti. The author most dear to him was Stendhal, to
whom—perhaps not surprisingly—he dedicates some pages in
Crowds and Power. What drew him to Stendhal? In his own
words: "He thought much, but his thoughts were never cold. . . .
All that he recorded and all that he shaped remained close to
the fiery moment of genesis."[2] Going by its title, Canetti's book
is about crowds and power: it has, however, a central inner kernel, a Stendhalian "fiery moment," which, like the glowing em-
bers at the heart of the fire, makes each line, each articulation,
each train of thought incandescent. This central kernel, however,
is never formulated, because the question that penetrates every
thought contained within the book like a watermark is "What is

man?" Like a great vision, this question renders this book vital even today, more than half a century later.

Looking at the book from this perspective, we can understand why it is so difficult to attribute a genre to the work. Canetti, in the middle of the twentieth century, reached back to a sort of genre which even at that time seemed anachronistic, and yet nonetheless formed part of a great European heritage. Beginning with the Greeks and the Romans, through to the major thinkers of the Renaissance and baroque ages, many had set this question before themselves, besieging it like a castle which yet no one had ever been able to capture. What is man? This is the question that impelled Montaigne, Hobbes, Luis de Vives and Pico della Mirandola, Thomas Browne and Robert Burton, as well as John Donne—whom, it is true, Canetti does not mention, but whose sermons on death, in my opinion, could well have been the archetypes for the most personal chapter of *Crowds and Power*, "Cemeteries." Many other similar predecessors might also be enumerated. But they have one thing in common: they have all passed out of intellectual fashion, just as the question has itself. Of course, not completely. Canetti still had, in his time, intellectual kindred spirits, although they were solitary wanderers, just as he was himself. Czesław Miłosz, Jorge Luis Borges, Béla Hamvas and Leszek Kołakowski, Maria Zambrano and Nicolás Gómez Dávila: they all traveled along divergent paths, all of them occupied with this same question, and all of them disinclined to constrain their own free modes of thought to the rigid grid system of academic disciplines. And they have something else in common with Canetti: they come not from the center of Europe but from its peripheries. They came from places where the susceptibility toward human passion had not yet been overwritten by that fearful malady—enabled through technical civilization—oblivion, and where a certain conviction was still alive, a conviction that perhaps humanity would not ascend to its greatest heights through the enlightened path of progress and development, but rather through the repetition of the ancient, so-called primitive acts in an ever more refined fashion. As Canetti puts it in the book: the European bourgeois of the twentieth century thinks that he stands above the African king, yet "his despots may use more effective means, but their ends often differ in nothing from those of these African Kings."[3]

What all these thinkers have in common, and what distinguishes Canetti's book, is the *openness to metaphysical questions*, which for two and a half millennia was the most powerful tradition in European thought, and which precisely became the most endangered in the twentieth century. That is why *Crowds and Power* was already anachronistic at the time of its first publication in 1960, and that is why it is even harder to imagine how it would be received in the American or European university of today. And yet its strength lies precisely in its openness. From the first page to the last, this book is distinguished by its capacity for amazement at the world. It is possible that ethnology would judge many of its pronouncements obsolete; that political scientists would not know how to connect this book to their debates and analyses of the everyday; that the science of psychology would see everything differently; and that the anthropologists would disagree with much in this book. And yet in his capacity for wonder, Canetti could give a lesson or two to these practitioners of science. A kind of lesson which even today is valid, and which even today would be worth learning. For in this, Canetti was (also) a mentor.

I quoted Canetti's assertion that the inner intentions of power holders are not much different from those of the ancient African kings, the formidable rituals of whom and cruelties of whom Canetti depicts with both horror and admiration. It is worth dwelling on this briefly. For with this thought, Canetti almost appears to be sending a message to someone. And this someone was none other than Hegel, whose name, however, does not turn up in his book. In fact, I am not sure whether Canetti ever read Hegel. Canetti, who was always disturbed by the "arrogance of concepts" and who always held examination of the individual phenomenon to be more important than that of generalizations, once said: "The conceptual interests me so little that even at the age of 54 I had not seriously read either Aristotle or Hegel."[4] Canetti made this statement a year before he published Crowds and Power. He placed the stamp of his antipathy toward the conceptual (Begriffliche) on the entire book—of which more later. For now let us remain with Hegel, whom Canetti almost certainly never read. In his Lectures on the Philosophy of World History (1837), Hegel also writes about Africa, and like Canetti, he too renders account of the cruelties of the African kings, their frightening rituals, the black heroes who dispatch their own lives with such ease, the bloodthirsty women, the cult of the dead, the executioners, the veneration of the golden and radiant sun, incomprehensible to Europeans. Although, in contrast to Canetti, he reaches an entirely different conclusion. Notably, he states that because of all the aforementioned and in contrast to Europe, history in Africa is not possible: "It is the land of gold, forever pressing in on itself, and the land of childhood, removed from the light of self-conscious history and wrapped in the dark mantle of night"—for this reason, Africa, in Hegel's view, could never contribute anything to human erudition. In the depths of Hegel's almost irritated repudiation of the ancient, archaic, and fixed phenomena found in Africa lurks the incomprehension of European (i.e., "rational") thinking confronted with inaccessible forms of being. Hegel describes the same scenes as appear in Canetti's book, but in terror. Of course, Canetti hardly found unconditional joy in those brutalities which, for example, could be experienced in the Kingdom of Dahomey. But in contrast to Hegel, he tries to understand them, and from his poetic style it can be deduced that he almost wants to experience them (things that otherwise he would consider frightening) for himself. In short, his terror does not culminate in repudiation, as with Hegel. At the end of the brief section where he discusses Africa, Hegel concludes, sighing deeply: "We shall therefore leave Africa at this point, and it need not be mentioned again. For it is an unhistorical continent with no movement or development of its own."[5] In con-

trast, in his book, Canetti returns to Africa again and again—
penetrating into its otherness ever more deeply, so as, at the end,
to reappear at the end of the tunnel—in Europe, in his own
present, where, looking around, he may pronounce: "His despots may use more effective means, but their ends often differ in
nothing from those of these African Kings."

Hegel and Canetti. One represents the peak of European
rationalism; the other is the suffering witness of European rationalism's numerous labyrinths and pitfalls—and, of course, of
its fruits. Hegel believes in expedient development, he believes
in the fulfillment of history, which is to say he believes in redemption for the sake of which all superfluous burdens—as,
for example, Africa—must be shed. Canetti, in contrast, has no
illusions in this regard. Although he is shockingly reticent in referring to the two world wars (he does so very infrequently), the
totalitarian regimes of the twentieth century, and the mass murders—unprecedented in history—which took place during that
time, his book is nonetheless a great pessimistic expression of
the viewpoint that man is irreparable, as he continually repeats
the same acts while employing ever more refined means. In the
view of the author of *Crowds and Power*, the European Enlightenment lost the potential for emancipation that lay within its re-
serves. From one chapter to the next, Canetti calls upon the great
ancient myths as his proof— myths from Australia to Alaska, from
Africa to South America, from Siberia to India. (It is interesting
to note that as far as Europe is concerned, he cites the mythic
world of the ancient Greeks and Romans relatively infrequently,

and when he does, he tends to mention the darker side of these myths.) All of this results in a characteristic methodological procedure: the parallels and the analogies with the modern age attest to either an open or a latent affinity, which represents a kind of identification. The Enlightenment tried to close itself off from myths as if they were a manifestation of immaturity. In Canetti's view, however, the European of the twentieth century has always lived in an ocean of myth, but without realizing that he does so. In this, this book is enlightening: it enlightens its readers in how the European bourgeois mistakenly thinks that he embodies the culmination of history and that his rationalism is the fulfillment of history. In conveying this message, *Crowds and Power* is of course not alone. Consider the work of Theodor Adorno and Max Horkheimer, *Dialectic of Enlightenment*, published in 1947; Canetti more than once exchanged ideas with one of its authors (Adorno) on the question of crowds and power. Similarly, in Paris, the exhibition *Le Surréalisme en 1947* was held; its catalogue contained an essay by Georges Bataille, "The Absence of Myth," in which the author declares the idea that we have gone beyond myths a delusion. On the contrary: even today we are the prisoners of a great myth, the myth that we no longer live within myth. "The decisive absence of faith is resolute faith. . . . 'Night is also a sun,' and the absence of myth is also a myth: the coldest, the purest, the only true myth."[6] There is yet another parallel to be found in Roland Barthes's *Mythologies*, published in 1957, three years before *Crowds and Power*, which similarly discovered in our everyday lives the most vital myths where we would least suspect. Adorno, Bataille, or Barthes were not "professional" researchers of myth; neither was Canetti. But they all drew attention to the nearly invisible spiderweb, comprising millions of threads thickly woven through the civilization of today, that can connect and associate us with the most ancient, the most primitive, the most repudiated of cultures and lifeforms. In *Crowds and Power,* Canetti asserts a similar connection with even more thoroughness and circumspection, if that is possible. His book can be read as an accusation against those who are still convinced of the supremacy of the white man of the twentieth century. Moreover, in 1970, ten years after the appearance of *Crowds and Power,* Canetti practiced a kind of "self-criticism" when he wrote that he felt he had betrayed the Bushmen by inferring from them the human being of today. He expressed it even more radically than he had in his book: "There have never been greater barbarians than us. One must seek humanity in the past."[7]

■

Ever since the year of its publication, many varied disciplines have tried to come to terms with this book. It has not lacked critics, just as it has not lacked admirers. Some see in Canetti the last of the polymaths; others emphasize his dilettantism. Any reader asked to state Canetti's exact area of expertise would be perplexed. Was he an anthropologist, ethnologist, historian, psychologist, historian of comparative religion, sociologist, or perhaps political scientist? He was all these and none. His scope of knowledge was worthy of astonishment, but so was his courage, as he simply never took notice of anything not directly pertaining to the object of his discussion. As opposed to the prudent and deductive logic of science, he entrusted himself to his instincts and presentiments — just like the Bushmen; I read his chapter on their intuitions as a kind of concealed autobiographical confession. One of the characteristics of intuition is that it never generalizes; it always attaches to a concrete object. This is the most characteristic — and for me, the most congenial — aspect of Canetti's book. When he was writing *Crowds and Power*, Canetti read a few lines from his favorite writer, Stendhal, every day, because according to his own admission Stendhal "allowed everything that was separate to remain separate, instead of trying to construct spurious unities."[8] Canetti was almost monomaniacally committed to the concrete, as he tried increasingly to distinguish the single and the individual, always paying heed to tangibility. I would not connect his personality with any one of the sciences, but instead consider him to be a phenomenologist for whom the individual branches of science merely served as raw material and objects of experimentation.

The determination of the two great themes of his book — crowds and power — clearly demonstrates his own characteristic procedures. For Canetti, the crowd was not a historical formation, nor was it a sociological or a political category, but instead it was a kind of obscurely eddying agglomeration which not only indicated human societies but was concomitant wherever life itself was manifested. As one of his American critics, Edward Roth-

stein, pertinently wrote: "Under Canetti's gaze, the crowd becomes an organism, a beast that crouches under the phenomena
of world history. The result is a sort of mystical primitivism."[9] For
Canetti, the crowd is an eternal constant, manifesting itself in
every age, and its most characteristic peculiarity is not necessarily
its largeness or its scale but the experience of space that accom-
panies it. The crowd provides the experience of *contact*; it offers
physical experience. As is stated in the book's opening sentence:
"There is nothing that man fears more than the touch of the unknown." Let us look away from the serious questionability of this
statement (and not think about infants, the dying, the solitary,
and all the others who yearn, more than anything else, for the
touch of another human being, no matter how unknown), to instead observe Canetti's methodology. Here is a living being, in
the present case a human being, who first and foremost is afraid.
He is afraid of being touched by someone, by an Other who will
step into the magic circle of his uniqueness. This Other has not
yet entered that uniqueness but can do so at any time—hence
the never-ceasing fear. How can one be free of it? We can do so
only by getting in front of it. How can this contact be avoided?
It can be avoided only if we do not distance ourselves from the
Other—for in every direction we are surrounded by Others, by
strangers—but come close to it. We must come close enough
for Otherness to cease. For this, everyone must be aggregated
together as Other. And now we have the *crowd*, in which others
do come into contact with me, but no longer as an individual;
the other does not touch me as a unique entity. "As soon as a man

has surrendered himself to the crowd, he ceases to fear its touch. Ideally, all are equal there."[10]

And yet we have not left the level of physical sensation for later. The experience of touch, of gathering together, the sense of my own individuality, as well as its loss. A phenomenological description of the crowd and its formation is enacted by means of value-free (*wertfrei*) statements. This confronts the reader of Canetti's book with a dilemma for which the author provides no solution. Is the crowd a positive or negative phenomenon? In Canetti's descriptions, it can be both or either. It saves one from the fear of touch, offers protection from the unknown. And yet at the same time it eliminates my own individuality—that very individuality I am afraid of losing through contact with others. The crowd annexes me, depriving me of my own chief characteristics. It does the best for me, even while it brings about the worst. This applies to individuality as well. If I wish, this is my greatest treasure, but it can also be my greatest burden. The crowd demolishes what Schopenhauer termed the *principium individuationis*—although Canetti, in a rather peculiar fashion, makes no reference to him, although one would be justified. Nietzsche introduces, in the interest of abolishing this precept, the Dionysian principle of intoxication: this is where the boundaries of the individual collapse, and the human being finds himself in the maternal embrace of existence. This will be the greatest value— it deprives the human being of individuality, which nonetheless can also be regarded as his greatest value.

I have intentionally mentioned Nietzsche's pathos-filled

words, for they are not far distant from Canetti's thoughts. Of course Canetti's use of language, his style—apart from a few exceptions—is not at all pathetic; instead it tends to be cautiously aloof. And yet at the same time, in relation to the crowd it grants validity to a thought deeply grounded in pathos: the crowd is not a human but a universal phenomenon. When people cluster in a crowd, they are not merely undertaking a political or sociological activity, they are mimicking each other. The Bushmen imitate the Africans, the Africans imitate the Europeans, and the Europeans imitate the Native Americans, who, for their part, imitate the Muslims—and all are alike in imitating animals, herds massing together for a variety of reasons—but animals imitate nature and all its phenomena. Canetti lists examples: imitation of fire, the sea, rain, rivers, the forests, wheat, the wind, the sands. And the book frequently mentions some of the most elemental manifestations of the crowd, power and survival—sperm and sperm cells. The crowd, the process of massing together, is not exclusively a human phenomenon; it is a cosmic one. From this it follows that a crowd does not simply mean that many people have gathered together; rather, that life within the crowd is inseparable from existence itself. The crowd is the *condition humaine.*

Historians, sociologists, and political scientists have not really known what to do with this interpretation of the crowd. But therein lies the key to why *Crowds and Power* could well be—despite its reception—one of the most significant books of the twentieth century. For example, a historian would first and foremost examine the differences or similarities between a Brazilian crowd of the sixteenth century, as it gathers to perform some kind of merciless ritual, and the crowd of two hundred thousand that gathered on Red Square on August 25, 1936, to demand the execution of Kamenev and his associates.[11] Or that same hypothetical historian would examine the link between an Islamic crowd of the eighteenth century, mourning and practicing self-mutilation, and a crowd of exuberant football fans in a stadium in our own age. A sociologist would analyze the composition of these crowds, the process of their becoming more dense or thinning out; attention would be paid to those trapped outside the crowd as well as to those at its center. A political scientist would observe the circumstances of the organization of the crowd, its timing, what sorts of precedents and antecedents existed to the formation of the crowd, and the question of why crowds form at certain times and not at others. And so on. Canetti writes conspicuously little about all this. He does, however, demonstrate that the crowd is a kind of unspoken *condition humaine*, delineating deep analogies between human beings, animals, and inanimate nature, all while articulating the great experiences of the twentieth century. And at the same time, without particularly touching upon these themes, he also interprets the experience of massification—which had never occurred to such an extent previously in human history—and the totalitarianisms that developed in parallel with it.

Crowds and Power does not speak *about* the twentieth century, but *from* the twentieth century, in the voice of that century. As indicated by the authors cited by Canetti, previous think-

ers had written *about* the crowd, and not only in the eighteenth
or nineteenth centuries but in the classical era as well. But the
experience of the crowd as an absolute mode of existence from
which there is no escape—because, with the help of effective
media, man can be reached even in his most solitary of refuges—
could be experienced and described only in the second half of
the twentieth century.

·

This brings us back to the question of power. What is the most
elemental manifestation of power? Canetti's answer is that
it devours the Other. What is necessary to devour something?
A mouth. And what is necessary for digestion? Teeth that can
grind. And teeth are good if they are smooth, hard, resistant—
and effective at creating order. Without smoothness and order,
power remains unconsolidated. What is ground up by the teeth
ends up in the oral cavity, itself a prison, though at the same time
it is an indispensable tool of power. After the oral cavity, the next
station is the throat that swallows—just as power swallows up
what it has subjugated. Then, in the stomach, the nourishment is
digested, and here the body definitively makes its own and renders internal (*verinnerlicht*) what had previously been alien to
it. And the final product is excrement, where the process of becoming one attains fulfillment: "Nothing has been so much part
of one as that which turns into excrement." For Canetti, the relation between man and his *excrementum* is an analogy for the
functioning of power: "Something alien is seized, cut up into

small bits, incorporated into oneself, and assimilated. By this process alone man lives; if it ceases, he dies."[12] These quotations are found at the beginning of the chapter "The Entrails of Power." Canetti also speaks about hands in this chapter. He speaks of the patience of the hand, of the finger exercises of monkeys, of the psychology of eating. But there are also things he does not speak about. For example, the exercise of power, the political nature of power, the division of power, the representation of power, the psychology of power. And Canetti does not discuss how the one who is devoured by power becomes an inanimate bodily part of power (its excrement), but nonetheless preserves vitality by the internalization of power, namely, the internalization, by the victim, of the gaze that enslaves him. The critics of *Crowds and Power* tend to find fault with its interpretations, calling on the work of Hannah Arendt for assistance, or the classic work of the Austrian F. A. Hayek, *The Road to Serfdom* (1944). I do not find this just. The sociologist, the political scientist, and the historian all differentiate; they prudently compare and distinguish. In contrast, Canetti's thought can be traced back to something quite different. But to what?

I believe that the examples taken earlier from "The Entrails of Power" demonstrate that Canetti was primarily trying to interpret and formulate a great vision in words. A vision arose in him concerning power. It was as if it were the result of a great dawning within him, a cathartic experience, similar to what Nietzsche experienced in Sils Maria when he conceived of the idea of the eternal return. And — just as the notion of eternal return can never be proven empirically—Canetti's vision of power could never hold up in front of the tribunal made up of historians, political scientists, or sociologists. But this does not in the least affect or influence its elemental truth. If we want to approach this book with the dignity it deserves, we will not insist on its providing us with partial truths, we will not weigh the political and sociological teachings that can be filtered from it; instead we will observe whether it has succeeded in accurately conveying and transmitting to the reader its own vision of the nature of power. What I said earlier about the crowd is also relevant to the question of power: this is a vision which could have reached Canetti only in the twentieth century; and in this case, he was not writing *about* power, but rather writing while looking out *from* the guts of power, as one of its *excrementa*. Canetti, instead of an exact historical analysis, offers the reader a description of the existential experience of power. For my own part, I would not compare his work with that of Hannah Arendt, but with Kafka's.

Canetti never employs the first-person singular, and yet his book is deeply personal. It is the vision he experienced that makes it such. During the nearly three decades he was working on *Crowds and Power*, Canetti continually strove to nurse this vision and keep it alive. Of what did his vision consist? This remains a mystery, just as Nietzsche's enlightenment must also remain an eternal mystery. But it is certain that the fear of the Other, of the Unknown played a crucial role in his vision, just as did the gut fear of being devoured. This vision makes his book not only deeply personal but a document of the twentieth century in each and every word. It was only in that century that a book like this could have been written, a century which considered itself the most developed in all of human history, and yet was the one that produced the horrors of the most monstrous dimensions.

In one of the chapters of *Crowds and Power*, the book's personal tone is thrown into particular relief. This chapter carries the revealing title "The Command." What is this command? For Canetti, it is not an abstract decision, but rather an achingly concrete manifestation, piercing like a thorn. The command—like a barb—is a spiritual formation which remains in the human being forever: commands, once they are executed, embed themselves forever in memory. And children are the most defenseless, he writes, his self-control somewhat loosening: "Those most beset by commands are children. It is a miracle that they ever survive the pressure and do not collapse under the burden of the commands laid on them by their parents and teachers. That they in turn, and in an equally cruel form, should give identical commands to their children is as natural as mastication or speech. . . . No child, not even the most ordinary, forgets or forgives a single one of the commands inflicted on it."[13]

The command is what unites every living being, whether animal or human. Such living beings are capable of survival only if they obey, if they fulfill the rules of the game dictated to them through these commands. If they did not do so they would fall to pieces, be destroyed. At this point, Canetti's phenomenological description is intertwined with a decisive value judgment (something that otherwise the author tries to avoid as much as possible). Namely, Canetti describes the command as that which is by definition evil. And yet, without the command, the world would not remain as it is. That pessimistic historical view, which in *Crowds and Power* can frequently be sensed, here gains decisive contours. At such moments, one comes across the traces of Canetti's concealed gnosticism. The world (or the cosmos, of which the human being forms as much a part as the animal or inanimate nature) is held together by something which can be designated *evil*. And yet I may perceive evil only if I have consciousness of the good. What would be this good?—a world in which there were no commands that yet would not fall apart from the lack of them. Can anything like that be experienced? No, says Canetti. But he suggests that—despite every rational principle to the contrary—such a world should exist. The dictatorship of commands must be shattered, he writes not as a historian or political scientist but with the voice of a preacher: "We must have the courage to stand against [the command] and break its tyranny. The full weight of its pressure must be removed; it must not be allowed to go more than skin-deep. The stings that man suffers must become burrs which can be removed with a touch."[14] And until this happens, we will be forced to endure the eternal endangerment of our own individuality; we may exist only as the excrement of power.

In accordance with the book's title, crowds and power speak of eternal nature. The vision, that Stendhalian "fiery moment," keeping the author's train of thought alive, was bound to its age—like an X-ray, it penetrates the twentieth century. The final objective of the book, however, is to accuse. *Crowds and Power* is an indictment against what both Emil Cioran and Canetti simultaneously referred to as flawed creation.

NOTES

Mass and Spirit

1. Walt Whitman, *Two Rivulets: Including Democratic Vistas, Centennial Songs, and Passage to India* (Camden, N.J.: Author's Edition, 1836), 19.

2. *On* is Greek for "being" (Trans.).

3. Ludwig Klages, *Der Geist als Widersacher der Seele* (Bonn: Bouvier Verlag, 1981), 711.

4. Taine, quoted in Carl Schmitt, *Politische Romantik* (Berlin: Duncker & Humblot, 1982), 40.

5. See J. Ritter and K. Gründer, eds., *Historische Wörterbuch der Philosophie*, 13 vols. (Basel-Stuttgart: Schwabe & Co.; A. B. Verlag, 1971–1984), 5:828.

6. Jacob Taubes, *Abendländische Eschatologie* (Munich: Matthes & Seitz, 1991), 37.

7. Elias Canetti, *Crowds and Power*, trans. Carol Stewart (New York: Continuum, 1973), 17.

Dostoyevsky Reads Hegel in Siberia and Bursts into Tears

1. See (in Hungarian): A. J. Vrangel, "Dosztojevszkijjel Szibériában," in *Istenkereső, pokoljáró. Kortársak beszélnek Dosztojevszkijről* (Budapest: Aurora, 1968), 137–156. In English, Vrangel's memoirs are partially included in Peter Sekirin, *The Dostoyevsky Archive: Firsthand Accounts of the Novelist from Contemporaries' Memoirs and Rare Periodicals, Most Translated into English for the First Time with a Detailed Lifetime Chronology and Annotated Bibliography*, (Jefferson, N.C., and London: McFarland,

1997). Hegel is mentioned in connection with Dostoyevsky and Vrangel's common studies in Joseph Frank, *Dostoevsky The Years of Ordeal, 1850–1859* (Princeton: Princeton University Press, 1990), 189.

2. Georg Wilhelm Friedrich Hegel, *Lectures on the Philosophy of World History*, trans. H. B. Nisbet (1899; Cambridge: Cambridge University Press, 1975), 191.

3. See Carl Schmitt, *Political Theology: Four Chapters on the Concept of Sovereignty*, trans. George Schwab (1922; Cambridge: MIT Press, 1985).

4. Fyodor Dostoevsky, *The House of the Dead*, trans. Constance Garnett (1861; New York: Macmillan, 1982), 19, 13.

5. Hegel, *Lectures*, 29.

6. Ibid., 25.

7. Ibid.

8. Ibid., 31–32, 212.

9. Ibid., 43.

10. G. W. F. Hegel: *Elements of the Philosophy of Right*, ed. Allen W. Wood, trans. H. B. Nisbet (Cambridge: Cambridge University Press), 373–374.

11. Hegel, *Lectures*, 172.

12. Carl Schmitt, *Political Theology: Four Chapters on the Concept of Sovereignty*, trans. George Schwab (1922; Cambridge: MIT Press, 1985).

13. Hegel, *The Philosophy of History*, trans. J. Sibree (Mineola, N.Y.: Dover, 2004), 91; Hegel, *Előadások a világtörténet filozófiájáról*, trans. Samu Szemere (Budapest: Akadémiai kiadó, 1979), 618.

14. Hegel, *Lectures*, 190.

15. Dostoevsky, *Notes from Underground*, trans. and ed. Michael R. Katz (New York: Norton, 1989), 21.

16. *Letters of Fyodor Michailovitch Dostoevsky to His Family and Friends*, trans. Ethel Colburn Mayne (New York: Macmillan, 1917), 57–58, 62, 65.

17. *The Complete Poetry and Prose of William Blake*, ed. David V. Erdman, rev. ed. (Berkeley: University of California Press, 2008), 201.

18. Katya Tolstoya, *Kaleidoscope: F. M. Dostoevsky and the Early Dialectical Theology*, trans. Anthony Runia (Leiden: Brill, 2013), 59; *Istenkereső, pokoljáró. Kortársak beszélnek Dosztojevszkijről*, ed. Gyula Ortutay and Ervin Pamlényi, trans. Klára Szőllősy (Budapest: Gondolat Kiadó, 1968), 111.0; Feodor Dostoevsky, *Crime and Punishment*, trans. Jessie Coulson (New York: Oxford University Press, 1998), 527.

19. Søren Kierkegaard, *Fear and Trembling*, ed. and trans. Howard V. Hong and Edna H. Hong (1843; Princeton: Princeton University Press, 1983), 42.

20. Lev Shestov, *Dostoevsky, Tolstoy, and Nietzsche (The Good in the Teaching of Tolstoy and Nietzsche: Philosophy and Teaching & Dostoevsky and Nietzsche: The Philosophy of Tragedy)*, trans. Spencer Roberts (Athens: Ohio University Press, 1969), 289.

21. Feodor Dostoevsky, *Memoirs from the House of the Dead*, trans. Jessie Coulson, ed. Ronald Hingley (Oxford: Oxford University Press, 1965), 129.

22. Dostoevsky, *Notes from Underground*, 88.

23. In Latin, *restitutio in pristinum statum*, "restoration to the original condition" (Trans.).

24. Dostoyevsky, *Notes from Underground*, 17; Dostoevsky, *House of the Dead*, 239, 241; Walter Benjamin, "Theses on the Philosophy of History," in *Illuminations*, ed. Hannah Arendt, trans. Harry Zohn (1950; New York: Schocken, 1969), 256.

25. Czesław Miłosz, *The Land of Ulro*, trans. Louis Iribarne (New York: Farrar, Straus and Giroux, 1984), 54.

The Globe-shaped Tower

1. *The Major Political Writings of Jean-Jacques Rousseau: The Two Discourses and the Social Contract*, trans. and ed. John T. Scott (Chicago: University of Chicago Press, 2012), 34.

2. Ernst Jünger: *Der Weltstaat—Organismus und Organisation* (Berlin: Ernst Klett Verlag, 1960).

3. *The Complete Poetry and Prose of William Blake*, ed. David V. Erdman, rev. ed. (Berkeley: University of California Press, 2008), 201.

4. Heiner Müller, *Jenseits der Nation* (Berlin: Rotbuch Verlag, 1991), 96–97.

5. Jean Baudrillard, *The Perfect Crime*, trans. Chris Turner (London: Verso, 1996), 96–97, 73.

6. Paul Virilio, "Gott, Medien, Cyberspace," *Lettre Internationale* (German edition) 35 (1995): 38.

Belief in the Devil

1. Quoted in Richard Friedenthal, *Goethe, His Life and Times* (New York: Routledge, 2017).

2. C. F. MacIntyre, *Goethe's Faust, Part I: A New American Version*, (New York: New Directions, 1957), 124.

3. Ibid., 52.

4. Pico della Mirandola, *Pico Della Mirandola: Oration on the Dignity of Man: A New Translation and Commentary*, ed. Francecso Borghesi, Michael Papio, and Massimo Riva (Cambridge: Cambridge University Press, 2012), 117.

5. *The Complete Poetry and Prose of William Blake*, ed. David V. Erdman, rev. ed. (Berkeley: University of California Press, 2008), 471.

6. Wolfgang von Goethe, *Elective Affinities* (Boston: D. W. Niles, 1872), 37.

7. Imre Kertész, *Fatelessness*, trans. Tim Wilkinson (New York: Vintage International, 2004).

8. Thomas Mann, "Deutsche Ansprache," in *Thomas Mann: Essays, Band 2* (Frankfurt am Main: Fischer Taschenbuch Verlag, 1977), 115–116.

9. See *Imre Kertész—Nobel Lecture* at https://www.nobelprize.org/nobel_prizes/literature/laureates/2002/kertesz-lecture.html (translated by Ivan Sanders).

Happiness and Melancholy

1. Leszek Kołakowski, *Metafizikai horror* (Budapest: Osiris, 1994), 23.

2. Œuvres de Saint-Just, représentant du peuple à la Convention Nationale (Paris: Prévot, Libraire-Éditeur, 1834), 218.

3. *Rapport sur le mode d'exécution du décret contre les ennemis de la Révolution, fait au nom du comité de salut public*, par Saint-Just, *le 13 ventôse, l'an second de la République* (France: Imprimerie Nationale, 1794).

4. Nicolas Edme Restif de la Bretonne, *Les nuits de Paris* (Paris: Hachette, 1960), 249.

5. Friedrich Schiller, "An die Freude (Ode to Joy)," trans. William F. Wertz, Jr., in Schiller Institute, *Friedrich Schiller: Poet of Freedom*, vol. 1 (New York: New Benjamin Franklin House, 1985).

6. Heinrich von Kleist, *Esszék, anekdoták, költemények* (Pécs: Jelenkor kiadó, 1996), 159.

7. Heinrich von Kleist, *An Abyss Deep Enough: Letters of Heinrich von Kleist, with a Selection of Essays and Anecdotes*, ed. and trans. Philip B. Miller (New York: Dutton, 1982), 91, 90, 92, 95.

8. Imre Kertész, *A boldogtalan 20. század*, in: *A száműzött nyelv* (Budapest: Magvető, 2001), 25–26, 35, 40–41 (trans. O.M.).

9. Georges Bataille, *My Mother, Madame Edwarda, The Dead Man*, trans. Austryn Wainhouse (London: Penguin, 2012), 31.

10. Rainer Marie Rilke, *Rainer Marie Rilkes Gedichte*, ed. Joerg K. Sommermeyer (Berlin: Orlando Syrg Taschenbuch, 2018), 100.

11. Goethe, *Wilhelm Meisters Wanderjahre*, (Berlin–Weimar: Aufbau, 1974), 32.

"For All but Fools Know Fear Sometimes"

1. Quoted in William Stigand, *The Life, Work, and Opinions of Heinrich Heine*, 2 vols. (London: Longman, Green, 1875), 2:358.

2. William Blake, "On Another's Sorrow," in *Songs of Innocence and Experience: With Other Poems* (London: Basil Montagu Pickering, 1866), 34.

3. Ludwig Klages, *Der Geist als Widersacher der Seele* (Bonn: Bouvier, 1981), 603–4.

4. Sigmund Freud, *Mourning and Melancholia*, trans. Shaun White-side, in *The Penguin Freud Reader* (London: Penguin, 2006), 404.

5. Ibid.

6. Klages, *Der Geist als Widersacher*, 604.

7. Michel Eyquem de Montaigne, *Essays of Montaigne*, trans. Charles Cotton, 10 vols. (New York: Edwin C. Hill, 1910), 1:172–73.

8. See as well Latin *spiritus*, "breath" (Trans.).

9. Friedrich Nietzsche, *Beyond Good and Evil: Prelude to a Philosophy of the Future*, ed. Rolf-Peter Horstmann and Judith Norman, trans. Judith Norman (Cambridge: Cambridge University Press, 2002), 89.

10. Walter Benjamin, *Illuminations*, trans. Harry Zohn, ed. Hannah Arendt (New York: Schocken, 2007), 256.

11. Søren Kierkegaard, *The Diaries of Søren Kierkegaard*, ed. Peter Rohde, trans. Gerda M. Andersen (New York: Carol Publishing, 1990), 19.

The Shadow of the Whole

Epigraph: Heinrich Heine, *Book of Songs*, trans. John D. Wallace (London: Chapman and Hall, 1856), 221.

1. *Kritische Friedrich-Schlegel-Ausgabe*, ed. Ernst Behler, Part 1, vol. 2 (Munich: Schöningh; Zurich: Thomas, 1958), 197.

2. Hermann Diels and Walther Kranz, *Die Fragmente der Vorsokratiker*, 3 vols. (Zurich: Weidmann, 1989), 1:215.

3. John Milton, *Paradise Lost*, book 8, available at the John Milton Reading Room, https://www.dartmouth.edu/~milton/reading_room/pl/book_8/text.shtml.

4. Ibid., book 10.

5. Mary Shelley, *Frankenstein; or, The Modern Prometheus* (Coradella Collegiate Bookshelf Editions), 174.

6. Marquis de Sade, *Justine und Juliette*, 10 vols. (Munich: Matthes & Seitz, 1990), 1:174; 8:180.

7. *Paradise*, canto 33, in *The Vision; Or, Hell, Purgatory, and Paradise of Dante Alighieri*, trans. Henry Francis Cary (London: Henry H. Bohn, 1856), 527.

8. Marquis de Sade, *Die hundertzwanzig Tage von Sodom oder Die Schule der Ausschweifung*, 2 vols., bound together (Dortmund: Harenberg, 1979), 2:217.

9. Ibid., 1:215.

10. *Novalis' ausgewählte Werke*, 3 vols., bound together (Leipzig: Max Hesses Verlag), 2:137.

11. G. W. F. Hegel: *Phänomenologie des Geistes* (Frankfurt am Main: Suhrkamp, 1970), 498.

12. G. W. F. Hegel, *Vorlesungen über die Ästhetik*, ed. Rüdiger Bubner, 2 vols. (Stuttgart: Philipp Reclam Jun., 1971), 1:229.

13. Quoted in Karl F. Grimmer, *Geschichte im Fragment. Grundelement einer Theologie der Geschichte* (Stuttgart: W. Kohlhammer, 2000), 253.

14. *The Complete Poetry and Prose of William Blake*, ed. David V. Erdman (Berkeley: University of California Press, 2008), 292.

15. G. W. F. Hegel: *Glauben und Wissen*, in *Sämtliche Werke*, ed. H. Glockner, Fr. Frommann, and G. Holzboog (Stuttgart: Fr. Frommann and G. Holzboog, 1958), 433.

16. August Klingemann, *Nachtwachen von Bonaventura* (Frankfurt am Main: Insel, 1974), 169.

17. Georg Büchner, *Danton's Death, Leonce and Lena, Woyzeck* (Oxford: Oxford University Press, 1998), available at googlebooks.com.

18. Christian Dietrich Grabbe, *Don Juan und Faust: eine Tragödie*, available at googlebooks.com.

19. Hans Urs von Balthasar, *A Theological Anthropology* (London: Sheed and Ward, 1982), 84.

20. Shelley, *Frankenstein*, 63–64.

21. See Dorinda Outram, *The Body and the French Revolution: Sex, Class and Political Culture* (New Haven: Yale University Press, 1989), 160.

22. Quoted in Abigail Solomon-Godeau, *Male Trouble: A Crisis in Representation* (London: Thames and Hudson, 1997), 122.

23. Johann Wolfgang von Goethe, *Wilhelm Meister's Journeyman Years; or, The Renunciants*, ed. Jane K. Brown, trans. Jan van Heurck and Krishna Winston (Princeton: Princeton University Press, 1989), 325.

24. See Mary Hillier, *Automata and Mechanical Toys: An Illustrated History* (London: Jupiter, 1976), 55, 58.

25. See Carol Ockman, *Ingres's Eroticized Bodies: Retracing the Serpentine Line* (New Haven: Yale University Press, 1995), 100–155.

26. See Terry Castle, *The Female Thermometer — Eighteenth-Century Culture and the Invention of the Uncanny* (Oxford: Oxford University Press, 1996), 141.

"Only That Which Never Ceases to *Hurt* Stays in the Memory"

1. Friedrich Nietzsche, *On the Genealogy of Morals*, trans. Walter Kaufmann and R. J. Hollingdale (New York: Vintage, 1989), 61.

2. Franz Kafka, "In the Penal Colony," trans. Willa and Edwin Muir, in Kafka, *The Complete Stories*, ed. Nahum N. Glatzer (New York: Schocken, 1976), 154, 148, 150.

3. Ibid., 150, 154.

4. A reference to Rilke's eighth Duino elegy.

5. *Letters Written by the Late Right Honourable Philip Dormer Stanhope, Earl of Chesterfield, to His Son, Philip Stanhope, Esq. . . . Together with Several Other Pieces on Various Subjects*, 4 vols. (London: J. Nichols and Son, 1804), 1:379.

6. Ibid., 1: 356.

7. Ibid., 1:323.

8. Ibid., 1:323, 2:28.

9. Heinrich von Kleist, "On the Marionette Theater," trans. Thomas G. Neumiller, *TDR: The Drama Review* 16, no. 3 (September 1972): 22–26, quote on 26.

10. *Letters Written by the Late Right Honourable Philip Dormer Stanhope, Earl of Chesterfield*, 2:28, 3:145, 1:332, 1:337.

11. Friedrich Nietzsche, *On the Genealogy of Morals*, trans. Walter Kaufmann and R. J. Hollingdale (New York: Vintage, 1989), 61.

12. *Letters Written by the Late Right Honourable Philip Dormer Stanhope, Earl of Chesterfield*, 1:308, 2:236–37.

13. Harold Bloom, "The Visionary Cinema of Romantic Poetry," in *William Blake: Essays for S. Foster Damon*, ed. Alvin H. Rosenfeld (Providence, R.I.: Brown University Press, 1969), 23.

14. See Dorinda Outram, *The Body and the French Revolution: Sex, Class and Political Culture* (New Haven: Yale University Press, 1989), 160.

15. Heinrich von Kleist, *The Marquise of O— and Other Stories*, trans. David Luke and Nigel Reeves (London: Penguin, 2004), 57, 93.

16. *Eric Rohmer: Interviews*, ed. Fiona Handyside (Jackson: University Press of Mississippi, 2013), 42.

17. On the many fine arts parallels, see "Angela Dalle Vacche: Painting Thought, Listening to Images; Eric Rohmer's The Marquise of O . . . ," *Film Quarterly* 46, no. 4 (Summer 1993): 2–15.

18. Quoted in Darcy Grimaldo Grigsby, "Nudity à la Grecque in 1799," *Art Bulletin* 80, no. 2 (June 1998): 311–35.

19. "Chateaubriand's Memoirs," *Blackwood's Edinburgh Magazine* (July–December 1850), 42.

20. See Dianne Hunter, "Hysteria, Psychoanalysis, and Feminism: The Case of Anna O.," *Feminist Studies* 9, no. 3 (Autumn 1983): 481.

21. Mary Shelley, *Frankenstein; or, The Modern Prometheus* (Coradella Collegiate Bookshelf Editions), 270–71.

22. See Sophia Andres, "Narrative Challenges to Visual, Gendered Boundaries: Mary Shelley and Henry Fuseli," *Journal of Narrative Theory* 31, no. 3 (Fall 2001): 261.

23. Shelley, *Frankenstein*, 174.

24. Béla Hamvas, *Karnevál* (Budapest: Magvető, 1985), 27–28 (trans. O.M.).

Sleep and the Dream

1. William Blake, Annotations to Swedenborg's "Wisdom of Angels Concerning Divine Love and Divine Wisdom," in *The Complete Poetry and Prose of William Blake*, ed. David V. Erdman (New York: Doubleday, 1988), 603.

2. Georges Bataille, *Guilty*, trans. Bruce Boone (Venice, Calif.: Lapis, 1988), 105.

3. Franz Kafka, *The Metamorphosis*, trans. Susan Bernofsky (New York: Norton, 2014), 3.

A Natural Scientist in Reverse

1. Achim von Arnim, *Die Kronenwächter*, in *Sämtliche Romane und Erzählungen*, 3 vols., ed. Walther Migge (Munich: Carl Hanser, 1962), 1:287.

2. "The Neckar," in *Poems of Friedrich Hölderlin: The Fire of the Gods Drives Us to Set Forth by Day and by Night*, trans. James Mitchell (San Francisco: Ithuriel's Spear, 2004), 46.

3. See F. G. Hartlaub, "C. D. Friedrichs Melancholie," in *Zeitschrift des deutschen Vereins für Kunstwissenschaft* 8 (1941): 272.

4. C. G. Carus, *Reisen und Briefe II* (Leipzig: Haberland, 1915), 29.

5. Jean Baudrillard, *The Perfect Crime*, trans. Chris Turner (London: Verso, 2007), 80.

6. Gotthilf Heinrich von Schubert, *Ansichten von der Nachtseite der Naturwissenschaft* (Dresden: Arnoldische Buchhandlung, 1808), 23.

7. F. W. J. Schelling, *Schriften zur Naturphilosophie*, in *F. W. J. Schellings Sämtliche Werke*, ed. K. F. A. Schelling, 14 vols. (Stuttgart: J. G. Cotta, 1856), 2:55.

8. Lorenz Oken, *Elements of Physiophilosophy*, trans. Albert Tulk (London: Ray Society, 1847), 16.

9. Heinrich Heine, *Ludwig Börne: A Memorial*, trans. Jeffrey L. Sammons (New York: Camden House, 2006), 32 (emphasis mine).

Kleist Dies and Dies and Dies

1. Heinrich von Kleist, *An Abyss Deep Enough: Letters of Heinrich von Kleist, with a Selection of Essays and Anecdotes*, ed. and trans. Philip B. Miller (New York: Dutton, 1982), 203.

2. Wolfgang von Goethe, *Elective Affinities* (Boston: D. W. Niles, 1872), 56.

3. Heinrich von Kleist, *Michael Kohlhaas: A Tale from an Old Chronicle*, trans. Francis H. King (New York: Mondial, 2007), 78–79.

4. Walter Benjamin, *Goethe's Elective Affinities*, trans. Stanley Korngold. Available at Scribd.com https://www.scribd.com/doc/2909355/Walter-Benjamin-Goethe-s-Elective-Affinities.

5. *An Abyss Deep Enough*, 202.

6. Quoted in *Heinrich von Kleist: Sämtliche Werke und Briefe*, ed. Helmut Sembdner (Munich: Carl Hanser Verlag, 1985), 2:888.

7. Quoted in *Heinrich von Kleists Nachruhm*, ed. Hemut Sembdner (Munich: Carl Hanser Verlag, 1996), 34.

8. Dr. F. B. Osiander, *Über den Selbstmord, seine Ursachen, Arten, medicinisch-gerichtliche Unterordnung, und die Mittel gegen denselben* (Hannover: Hahn, 1813), 300.

9. Gotthold Ephraim Lessing, *Emilia Galotti*, in *Four Georgian and Pre-Revolutionary Plays: The Rivals, She Stoops to Conquer, The Marriage of Figaro, Emilia Galotti*, ed. David Thomas (London: Macmillan, 1988), 289.

10. Eduard von Bülow, *Henrich von Kleist's Leben und Briefe* (Berlin: W. Besser, 1848), 73.

11. Georges Bataille, *Inner Experience*, trans. Stuart Kendall (Albany: State University of New York Press, 2014), 78.

12. Friedrich Nietzsche, *Unzeitgemässe Betrachtungen*, III. 3, in Nietzsche, *Sämtliche Werke*, ed. Giorgio Colli und Mazzino Montinari, 15 vols. (Munich: Deutscher Taschenbuch Verlag; Berlin: de Gruyter, 1980), 1:352.

13. Robert E. Helbling, *The Major Works of Heinrich von Kleist: A Study*, (New York: New Directions, 1975), 27.

14. *An Abyss Deep Enough*, 98.

15. Sir Thomas Browne, *Religio Medici and Hydriotaphia, or Urne-Buriall*, ed. Stephan Greenblatt and Ramie Targoff (New York: New York Review of Books, 2012), 50.

The Fatal Theater of Antonin Artaud

1. Antonin Artaud, *Oeuvres complètes*, 26 vols. (Paris: Gallimard, 1979), 5:145–46 (all quotations from this source trans. O.M.).

2. Antonin Artaud, *Collected Works*, vol. 4, trans. Victor Corti (London: John Calder, 1974), 14.

3. *The Diary of Anaïs Nin*, vol. 1: 1931–34 (New York: Swallow Press, 1966), 191–192.

4. Quoted in J. H. Matthews, *Theatre in Dada and Surrealism* (Syracuse: Syracuse University Press, 1977), 31.

5. Artaud, *Oeuvres complètes*, 5:15, 5:147.

6. Ronald Hayman: *Artaud and After* (London: Oxford University Press, 1977), 31; Susan Sontag, "Approaching Artaud," in Sontag, *Under the Sign of Saturn* (New York: Farrar, Straus and Giroux, 1981), 22.

7. Nicola Chiaromonte, "Antonin Artaud und sein Double," *Merkur* 26, no. 293 (September 1972): 873.

8. Roger Blin et al., "Antonin Artaud in 'Les Cenci,'" *TDR: The Drama Review* 16, no. 2 (June 1972): 91–145 (91).

9. Artaud, *Oeuvres complètes*, 4:104.

10. Antonin Artaud, "*Mise en scène* and Metaphysics," in *Antonin Artaud: Selected Writings*, trans. Helen Weaver, ed. Susan Sontag (Berkeley: University of California Press, 1998), 234, 235–36.

11. Ibid., 235–36.

12. Matthews, *Theatre in Dada and Surrealism*, 55, 64.

13. Artaud, *Oeuvres complètes*, 4:98; Theodore Folke, *The Theatrical Theory of Antonin Artaud* (Lund: University of Lund, 1971), 18 (typo of "puter" for "outer" silently corrected).

14. Artaud, *Oeuvres complètes*, 5:196; Hayman, *Artaud and After*, 45.

15. Artaud, *Collected Works*, vol. 4, 20.

16. Martin Esslin, *Artaud* (London: Fontana/Collins, 1976), 76.

17. Antonin Artaud, *The Theater and Its Double*, trans. Mary Caroline Richards (New York: Grove, 1958), 130; Artaud, *Collected Works*, vol. 4, 89.

18. Jerzy Grotowski, *Towards a Poor Theatre* (New York: Simon and Schuster, 1968), 121.

19. Artaud, *Collected Works*, vol. 4, 47; Artaud, *Selected Writings*, 223.

20. Artaud, *Collected Works*, vol. 4, 54–55, 54.

21. Ibid., 32.

22. Ibid., 54; Hayman, *Artaud and After*, 81.

23. Martin Heidegger, "The Origin of the Work of Art," in Heidegger, *Poetry, Language, Thought*, trans. Alfred Hofstadter (New York: Harper Perennial Modern Classics, 1971), 24.

24. Artaud, *Collected Works*, vol. 4, 6; Hayman, *Artaud and After*, 91, 61–62.

25. Quoted in Joachim Fiebach, *Von Craig bis Brecht* (Berlin: Henschelverlag, 1975), 178.

26. Blin et al., "Antonin Artaud in 'Les Cenci,'" 133, 97.

27. Artaud, *Collected Works*, vol. 4, 31.

28. Matthews, *Theatre in Dada and Surrealism*, 152.

29. Artaud, *Oeuvres complètes*, 4:14.

30. Nikolai Nikolayevich Evreinov (1879–1953) was a Russian director and dramatist (Trans.); Artaud, *Selected Writings*, 59.

31. Artaud, *Collected Works*, vol. 4, 6; Artaud, *Oeuvre complètes*, 8:286; Folke, *The Theatrical Theory of Antonin Artaud*, 46.

32. Hayman, *Artaud and After*, 67, 105.

33. Artaud, *Collected Works*, vol. 4, 4–5.

34. Antonin Artaud, Letter to Paule Thévenin, February 24, 1948, in Artaud, *Selected Writings*, 585.

35. Edward Gordon Craig, *On the Art of Theatre* (London: William Heinemann, 1911), 84.

A Capacity for Amazement

1. Elias Canetti, *Nachträge aus Hampstead: Aufzeichnungen 1954–1971* (Munich: Carl Hanser, 1994), 32.

2. Elias Canetti, *Crowds and Power*, trans. Carol Stewart (New York: Continuum, 1973), 277.

3. Ibid., 411.

4. Quoted in Roberto Calasso, "Bibliographische Bekenntnisse," in *Einladung zur Verwandlung. Essays zu Elias Canettis "Masse und Macht*," ed. Michael Krüger (Munich: Hanser Verlag, 1995), 23.

5. G. W. F. Hegel, *Lectures on the Philosophy of World History*, trans. H. B. Nisbet (Cambridge: Cambridge University Press, 1975), 174, 190.

6. Georges Bataille, "The Absence of Myth," in *Writings on Surrealism*, ed. and trans. Michael Richardson (London: Verso, 1994), 48.

7. Quoted in Henning Ritter: "Als hätte einer allein die Griechen entdeckt, und niemand achtete darauf," in *Einladung zur Verwandlung*, 11–21 (13).

8. Canetti, *Crowds and Power*, 277.

9. Edward Rothstein, "Dreams of Disappearance: The Secret Life of Elias Canetti," *New Republic*, January 8 and 15, 1990, 36.

10. Canetti, *Crowds and Power*, 15.

11. Leo Borisovich Kamenev (1883–1936), was one of the members of the first Politburo and brother-in-law of Leon Trotsky; his execution, along with that of Grigory Zinoviev, signified the beginning of the purges under Stalin's rule (Trans.).

12. Canetti, *Crowds and Power*, 210.

13. Canetti, *Crowds and Power*, 306.

14. Ibid., 333.

CREDITS

The credits page constitutes a continuation of the copyright page.

Earlier versions of the following essays were originally published in Hungarian; some have been substantially revised for the English translation.

"Tömeg és szellem" (1995)

"Dosztojevszkij Szibériában Hegelt olvassa, és sírva fakad" (1997)

"A gömb alakú torony" (1998)

"Az ördögbe vetett hit" (2012)

"Boldogság és melankólia" (2007)

"Csak a bolondok nem félnek semmitől sem" (2007)

"Az Egész árnyéka" (2003)

"Csak ami nem szűnik meg fájni, az marad meg az emlékezetben" (2015)

"Az alvás és az álom" (2003)

"Egy fordított természettudós" (2004)

"Kleist meghal és meghal és meghal" (2000)

"Antonin Artaud halálos színháza" (1990)

"A csodálkozás képessége" (2010)

Excerpt from Friedrich Schiller, "An die Freude (Ode to Joy)," translated by William F. Wertz, Jr., President of the Schiller Institute, in Schiller Institute, *Friedrich Schiller: Poet of Freedom*, vol. 1 (New York: New Benjamin Franklin House, 1985). Used by permission.

Excerpt from Friedrich Hölderlin, "The Neckar," in *Poems of Friedrich Hölderlin: The Fire of the Gods Drives Us to Set Forth by Day and by*

LÁSZLÓ F. FÖLDÉNYI (b. 1952) studied English and Hungarian literature and the philosophy of art in Budapest and spent several years in Germany and the Netherlands. He is now a professor at the University of Theatre, Film, and Television, Budapest, and holds the chair in the theory of art. His books on literature, art, and the history of ideas have been translated into more than ten languages. He has won many literary prizes in Germany und Hungary, including the highest state honor in Hungary, the Széchenyi Prize. In 2009, he was elected to the Deutsche Akademie für Sprache und Dichtung. He lives with his American-born wife, an architect, in Budapest, and has two daughters and a son.

OTTILIE MULZET, a translator and literary critic, has translated the work of László Krasznahorkai, Szilárd Borbély, and Gábor Schein, among others. Recent translations include *Baron Wenckheim's Homecoming*, by László Krasznahorkai, and *Final Matters: Selected Poems, 2004–2010*, by Szilárd Borbély; forthcoming translations include *The Bone Fire*, by György Dragomán, and *Autobiographies of an Angel*, by Gábor Schein. Mulzet is also editing an anthology of contemporary women's poetry from Hungarian, and is the editor of the Hungarian List at Seagull Books.